D1431140

THE YEARS OF THE LOCUST
(America, 1929–1932)

THE CAPITOL : JULY, 1932

Bonus Marchers from California Keep the Death Watch over Congress

THE YEARS
OF THE LOCUST

(America, 1929-1932)

GILBERT SELDES

*The contemplation of things as they are, without
substitution or imposture, without error
or confusion, is in itself a nobler
thing than a whole har-
vest of inventions.*
—BACON

BOSTON · 1933

LITTLE, BROWN, AND COMPANY

Copyright, 1933,

BY GILBERT SELDES

———

Published February, 1933
Reprinted February, 1933

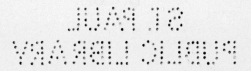
PRINTED IN THE UNITED STATES OF AMERICA

TO

A. H. S.

CONTENTS

ILLUSTRATIONS

PART ONE: FROM DAY TO DAY

CHAPTER ONE

THE SHAKE-OUT

ON the 13th of September, 1931, at the opening of George White's Scandals in New York, Mr. Rudy Vallee, awkwardly appearing before a public prepared to resist the blandishments which had made him a popular crooner on the radio, lifted up his voice, a little, and sang a song, the burden of which was, Life is just a bowl of cherries. Like another famous song derived from the vegetable kingdom, this one was not musically important; it thumped along, as undistinguished as the singer's Maine Stein Song, but he sang it as softly as he had sung "I Kiss Your Hand, Madame." The words were simple:

> "Life is just a bowl of Cherries.
> Don't make [1] it serious.
> Life's too mysterious. . . ."

Yet the song was, in a small way, epoch-marking, if not epoch-making. For the first time, America was dispraising God in its psalmody. The phrase, "a bowl of cherries", came into common use because it expressed a common state of mind. The bottom had fallen out of the tubs into which America had poured its hopes and its faiths; the great horn of plenty had voided itself and all that was left of its unimaginable riches was a bowl of cherries.

---

[1] So Mr. Vallee sang it. Miss Ethel Merman, a distinguished shouter in the same production, sang "don't take it serious", giving joy to the critics. The published version has "make."

Other borrowings from the vegetable kingdom were also popular. From E. B. White's caption for Carl Rose's drawing in the *New Yorker* ("I say it's spinach and I say the hell with it") were taken the first four words to indicate a profound disbelief in the promises and prophecies of those in authority, and from the habits of the ancient army the sound known as the "bird", the "Bronx Cheer", but most popularly as the "raspberry", came into universal use. The sound had been shown, effectively, in the silent movies, but as late as the end of September, 1929, it was so offensive to public morals that it led to arrest [2]; the talkies gave it increased currency; as an expression of vulgar contempt the sound is incomparable and those who could not purse their lips or frame their tongues to utter the sound itself familiarly used its name.

That God's Country, the land of simple faith and buoyant optimism, had turned sour, cynical, disbelieving, and a little nasty was all the more remarkable because in October, 1929, nothing had happened; nothing, that is, except a technical correction of the mild excesses of the Stock Market. For a day or two it seemed that the break which a few crafty observers had foreseen and predicted had occurred. On October 19, the big board and the curb had traded over five million shares in a short session and had recorded drops of five to forty points, wiping out values estimated at over three billion dollars; five days later thirteen million shares were traded on the Stock Exchange in spite of the almost unanimous opinion that "the technical position of the market had been sufficiently cor-

---

[2] A detective in New York City arrested Prescott Robinson, a surface car track-walker for giving the raspberry to Grover Whalen, Commissioner of Police, the splendor of whose vehicle annoyed the humble worker. The commissioner did not, however, prosecute. The complete reversal of fortune which gives so much pleasure to the thoughtful mind did not come until late in 1932, when Mr. Ben Stein, having directed a Bronx cheer at Patrolman Van Coney in Cincinnati, was jailed; he sued for damages and got them — $500.

rected" and the offers of "attractive purchases" by many brokers. Publicists who were presently to say that "everybody" had been speculating [3] reverted to a pre-war concept of Wall Street "functioning as a separate phenomenon, without effect on or relation to the economic and financial system of the country"; but their reassurances were worthless. On October 24 occurred "the blackest day" and the "darkest hour" of the market, yet it was the darkest hour before the dawn, which came at 1:30 P.M., Eastern Standard Time, when Mr. Richard Whitney proceeded to the trading post of United States Steel, and seeing that stock falling to 195, offered to buy 25,000 shares at 205. It was promptly understood that this extravagance — an unnecessary payment of $250,000 — was ordered by a group of bankers, the most powerful in America, and that it represented their belief that not only Steel, but all other substantial stocks, were selling at absurdly low prices; or, to put it another way, that these bankers, being in business for money, believed Steel would go to at least 206 and stay there. It was the first of many errors.

The following day drove home the lesson that nothing exceptional had occurred.

BANKERS CHECK STOCK COLLAPSE: BUSINESS STEADY, SAYS TREASURY

ran the headlines and this theme was developed in elaborate counterpoint by publicists, bank presidents, and public officials until the news of the economic stability of the country reached the White House and was, from the White House, broadcast to the people at large.

That nothing had occurred soon became a fixed dogma,

[3] This is an item in the "classic" explanation of the years 1929–1932, and is entirely misleading. For an examination of the actual number of individuals in the market, see page 307.

the substructure upon which an enormous and rickety edifice was built. It was, however, all façade and when it fell the shock to the American people was infinitely more serious than the collapse of the Stock Market. Since it was an emotional collapse, not a financial one, no graphs exist to chart its ups and downs. It is part of the plan of this book to prepare such a fever chart of the thoughts and feelings of the American people and to superimpose it upon the charts of stocks and car loadings and production which have become so familiar in the financial pages of our newspapers.

For this purpose it is important to note how the foundations were laid and I might as well say at once, to be done with it, that fatuous and false as these reassurances and later predictions have been, I do not quote them in any spirit of mockery. That has been perfectly done in the Oh, Yeah booklets; perfectly because their only commentary on speech is the cold silence of fact. These books and a number of studies similar in tone were gadflies, stinging the public into remembering what their leaders had told them, warning the sluggish horse to be ready with the raspberry when further promises were made. Yet something remains to be said for the publicists, the great merchants of confidence. It is not only that they were defending their own. They were, in a sense, wise during the event, whereas we can only be wise after the event. A clairvoyant observer might have known that when you washed all the billion-dollar colors out of a woolen dress, the dress would shrink; that the collapse of the market must have some repercussion on industry; that the market break did not come unheralded and without distant causes; that years might pass before the nervous effects of the shock would pass. Yet even such an observer would have been a bad public servant if in the first days of November he had shrieked hysterically that all was lost, including honor; many things will not be forgiven Mr. Hoover, but the most unforgivable thing he did not do:

he was not panic-stricken and he brought no further panic to his country. The bankers pretended that the country "could take it"; naturally they wished to believe that a country which had absorbed so much bad financing could stand a little loss. The President was under a moral obligation to be reassuring; for him to have been anything else is unthinkable.

The error crept in much later when it became clear that some of our most effective leaders not only offered us false economic doctrines, but preferred to believe them and were attempting to conduct the business of the country as if the lies were great economic truths. In that effect they came close to wrecking the mind and the spirit of America. Came close, I say, because they haven't finished; they may still succeed.

They began with the mumbo jumbo of the Stock Market. It was a technical situation; liquidation had gone on; the bears had achieved a "shake-out" of the public speculators, leaving the market where it belonged, in the hands of the professionals; a squeeze play had been pulled; it was "a frightened market"; Mr. Lamont "pointed out that the collapse of certain stocks was due to the technical condition of offers and no bids." "The tardiness of the ticker was blamed for the panicky selling." The reaction (against high price levels) had overrun itself, according to Charles E. Mitchell, one of the five bankers who had inspired Mr. Whitney's cry for expensive Steel. The losses were paper losses; it was a security panic, said Colonel Leonard P. Ayres, "with no economic basis"; and an anonymous official of the Treasury said "the market had been overextended"; in the shake-out it had "freed itself of a tremendous amount of margin trading."

This was Point One: the mysterious market had acted in its usual way. The numbers were bigger; more shares were sold and the prices fell in more spectacular bounds. The country which for five years had been cajoled and browbeaten into speculation was being told that it had nothing to fear and little to do with the market. There was even a suggestion, with a faint tone of reproach, that the comparatively unimportant event in the market might have the important result of turning minds and money back to their normal channels, namely, to work and to sound investment. Advisers to Mr. Hoover assured him that "the very salutary and inevitable deflation of a highly unhealthy situation would enable national industry to go forward on a surer footing." (Economic advisers are given to a style which might itself bear deflation.)

At the very beginning a few serious words were said. A few people suggested that the prices of stocks were being reduced so that they corresponded to the earnings on those stocks and to the general prospects of business; confident that prices would not go lower, they said that if prices *should* go lower, business and industry *might* suffer. The idea that the earnings of a company had any relation to the price at which the company's stock sold was never taken seriously by speculators, but for investors it had some sense; an old assumption that a stock should sell at ten times its earnings had, however, been blown up by a casual remark of John J. Raskob that fifteen times earnings was a reasonable standard, at least for General Motors. So that Professor Irving Fisher, witnessing the crash, could say, with no hesitation, that "the market will recover because the crash carried the price average of individual stocks down to ten or eleven times their earning" — down, that is, to the level considered normal only a few years earlier.

These were the words of the cautious men and the doubters. For the rest, men of business and politics were proud to agree that "the tremendous development of industrial and natural resources and the solidification of banking interests made the United States probably the only nation in the world which would withstand the shock of a three billion dollar paper loss on the Stock Exchange in a single day without serious effect to the average citizen", and that there was too much wealth in the country for the situation to become serious. If the bankers and brokers were not to be trusted, the industrialists were ready with encouragement: Walter C. Teagle of Standard Oil of New Jersey did not "regard any corrective movement (in the market) as symptomatic of the trade movement"; the president of Swift and Company thought that "the decline in stocks will have no effect on the fundamental soundness of business conditions"; the head of a great department store in Chicago held that the readjustment in stock prices would be helpful to the business situation, if only the readjustment were not too drastic; Robert Dollar preferred the decline to "a big rise in prices"; R. E. Wood, of Sears, Roebuck, said simply that "we are going to do the biggest business in our history this month." So industry stood behind finance.

Behind industry stood the Government. I have already quoted the anonymous guides from the Treasury; irresponsible they may have been, since they were anonymous, but if the responsible heads of the Treasury wished any contrary opinion to prevail, the newspapers were open to them. The next step toward final authority brings us to the Federal Reserve Board which had, for a long period, left money free for speculation. The board held two "extended meetings" and continued its policy of masterly inaction, deciding "that the avalanche of selling on the New York Stock Market . . . had not resulted in a situation serious enough to call for any immediate formal declaration. . . . One of the highest officials expressed the opinion that the break 'would not prove disastrous to business and the prosperity of the country'."

The question was officially settled when, on October 26, the newspapers carried word from the President that "the fundamental business of the country — that is, the production and distribution of commodities — is on a sound and prosperous basis."

On the first Sunday after the crash, the Church, seeing opportunity in the fall of its great enemy, announced that "the gambling craze practically means an attempt to get something for nothing — to secure a far higher reward for an investment than it really deserves. . . . This is not according to the mind of Christ." Mr. Raskob's standard of fifteen times earnings was thus rebuked by the Right Reverend Frank Theodore Woods.

It was further rebuked during the following week when, despite (or as later defenders insisted, to spite) the President, the selling of stock continued, lopping off twenty, thirty, even sixty of the luxurious points accumulated during the past ten years and coming to a beautiful climax on Tuesday, October 29, when in a *dégringolade* of liquidation over sixteen million shares were traded and America lay back exhausted to marvel at its own magnificence. Nothing like it had ever been seen before; it was the record, millions of times more exciting and expensive than flagpole sitting. We had beaten the world again and the only question was what it would cost us.

The immediate answer was that we could pay the bill. America was marvelous. The Stock Market had gone to hell and new projects were forming everywhere, new buildings, new enterprises. A few malcontents committed suicide or went bankrupt, but Doctor Julius Klein, Assistant Secretary of Commerce, knew, and told, that only four per cent. of the families of America were at all affected and business men announced that they were buying stocks. Just as the first announcements of fundamental soundness made their way to the Chief Executive, so the announcements of new buying made their way to the patriarch of business and John D. Rockefeller, Sr., made a statement as calm and as reassuring as Hoover's own: "My son and I have for some days past been purchasing sound common stock." The Stock Exchange was closed by its governors for the better part of a week.

Everything was all right. Nothing had happened.

CHAPTER TWO

BLINDFOLD

SOMETHING had happened. Incomparably realistic, disabused, and cynical, *Variety* ran the news under a great headline: [1]

WALL STREET LAYS AN EGG!

If I were writing a diary of the depression, or a play, I should have to postpone this revelation; history and the theory of dramatic suspense worked together, and it was many months before America knew what had hit her. I sacrifice suspense in favor of emphasis on a single point: the discrepancy between fact and fiction had a profound effect on the minds and hearts of the American people; the way we took the depression, the means we chose to extricate ourselves, our attitude toward charity, our feelings about Russia, our alternating trust in and suspicions of our leaders, and a hundred more obscure and subtle shades of feeling all were determined by this one thing, *that we were not permitted for many months to confront the reality of our situation.* "The contemplation of things as they are," wrote Sir Francis Bacon in one of the noblest utterances of thinking man, "without substitution or imposture, without error or confusion, is in itself a nobler thing than a whole harvest of inventions." It is not only a supreme satisfaction to see things as they are; it is an essential thing for the health of a community.

The practical effort of industry and government in the days

[1] To lay an egg: to produce an elaborate and expensive and instant failure in the theater.

following the market crash was to keep things as they were; the psychological effort was to lull people to sleep (for sixty days) in the hope that by the time they awoke, the conditions of September, 1929, would have returned. Underlying both of these attempts was the assumption that nothing of importance had happened to the American system of life.

The reality was this:
The crash which came in 1929 was a natural outcome of the American system of industry, finance, politics, and social life;
It was not inevitable;
It was predictable, it was predicted, and slight efforts were belatedly made to head it off;
It required an immediate and summary change in the American way of living if its results were not to be disastrous.

These items are now familiar to all except those who cling obstinately to the classic explanations; had they been acknowledged before, say January, 1930, the progress of the depression would have been different. I do not say that we should have suffered less from want of food and lack of occupation; but emotionally we should have been healthier, standing firm in the contemplation of things as they are.

For purposes of comparison, here is the classic theory, expressed during the presidential campaign by ex-President Calvin Coolidge, in the *Saturday Evening Post* (of September 10, 1932):

"In the winter of 1928–1929 it was apparent that the country was engaged in too much speculation. I was alarmed at it and kept in contact with the Federal Reserve Board, which is an independent bipartisan body established under the last Democratic administration. I understood they were using their influence quietly, as was necessary, to check speculation, and for that reason they favored raising the interest rates, which had

STAGE | BROADWAY | SCREEN

VARIETY

PRICE 25¢

Published Weekly at 154 West 46th St., New York, N. Y., by Variety, Inc. Annual subscription, $10. Single copies, 25 cents.
Entered as second-class matter December 22, 1905, at the Post Office at New York, N. Y., under the act of March 3, 1879.

VOL. XCVII. No. 3   NEW YORK, WEDNESDAY, OCTOBER 30, 1929   88 PAGES

WALL ST. LAYS AN EGG

Going Dumb Is Deadly to Hostess In Her Serious Dance Hall Profesh

A hostess at Roseland has her problem. The paid steppers consider their work a definite profession calling for specialized technique and high-power saleswomanship.

"I've seen you gals sell your personality," said one. "Each one of us gals has our own clientele to cater to. It's just like selling dresses as a dame—you have to know what to sell each particular customer.

Some want to dance, some want to kid, some want to get sopsy, and others are just misunderstood husbands."

Upon applying for hostess jobs at Roseland must be 21 or older. They must work five nights a week. They earn strictly on their own, no salary going with the job and the house collecting 25 cents on every 25 cent ticket. To keep her job, a girl must turn in at least 150 tickets a week during the cold season and 200 in the summer months. In a dull week girls buy their own tickets to keep up the record.

It's a bother wishes to sit out a dance, he must pay for the privilege. "Buying-out time" sells at eight tickets an hour, or $2.00. It's usually a free sport who will come across with less than $2, many kicking in heavier for a little genial conversation.

The girl who knows her professional dancing trade will keep an eye out for potential "sitter down," overtime their hobbies and talk heart, line a whole string of tickets. In this way star no, only earns money easily, but saves wear and tear on her evening dresses and slippers.

But money rolls in if she has a good line. One of the most profligate gals at Roseland takes this part of her work so seriously that she reads up on current events (sports and stock market included) and has a smattering of current literature and art.

There are two types of hostesses at Roseland," she said, displaying high-brow leanings. "They are the mental and the 'physical.' Surprisingly enough the physical ones are not those who make the most money. One customer will buy tickets from them at the most. They rely on their sex appeal and go dawn between dances—and that's the surest way to lose a partner going dumb.

Mental Girls

"The mental girls, being good conversationalists, can wise-rack a

Hunk on Winchell

When the Walter Winchells moved into 204 West 55th street, late last week, June, that's Mrs. Winchell, selected a special room in Walter's exclusive sleep den for his late hour nights. She shunned the Winchell skidoo when her husband drew in at his usual eight o'clock the first morning.

At noon, Walter's midnight, his sound proof room was penetrated by so many high C's he awoke with but four hours of dreams and a grouch. Investigated at once, after having signed the lease, of course.

Right next door, on the same floor, is the studio of the noted vocal instructor, Kinney. Among his pupils are Ona Munson, Irene Delroy and Marjorie Peterson. They love Winchell like you love carbolic acid.

And Miss Munson is reported to have requested that an amplifier be started hereafter when she runs up the scale.

Demand for Vaude

Springfield, Ill., Oct. 29.
Petitions requesting Publix theatres to resume vaudeville in Decatur, Ill. are in circulation in that city.

Petitions specify that vaudeville at one or more of the three larger Publix houses, would furnish employment to a number of Decatur musicians and stage hands and provide larger variety of local entertainment.

Paul White, Publix manager in Decatur, states that he believes vaudeville will find a place to Decatur before the season is over.

Pickpocketing Dying Out

Chicago, Oct. 23.
Some 1,800 old pickpockets who used to make Chicago what it was are no more. A confidential list in the hands of government operatives now allows them to be operating in

DROP IN STOCKS ROPES SHOWMEN

Many Weep and Call Off Christmas Orders—Legit Shows Hit

MERGERS HALTED

The most dramatic event in the financial history of America is the collapse of the New York Stock Market. The stage was Wall Street, but the onlookers covered the country. Estimates are that 22,000,000 people were in the market at the time.

Tragedy, despair and ruination spell the story of countless thousands of marginal stock traders. Perhaps Manhattan was worst hit in the number of victims. Many may remain broke for the rest of their lives, because the money that disappeared via the ticker tape was the savings of years.

Many people of Broadway are known to have been wiped out. Reports of some in show business losing as much as $300,000 is not hearsay. One caustic comment is that was that the theatre is enough of a gamble without the people to venture into Wall street.

Prominent showmen, several identified with the picture industry

(Continued on page 84)

FILTHY SHOW OF SHUBERTS GOOD FOR SCREEN

Chicago, Oct. 29.
Shubert's latest musical of their "Night" series, now in Chicago, is so filthy that one of the cast admits embarrassment while in the performance.

The second act of this scramble is called "Broadway Nights," is the

(Continued on page 81)

Kidding Kissers in Talkers Burns Up Fans of Screen's Best Lovers

Talker Crashes Olympus

Paris, Oct. 29.
Fox "Follies" and the Fox Movietone newsreel are running this week in Athens, Greece, the first sound pictures heard in the birthplace of world culture, and in all Greece for that matter.

Several weeks ago, Variety's Cairo correspondent cabled that a cinema had been wired in Alexandria, Cleopatra's home town.

Only Sodom and Gomorrah remain to be heard from.

HOMELY WOMEN SCARCE; CAN'T EARN OVER $25

No homely ones on Broadway!
And now it looks as if Crosby Gaige may have to postpone production of "One Beautiful Evening" because the Main Stem is devoid of the non-beauts required for the casting of the show.

Arthur Lubin, caster for the producer, for several weeks has been trying to land the right type of women. A most unusual piece, the drama has an all-women lineup, and, although as many as 23 are needed, all must be homely—and middle age or over, except for two who can be young.

Vera Caspary wrote the play, and it centers about conditions at a club for girls where requirement of residence demand that the girls must not earn over $15 per week in order to live under its roof.

That's why they must be homely.

Ads for Execs

Chicago, Oct. 29.
Newspaper ad calling for potential executives for the Publix-B. & K. organization here, drew heavy response, with over 200 applicants. From all walks of life, with sev-

Boys who used to whistle and girls who used to giggle when love scenes were flashed on the screen are in action again. A couple of years ago they began to take the love stuff seriously and desired, but the talkers are reviving the ha ha for film osculators.

Heavy loving lovers of silent picture days accustomed to charming audiences into spasms of silent ecstasy when kissing the leading lady are getting the bird instead of the heartbeat. The sound accompaniment is making it tough.

Such a picture romancer as John Gilbert is getting laughs in place of the sighs of other days, and the flaps who still think he's grand are getting sore. One little flap had it up picked by an usher when making a commotion during a Gilbert picture at the Capitol, New York. The person sitting next to her, like many others in the house, tossed Gilbert's passion lightly. The girl jumped to his defense and started to bawl out the Gilbert derider.

Not only has Gilbert received the bird lately, but all of the other male screen players who specialize in romance. Charley Farrell in "Sunny Side Up" draws many a giggle from his mush stuff.

In the silents when a lover would whisper like a ventriloquist lips apart and unmoved, and roll his eyes passionately, preparatory to the clinch and their kiss, it looked pretty natural and was believable. The build-up to the kissing now makes a gag of the kiss.

When the kiss is within reaching point, the laughs are out of order. It's burning the impassioned female fans to see their favorite kissers kidded when a-kissing.

In Reverse

Burns the only type of love stuff received at intervals now advent of the talkers in the comedy love scene. The screen comics are becoming the heavy lovers and the heavy screen comedians.

The normal kiss, delivered with the usual smack, sounds like an explosion. For that reason clinch scenes in the early talkers had them ending in the ozone.

Toning down that kissing to make it noiseless has made busy kissers of the screen's best lovers, who, audible or silent, the kisses are getting laughs that don't belong.

to be done carefully to avoid injuring nonspeculative business. This action had some effect in the early spring,[2] but in the summer of 1929 a fresh wave of speculation started. At this same time the business world was shocked by the failure of a large concern in England, and general business in this country began to recede.[3] This brought on a heavy liquidation which resulted in a violent decline in the stock market in October and November.

"This shock was finally absorbed, and in the late winter of 1930 there were many indications of a business revival. About this time there came a world-wide crash in agricultural products. As the season advanced, a large part of the country found itself suffering from a lack of rainfall, which extended over a wide area reaching from the Atlantic seaboard to the Rocky Mountains. In the late fall of 1930 world agricultural prices were thrown into another violent decline by the dumping from Russia. In the spring of 1931 the economic condition of Austria and Germany broke down. Their governments and their banks were unable to meet their obligations. Because they were borrowers of considerable money from our banks, this resulted in something of a bank panic in the United States. People began drawing out their deposits until the estimated amount of hoarding reached $1,500,000,000. Meantime, the disaster in Germany caused other European countries to start withdrawing their foreign balances. The Bank of England had such large losses of gold that that country was forced off

[2] The raising of the rediscount rate, to which Mr. Coolidge alludes, actually took place on the 8th of August, 1929 — the first raise since July 13, 1928. "Early spring" seems to be a slip.

[3] In a special bulletin, made prominent by the signature of Charles E. Mitchell, then a director of the Federal Reserve Bank of New York, the National City Bank indicated that by April 18, 1929, "the existing credit situation is already having its effect upon business and threatens to undermine the natural and justifiable prosperity of the country to an increasing degree unless a corrective is promptly found."

the gold standard in the latter part of September. Heavy with-drawals were being made from the United States. Europe was filled with rumors that we could not maintain our gold stand-ard. Consequently credit became contracted and banks were failing by the hundreds. Because of the decrease in the volume of business, the revenues of the Government decreased, causing a large deficit, which brought further alarm both at home and abroad, and further liquidation. All these adverse circum-stances, through their effect on industry, commerce and agri-culture, resulted in a constant increase of the number of un-employed in this country. . . .

"It will be observed that all these causes of depression, with the exception of the early speculation, had their origin outside of the United States, where they were entirely beyond the con-trol of our Government. If the advantages and privileges of prosperity were abused by overspeculation, it was something in which the great body of the people were engaged, through one method or another, to such a degree that they did not heed the warning efforts of the Federal Reserve Board."

This is, to be sure, a campaign document, but it is worth seeing how the classic theory is turned into the classic defense:

"When men in public office have to meet a crisis which they did not in any way create, the measure of credit or blame which should attach to such officeholders is not the intensity of the crisis, nor the danger or damage that results from it, but the manner in which they meet it and the remedies which they apply to it."

The beneficiary of Mr. Coolidge's analysis was not hostile to these ideas. In June, 1931, Mr. Hoover committed himself to the principle that "the main causes of this depression came from outside the United States", and in August, 1932, he put forth the corollary that "after a year of world-wide depression we (the United States) came into the first quarter of 1931 with strong evidences of our recuperation. . . . The signs of resumption of industrial activity and employment gave us the right to hope that the country was righting itself. Then there came to us a concentration of catastrophes from abroad such as we have not experienced in the whole of our economic history . . . a host of new forces of destruction."

The search for a scapegoat, the witch hunt, is not only a terrifying element in all religions based on superstition; it occurs inevitably when disaster unsettles the minds of men. Wicked old Europe was not the only one chosen as villain for the melodrama which our leaders made out of the American tragedy; we shall come to others presently. But as this book is bound to be largely a record of illusions and phantasms, of disorderly imaginings and delusions, I prefer to deal for a few minutes with the reality which sane minds discovered, usually too late.

It suits the odd purposes of Mr. Lothrop Stoddard to exaggerate the guile of the Soviets, so that the emotional adjectives in the following may be discounted; the facts remain:

"One of the high lights of the Congress (of the Third International, held in Moscow in 1928) was a prediction that the capitalist world was on the verge of a prolonged economic depression. With almost uncanny accuracy, the Communist leaders, *noting the downward curve of commodity prices which had recently begun,* deduced therefrom the approach of a major economic crisis which would last several years, presumably reaching its maximum intensity by 1932 or 1933. By-products such as mass unemployment, currency and credit disturbances, and a general increase of unrest were likewise foretold. . . ."

I have italicized the significant fact.

There must have been a fact, although I cannot name it,

which suggested to foreigners, and particularly to the French, to sell United States Government securities just before our market broke. It may have been the fact that the prime industry of the United States, the motor car, had passed its peak of production in April, and that production of new Fords alone kept up the statistical level, all the other manufacturers together showing a loss of ninety thousand cars in August, 1929, as compared with August a year before. Perhaps the logical French turned from motors, which may still be regarded as partly a luxury, to such a fundamental necessity as building and discovered that only three quarters as many structures were rising in August, 1929, as had risen in August, 1928. Perhaps they had listened to Roger Babson, whose prediction of a break lost impact because of his chronic pessimism about the market, but who was partially justified by a decline in August; perhaps the French, having an ocean between themselves and us, had noticed that after a hesitant warning issued in February, the Federal Reserve Board had finally put a check on speculation [4] on the eighth of August and that the great "blue chip" stocks had dropped ten and fifteen points in a fury of selling the next day; perhaps the French remembered that this was the second break in four months in a market which Americans believed rising without interruption and destined so to rise for ever. Perhaps they were merely as cautious as Mr. Coolidge who, in private life, was not so belated in action as he had been in office. As President, responsible for the well-being of the entire country, he was, according to his own confession three years later, "alarmed" and "kept in contact", but at the same time he let it be known that the vast loans made to brokers and dealers by the Federal Reserve Bank seemed to him a "natural expansion of business in the securities market, and [he] sees nothing unfavorable in it." Later, as a private

[4] By raising its rediscount rate — a mysterious but effective method.

citizen, however, he acted: he sold his shares, a small number, of United States Steel before the break came.

I am listing here those signs and portents which might have given a wise man pause. The signs pointing the other way were, no doubt, reassuring enough. Steel, the great barometer, was booming; the market, in its May and August breaks, had only recoiled to leap farther; railroads, at least some of them, were earning more money, although their gross was less; who would bother about the gross (which implied things about the general state of industry) when the net was so good? We were in the midst of a boom and the direction of a boom is upward.

Examine, then, the boom itself. Mr. Stuart Chase, writing before the panic, with little revision to make after it, is "convinced that prosperity is a fact of commanding proportions", yet has to make reservations:

Prosperity is limited to the Middle Atlantic, East North Central, and Pacific States; the rest, says the National Bureau of Economics, have not prospered.

Even in the prosperous States, the farmers fail.

"The small business man, the independent storekeeper, the wholesaler, many professional men and women, have failed to keep income on a par with the new standards of living."

Unemployment exists; in the decade 1920–1930 more than half a million men and women have been added to the list through "technological unemployment."

Coal, textiles, leather, boots and shoes, shipbuilding have not shared in prosperity.

The railroad equipment industry has been failing — an ominous sign, since it points to the future.

And finally we have excessive bankruptcies on one side and "millions of unskilled workers . . . teetering on the edge of a bare subsistence. . . ."

The moral argument is that no nation can be called prosperous which leaves two million men [5] out of work (most of them willing to work), condemns to comparative failure one quarter of its entire population (those living on farms), and gives to nine out of ten families an average annual income which barely covers the cost of living ($2,200 per family against an estimated minimum of $1,920) and to its workers an average wage ($1,384) considerably below the requirements of decency. The moral argument can go further and inquire whether such a society is fulfilling its function; the moral argument can go anywhere. For my purpose the economic argument is more than enough; it uses the same figures, but for a different purpose. The two million unemployed, the thirty million complaining people on the farms, the ninety per cent. with only the meanest margin over the bare necessities of living, were all flaws in an economic demonstration which was something new and strange in the world.

I can put this new formula into simple, no doubt inexact terms, without the use of statistics or the professional language of the sociologist. It is this: thirty years ago the yacht of the millionaire represented the hunger and misery of ten thousand men, women, and children; he *had* because they lacked; he enjoyed because they suffered. Five years ago the yacht of the multimillionaire, a far more resplendent and luxurious and wasteful craft — represented the putt-putts and Fords and radios and electric refrigerators of ten thousand families. He had *because they had;* he was rich only because they were prosperous; he luxuriated because they lived, a little beyond their means, in comfort, on the installment plan. I do not know whether either the rich or the poor ever expressed this difference to themselves in words; but they lived

---

[5] All figures for unemployment, before and after the crash, are inaccurate — as if we hated the thought so much that we would not bother to get statistics. I have used those which seem most nearly correct and, sometimes, those generally accepted.

with this difference in mind, the subtle proof being that in the
two decades between 1910 and 1930 the rich man had ceased
to be a bad man; the cruel tyrant of commerce had passed
not only from the stage and the novel, but from the public
mind. In his place stood the benevolent friend of labor who,
in the 1920's dedicated himself to Service. The little Fords and
Chevrolets ran alongside the Lincolns and the Packards on
broad, four-lane highways, and the man in the Ford did not
think that the Lincoln represented excess profit; he knew that
the man in the Lincoln had made the Fords possible.

The conflict between the rich man and the poor man has
always been confused in America because of the comparatively
rapid shifting from one class into another and because of the
real, or imagined, freedom of opportunity. In the past ten
years this new thing was added, that the poor man, becoming
a little easier in money and much easier in credit, no longer
accused the rich man of "grinding the faces of the poor" or
living by the sweat of their faces. The rich man, especially if
he remained in business, was also aware of a changed relationship. He knew his riches depended upon the goodwill of a
public far more numerous and infinitely more capable of spending money than it had ever been. The development and advertisement of business ethics, the work of the Rotarians, the
emergence of the public relations counsel to a position of
actual influence, the chatter about Service, and even the
election of a business man to be President of the United States
are all phenomena of this era, all indicating a new urgency in
the mind of the industrialist to create a pleasant image of
himself in the public mind.

For the first time, the masses in America were important
not as laborers, but as customers, and their importance could
not be exaggerated. No capitalist, inspired by noble ideals of
the brotherhood of man, had ever proclaimed that the laborer
is always right; but that the customer is always right became

a commonplace in American business and it carried not a grain
of hypocrisy. The customer was right because the whole structure of industry rested upon him. The problem of labor grew
dim and vague: the American Federation of Labor became
a conventional supporter of government and industry, hardly
distinguishable in policy from the Chambers of Commerce
and the associations of manufacturers; the Industrial Workers
of the World broke down; the threat from Russia was dissipated; on the surface, the economic problem seemed to have
been solved for the first time in human history, and seemed
so not only to us, but to others — Germany, says Professor
Bonn, believed that in America "by the agency of a reasoning
intelligence, had been achieved the miracle of a permanent prosperity which no crisis could destroy." The miracle was the
creation of the human being as a buyer, a consumer, one who
ate up all the porridge in the world and cried for more.

It was not "reasoning intelligence" that worked this temporary miracle, it was the end of a great romance: the winning
of the West, the magnificent physical adventure of America
which lasted a hundred years. The capital fact of American
history is that the land rush ended in the 1890's, the supply
of good free acreage was exhausted, the Homestead Act became
an anachronism and its importance dwindled, making way
for the Sherman Act, the McKinley Tariff, the Income Tax
amendment, the whole body of laws regulating commerce and
industry and, incidentally, giving to commerce and industry
an unexampled liberty of motion. The disappearance of the
frontier and of free lands beyond it is so fundamental that it
is hardly mentioned in the textbooks on American history;
it has changed our literature, our habits of life, and our speech;
it is probably one of the reasons why we went to war with
Spain and could be brought into the Great War, since our
faces had turned from the West; and it can be listed among

the causes of the depression because we were not aware of what had occurred and tried too long to live as if nothing had changed. We tried to live as if we were still an expanding country, in which freedom and mobility are the most desirable things; but we were not expanding as we had for a century. The pioneer, after he has cleared his land, uses a plough; in industry, we kept on using dynamite, and were blown up.

The machinery for large-scale production [6] came to perfection shortly after the conquest of the frontier was complete. This meant that the machine could produce more skillfully and in greater volume than the laborer, and this, in turn, meant that the worker was thrown out of his job precisely at the time when there was no more free land upon which he could settle. From the long seduction of the frontier to the grim hardship of daily life with the machine, the American was compelled to turn. His resentment, the difficulties of new adjustments, brought about psychological effects ranging from delusions of grandeur to childish tantrums and these, in turn, formed the emotions and the nerves with which we were supplied when we had to confront the current depression.

If I skip over world events, a paragraph to each, it is because the emotional effects can be seen all the better if the details are omitted. The effect of shock, for instance, is greater in America because America is neither sceptical nor cautious. "The American people," said ex-Governor Smith, "never carry an umbrella. They prepare to walk in eternal sunshine." For a hundred years sunshine lay over the Western plains; after, it was obscured in factory smoke. But for thirty years in a new century we lived as buoyantly and as optimistically as ever, because we had discovered a new frontier within the old: the

[6] The method was nearly as old as our government; Eli Whitney offered to supply guns *with interchangeable parts* to the nation before 1800.

frontier of buying power. When the need for railroad track came to an end, we turned to motor cars and *created a demand* for them; if coal could no longer make us rich, we *created demands* for oil and gasoline; if cotton was no longer king, we *created a demand* for silk; if wheat rotted, we *created a demand* for candies, cigarettes, and laxatives; if there were too many theaters, we *created a demand* for radios. We invented new things to make and to sell and invented new ways of selling them; virtually we created a new nation of buyers. The economists call this the gradual swing from producers' industries (steel, building materials, textiles, machinery, railway equipment) to consumers' industries (luxuries, radios, motor cars, silk, etc.). In our human terms it is a change from natural *needs* to created *demands*. A difference that shines even from the printed page is that these new products were made to be bought either in quantities or repeatedly, and in either case, were *made to be thrown away*.

Only twenty years after Woodrow Wilson stigmatized the automobile as the most provoking single cause of social discontent in America, the "ideal" of two cars in every garage was seeping down from the manufacturers to the consumer; it was a necessity; one owed it to America to possess two cars, not merely as a convenience (they were rapidly ceasing to be anything more than an occasional pleasure, owing to congestion of city streets and highways), but as a symbol of success. Yet two cars in every garage was not the end; the end was at least one car junked a year, its carcass thrown beside the road until a great new industry of destroying motor cars came into being to keep pace with the industry of manufacturing them. Radio, second of the two ladder industries upon which America mounted to prosperity, was also a junking industry, and this year's model was as important in the home as on the road. (Two radios in every house was just beginning to suggest itself when the market broke.)

In the mind of the industrialists there were two problems: how to make the customer buy and how to make it possible for him to buy. The first is a purely human problem, the second economic; both were solved in spectacular ways.

"Our chief job in research is to keep the customer reasonably dissatisfied with what he has," said Charles Franklin Kettering, president of General Motors Research Corporation, before the crash, and in the midst of the depression he embroidered the theme: "When we continue to produce the same things, the same model indefinitely . . . the people don't want to buy it. . . ."

The first statement, completely realistic, trimmed of all the grandeur of Science and Service, is refreshing. Dissatisfaction was to be moderate; that is, it must not extend to the whole genus of motor cars; not even to the species Chevrolet; but to the sub-species under examination: last year's model. The inculcation of a reasonable dissatisfaction led to improvement in engine and in braking; to refinement in comfort and to greater delicacy of body lines; to better springs, self-starters, balloon tires; it led also to freak inventions and to an infinity of gadgets. The principle remained good. Taken with the solution of the second problem (how to make purchasing power available) it meant: The car which you will barely have paid for at the end of a year will be just the car for you to trade in (or throw away) when the year is over.

This brings us to the foothills of the vast mountain range called high-pressure salesmanship. The methods are so well known that we may as well take a deep breath and decide not to go over the ground again, choosing a detour in which the first step may be called the Path of the Satirists. The ten triumphant years of American business were also the ten years of American satire, from "Main Street" and "Babbitt" to "Beggar on Horseback", from Mencken to *Ballyhoo*. About this satire the best thing that can be said is that the victims took it in better part than the satirists themselves: the men and women abused in "Main Street" because they could appreciate nothing finer than their own dull lives, were the very men and women who made "Main Street" a best-seller; the Rotarians called each other Babbitt in jest; the slaves and masters of Big Business enjoyed the satire on big business; advertisers rejoiced in the harsh burlesque of advertising in *Ballyhoo*. The implication is that business "could take it"; something either powerful or good enough to withstand the impact of the angry satirists gave business the power to resist and even to persist in such stupidities as obviously false and paid-for endorsements long after they had been exposed. Not finding it possible to believe entirely in the intelligence of business men, I have to assume that the satirists' thrusts came up against something peculiarly solid and sound; and the analyses of business after the crash prove that this is right. For the two things upon which the critics concentrated their heaviest attack — Service and "being in conference" — are variations of the two things chosen by analysts of business technique as the great contributions of the last decade and the great hope of the future of business if it is to survive at all. That both were riddled with bunk is as certain as that human beings are greedy little hypocrites. But the idea of Service is the first intimation, in the general run of American affairs, that industry may exist for something beside profit; and the idea of going into conference is a definite recognition of the end of the one-man tyranny in business, pointing to the technologists' ideal of management divorced from ownership. These two things — diminishing the profit motive and enlarging the field of the technologist — are always set down, in that order, as the fundamentals of good business in the future; without them, the experts agree, business can hardly expect to have a future at all. The satirists were right enough to expose the extravagances of both; but I doubt whether they ever imagined that realities of the first importance lay behind them.

The second stage of the detour around the art of selling has to do with junking. A few years ago Mr. Stuart Chase wrote a book called "The Tragedy of Waste", a few chapters of which were printed in the *New Republic*. I recall my surprise when the late Herbert Croly, the editor of the magazine, said in a casual conversation that he wished Chase had chosen a less melodramatic title and went on to a speculation which most people would consider treachery in one of the *New Republic's* editors. Briefly, he wondered whether it was right to apply the moral term, tragedy, to the economic phenomenon of waste; he wondered whether being wasteful might not be a fairly good thing, a natural and defensible way of living. Then he shrugged his shoulders and went to lunch, to discuss the morals of other economic problems.

In writing a play you allow yourself none of the doubts an editor may enjoy. "The Apple Cart", by Bernard Shaw, had for villain an imaginary institution, Breakages, Ltd., which was virtually the ruler of England. Breakages, Ltd., had the monopoly of junk and it was the duty of manufacturers to make cars and shoes and fountain pens and tables and pianos which must rapidly fall to pieces; the whole purpose of industry was to create ultimate rubbish; to make a safe or a book which resisted destruction was a crime against the social order. The human body may be conceived as a machine which creates poisons, many of which are thrown off; and the industrial body may be conceived as a machine for making rubbish, part of which serves a useful or agreeable purpose in its progress toward the junk heap. It sounds wasteful, uneconomic, immoral; but if prosperity depends on the manufacture of nine million motor cars a year and only six million can be sold, three million must be made to be junked. Mr. Edmund Wilson's description of the physical process adds a new small circle to Dante's Hell:

"The old automobiles sent in on little cars are like disemboweled horses at the bull ring whose legs are buckling under them. A fiend in blue glasses on a high throne on an enormous blue chariot or float causes it to move horizontally back and forth before the white-glowing mouths of the furnaces, feeding them the flattened cars like so many metallic soft-shell crabs — ramming each one in with a sudden charge, dropping it quickly with a twist. There are not many mouths big enough yet to accommodate a whole car at one gape, and pending the completion of ten hundred-ton furnaces specially designed for the consumption of old cars — fifty thousand of which have been melted up since the April before last — they are being chopped up for the small-mouthed furnaces by a thousand-ton electric shear, which reduces chassis, springs, wheels, fenders and all to a junk fodder of iron spines and bent tin shells, like horseshoe crabs cut up for pigs. When you put on blue glasses and gaze through the blinding golden hole in the furnace door, where the old cars are being digested with such condiments as limestone and pig iron, you see only a boiling livid lake vibrating with pale and thickish bubbles.

"Twice a day the old liquefied cars are poured out through the backside of the furnace into receptacles like huge iron buckets, below where the charging floor drops sheer — a thunderous hissing, a hot stink, the voiding of a molten feces of gold burned beyond gold to a white ethereal yellow, a supreme incandescence, while an explosive spray of snow-crystal sparks bursts like tiny rockets on the air. In the arena below the gallery, during the pouring no human beings go. Giant cranes advance along the ceiling and picking up the vats of golden soup with hooks, lift them across the great empty barn and tip them up into other vats, when the liquid runs down through holes in the bottom into cylindrical ingot molds. Eleven hundred tons of steel a day."

It is not true that goods sold under high pressure were necessarily inferior to goods sold without lies, subterfuge, and lyric advertisements. Even the motors made to be junked were good motors and could and did run more than a year; many of them crept back, from God knows where, to the highroads in 1932, looking unbelievably ugly, but keeping pace with the new models. Yet the connection between pressure and junking was close. If the advertisers spent a billion and a half dollars a year they had to trust to the beneficent god, Obsolescence, to bring them returns. Mr. Howard Scott's Technocracy group has discovered that to-day a motor car could be manufactured which would last a lifetime; and that if such a car were made, the motor industry of the United States would run at full capacity for five years and then be compelled to shut down for sixty. If ten million dollars were spent to advertise Lucky Strikes in a year, the return could not come entirely from smokers seduced away from Camels and Old Golds, which were advertising about as much; the social advantages of smoking for women had to be suggested; another ten million for razor blades, with no fresh source to tap, contented itself with advising that blades be used up twice as fast, with two shaves a day. To throw a thing away after it was once used became a habit, with napkins, towels, handkerchiefs,[7] drinking cups, plates, beverage bottles; to change shirt, stockings, garters, shoes, more and more often became a social necessity.

Gradually "selling points" took the place of quality; it was inevitable, since a plate which is used once is naturally made of cheap material and not of rare china, and a car which is expected to be turned in for a fifth of its value at the end of

[7] Glass, fine linen, plate — the very symbols of respectable riches, the treasured heirlooms of the past.

a year must exhaust four fifths of its value in that time: its looks, its novelty, its prestige. If a moralist were to say that the process is wasteful, an industrialist might answer that to put a ten-year engine into a one-year car is waste on a much greater scale; and if he were an immoral industrialist, he might add that even in a motor car beauty should be its own excuse for being. He could truthfully say that the turned-in car offered the only method of supplying any kind of car at all to those too poor to buy new ones, and that the system *worked*. That is, until the end of 1929.

In the middle of 1932 the National Quality Maintenance League was aware of all the arguments on both sides and prepared an educational campaign "to boost values, to calm down advertising writers." It carried on an attack on "high styling" in textiles, shoes, hosiery, handbags, underwear, and the like, on the ground that until styling, with its extremely rapid changes, is held down to reasonable limits, women will not buy for permanence and quality. That quality and style, value and advertising, can be at odds is an idea not heretofore admitted into American business.

If the advertisers are to be calmed down, they will forsake their two gods: the promise and the threat. Both of them are based on the soundest principle in advertising: the principle of association, by which a cup of coffee is shown on the salver of a distinguished butler and a stiff collar always around the strong neck of at least a minor executive, while the improperly washed or gargled, and those lacking correct hose supporters, languish in gloom, watching others dancing with carbolized bodies, disinfected throats, and neat stockings. Social and commercial satisfactions took the place of personal ones; that you could use the same cold cream as a good duchess or a moderately good queen was a better argument than that the cream itself was good for you. The implied promise of rising in the social scale (for women) or in the business world (for men) became a brutal threat when the negative was marked: ostracism and, what is worse, bankruptcy met those who failed in their duty by the advertisers. Even economy had to be made smart and in thirty years Macy's changed from "the attractions of our stores are their low prices" to "it's smart to be thrifty." The instinct for bargains persisted through boom times, but the warnings against mere bargains were constant and were coupled, again, with threats: your life was in danger with cheap or old-fashioned brakes, without chains, without fire-proofing; the lives of your dear ones were embittered without certain forms of insurance; you were in danger of poisoning if you lacked the right kind of refrigeration; your clothes would be torn by cheaper, but inferior, washing machines; it was understood that no good would come from the milk of a discontented cow.

The methods of selling varied. Brushes and silk stockings you might not be able to get unless you telephoned to, or could not resist the blandishments of, "personal salesmen." Motor cars, of certain makes, were thrust upon you by managers who would lose their agencies if they did not sell a certain quota. By buying one package of Camels, you were eligible to try for a prize of $25,000; by supplying a missing line from a limerick, heard on the radio, you could win somewhat lesser advantages. The importance of selling was never more conspicuously proved than in the years 1920 to 1930, when the whole business of broadcasting became an adjunct to the business of creating customers — largely through an error made by Mr. Hoover, as Secretary of Commerce. Averse to publicity himself, and superficially unaffected by it, Mr. Hoover maintained that no legislation was necessary, as the American people would never stand for advertising on the air. Mr. Hoover is, in fact, one of the few notable Americans who remains sceptical of advertising. In an address to the very gods of the art, the Association of National Advertisers, in 1930, he said, "Advertising . . . is the vocal organ by which industry sings its songs of beguilement. . . . You have stirred the lethargy of the old law of supply and demand. . . . Your latest contribution to constructive joy is to make possible the hourly spread of music, entertainment, and political assertion. . . . The public has come to include you in the things we bear in life." Irony is rare in Mr. Hoover's utterance and it is interesting that he should have chosen advertising as one of his few victims.

CHAPTER THREE

The Panic before the Crash

Threatened, seduced, and inspired to buy, the American people in twelve years spent nearly seventeen billion dollars more than they earned;[1] allowing for errors in calculation and such concealed earnings as come from odd jobs, bonuses and bribes, racketeering, and trade-in allowances, ten billion dollars still remains as excess of expenditure over income. This is the conclusion of a survey made by the *Business Week,* guided by Doctor Virgil Jordan. It suggests that the American people were going into debt and with that suggestion I will not quarrel. I will only place beside it another figure of indebtedness which being some fifteen times greater may be a little more impressive. That is the debt into which the United States as an industrial concern had fallen, our total amortizable debt; the figure is two hundred and eighteen billion dollars. This is the sum arrived at by Mr. Howard Scott in his "Energy Survey of America"; Mr. Scott adds that interest, amortization and taxes will this year take about three fourths of the national income. A great part of this debt is, no doubt, in the form of bonds, so that we may prefer to say that industry has divided its ownership and pays profits to millions of people. Yet the fact is there: the debt against American industry as a whole,

[1] So phrased for purposes of shock only; the figure includes savings and taxes as well as what we usually call spending; but the gap between income and expenditure is so great that even these qualifications do not make it any easier to understand. Doctor Jordan says that when we leave the facts "and attempt to explain this paradox we frankly enter the field of fantasy and speculation."

the amount of cash it would have to pay in order to owe nothing, is over two hundred billion dollars and that sum is, by present standards, greater than the value of all the industry in the United States put together.[2] Individually Americans have cheerfully gone into debt; towering over the sum of these debts is the debt of the corporate industry upon which the country depends for its prosperity. (We are not alone in this predicament; it has been estimated that the total debt of Great Britain also has outstripped its total national wealth.)

Surveying the pre-panic years, Charles E. Persons concludes that "producers have been selling a volume of goods equal in value to the total national income *plus 5% or 10% of new debt* created." Mr. Lawrence Dennis says, "we financed by the creation of some seventy-two billion dollars of interest-bearing debt . . . a perfectly splendid internal credit boom"; yet Mr. Dennis does not hold that we lived beyond our income — we have lived only beyond the earned income, not the potential income of the people, and he concludes that we must find a way to earn all we can produce. But no analyst of the situation doubts the figures: we went enthusiastically into debt and are now head over ears in debt; we are suffering because the way in which we got into debt no longer works; if we could still borrow, we could still be prosperous. In other words, our credit is gone.

Most of us who have timidly accosted a second vice president in a bank and murmured, shamefaced, the names of the few shares of stock we still held, and talked about our salaries, and mentioned our life insurance, know perfectly well that our credit is gone, but we aren't aware of the blessing it has left behind. We cannot go into debt; at least, not on the scale to which we had become accustomed. It seems cruel that just as our incomes diminish, we should be compelled to live within them, but that is, apparently, the price we pay for a little

[2] Changed for the better toward the end of 1932.

extravagance before. Yet if the banks are hard-hearted
prefer to stay liquid, one thing remains (above the level o
pawnshop and the Morris Plan): installment buying, so
wardly and accurately called "the hire-purchase system" in
England. On the merits of the installment plan, the economists
are divided, but all other human beings who have wanted anything, from a stamp album to a yacht, before they had the
money to pay for it, are united. And they have conquered.
By buying through acceptance corporations and the like, they
have paid perhaps ten per cent. more than a cash price (and
lost the four per cent. their money might have earned in
savings banks if they had waited); but they have had their
pianos and refrigerators and vacuum cleaners and washing
machines; and a foreigner, a good economist, assures us that
"of all the achievements of 'permanent prosperity', hire-
purchase stood the crisis by far the best." [3] Because it seems
likely to continue, one or two of its significant features may be
mentioned.

One point is that the price of the installment-plan commodity had to be brought down to a low level; and that means
that the extras (for insurance and credit) may have been, or
could have been, wiped out by the lower cost of production.
Another is that the money which went into installment buying was taken either from savings or from other forms of
buying and most observers assume that people kept on saving
after they started to pay installments. And, finally, installment
buying was the most prodigious single step in creating the
new buying public, the public that bought a thing not to use
it, but to use it up.

In the first place, it appealed to the growing class which
has no tradition of ownership or permanence. The Negroes who
had drifted northward and into industry since 1914 were only
part of the new buying population which included all those

[3] M. J. Bonn: "The Crisis of Capitalism in America."

who had begun to be at all easy in their lives with the uprush of employment and wages. They rented apartments, flats, or small houses and lived in them a year or two and as soon as they had exhausted these habitations, moved on; for them it was natural to rent anything from a house to a ten-piece suite of furniture or an electric toaster, although in the latter instances they called the system installment buying. Actually they rented for a year or so, and if the toaster was still good at the end of that time, ownership represented their idea of velvet. On the other hand, for those with a strong instinct of possession, the installment plan cut away the misery of rent, because they could fix their eyes on the moment when the last installment was paid — the very moment when others were preparing to turn in the old car, sewing machine or radio as advance payment on a new one. It is a nice problem in psychology to judge between the two attitudes toward installments, the emphasis on the early period of payment and the emphasis on the latter period of free ownership. It is only my guess that to a majority of buyers, installment payments tended to become a form of rent. A cheerful friend of mine who had followed the usual custom of buying a second-hand car on installments and turning it in for a new car, also on installments, said to me, "We're going to do this every year for the rest of our lives."

The substitution of the word "credit" for the word "debt" [4] and the universal habit of living on next month's salary created the proper atmosphere for installment buying;

installment buying added to high-pressure salesmanship created the demand for goods;

new methods of manufacture created the goods;

new methods of financing enabled industry to pay enormous total sums in wages;

[4] Credit is the same thing as debt, says Professor F. Cyril James. Thomas Paine's definition was "Credit is suspicion asleep."

wages added to credit bought goods and rolled up profit for the manufacturers;

profit, snowballing up, had to be invested and was turned into more and more productive channels and, with the prospect of an infinite number of customers, led to more and more credit.

At this point the structure collapses.

The Malthusian theory supposes that food increases by simple multiplication while population increases by squares. At a given time there are, let us say, two hundred human beings and two hundred bushels of wheat, which is all they need; a generation or two later there will be four hundred people and four hundred bushels of wheat; again enough; but the third time there will be sixteen hundred people and only eight hundred bushels and thereafter the disparity becomes ever greater. Something like this seems to have occurred in the race between customers and production; every new factory created customers by paying out wages, but it also created new factories out of profits and credit, and these new factories created things to sell faster than they created wages. In J. A. Hobson's terms, the paradox of plenty — starvation with full granaries — is due to excessive saving, that is, to putting too much money into production. Mr. Stuart Chase similarly holds that the spendthrift millionaire, bugaboo of social reformers two generations ago, is not nearly so menacing a character as the millionaire who reinvests interest, income, and profits in further productive activity. Mr. Lawrence Dennis and Professor James both suggest that in order to keep production going, we have to pay out enough in total wages to equal the price of total products. There are dozens of ways of phrasing the problem. One of the simplest is to say that we went into debt in order to build factories which would sell more or less perishable things to people who would go into debt to buy them; when we had built too many factories and people had gone into debt as far as they dared, we could no longer sell what we made; and therefore could no longer borrow money with which to finance new factories and new payrolls; so, with vast stocks of raw materials and finished goods on hand, we collapsed.

It must be clear that the financial crash in October of 1929 was not an event totally independent of all these circumstances, as if it were an eclipse of the sun, with which the people on the earth had nothing to do. The early theory, that the Wall Street crash came because of speculation (in which we were all engaged) and that industry was carried down in the debacle, was cherished by bankers who had turned into merchants of securities; it was easy to believe because a vast, complicated machinery of credit existed about which most people knew nothing. But the operations of ten thousand shoe clerks and messenger boys, buying their tens and fifties of Goldman Sachs or Continental Can, putting them away and trying hard to pretend they were forgetting them, or selling at a two-point rise — these were not enough to break down the whole industrial system. The system broke down because it was not checked, because it carried with it the seeds of destruction. Wall Street was a phenomenon of Pittsburgh, Grand Rapids, New York, High Point, Detroit, Des Moines — of every city in which a factory expanded before it had a market. The situation was made infinitely worse when the business of selling securities took on the character of industry, when the happiest ambition of a college man's days was to become a prominent bond salesman, and when banks gave up the function of caring for money and credit, and, establishing subsidiaries, brought pressure salesmanship to the highest point by forcing everything from bonds to the most speculative of stocks into the hands of their patrons.

The complexities of brokers' loans and the call market, the whole system by which stock-market financing was accomplished, is far too technical for me to explain. I want only to connect the boom in stocks with the boom in industry — an object which would be superfluous if the connection were not so earnestly denied. Even at first glance a connection is seen, for some of the most spectacular stocks were in the very industries which profited most by the creation of the new consumers, such as radio and certain motors. Again, these stocks were bought not for use, but to be used up — that is, traded in for better stocks at the most favorable opportunity. They were seldom bought outright, but were rented — a first installment being paid down in the hope of selling before another would be required. And they were bought on credit. Mr. Dennis notes that "the players on the stock market were paying interest on six to eight billion dollars of security loans." And Doctor Jordan, reviewing the panic a few months after it began, wrote, "Many business concerns became investment trusts and banking institutions. They borrowed money from individuals who borrowed it from banks; they loaned it in the call market to enable people to buy their own and others' securities; they traded in securities themselves. They made larger profits, not so much by producing and distributing goods as by producing and distributing more securities and by borrowing and lending more money." In all fairness it should be said that the banks were not behindhand and made themselves adjuncts of the Stock Market as whole-heartedly as possible.

It is interesting to note that Doctor Jordan, a year later, summarized the depression (not the Wall Street crash) with only casual reference to the market. The summary, in technical terms, holds that the disaster "was caused fundamentally by uncontrolled financial influences, operating through our investment machinery, security markets, and banking system, which resulted successively in (*a*) a vast over-expansion of construction and plant capacity based on excessive corporate savings and security flotations supported by uncontrolled expansion of bank credit; (*b*) a temporary and abnormal stimulation of consumer purchasing power and export trade, and increased corporate and speculative profits; (*c*) excessive accumulation and reinvestment of corporate surplus in plant extension or speculation; (*d*) subsequent sharp contraction of consumer purchasing power, decline of prices and profits, deflation of capital values, increase of debt burdens, liquidation of credit, debt defaults and numerous moratoria."

In "The Future of Business Cycles", Carl Snyder, statistician of the Federal Reserve Bank of New York, writes in the same general vein:

"It is the fashion of the superficial to ascribe this decline in business to the tremendous crash in the stock market. As a matter of fact, a tendency to decline had shown itself some time before the panic. . . . There are reasons for believing that the declining course of trade would have been much the same . . . had there been no stock-market panic. It is, indeed, difficult to believe that stock-market gambling, even on such a colossal scale as last year, could so dominate the vast business of a nation of 120 millions, whose production and trade is now equal to nearly half the total for the commercial world. The forces that determine the ups and downs of this incredible volume of trade lie deeper."

Since I am sceptical of the theory that "everybody was in the market", I shall omit any picturesque description of the great days in the Street. It is, of course, perfectly true that a country taught to respect securities through the operations of the Liberty Loan campaigners, and supplied with much money, swept into the market and that the number of speculators multiplied many times. Of all the details, however, I must choose only the most significant. The great powers of America blessed the market, to wit: industry, advertising, the President, the Church, and the bootleggers. For example:

Mr. John J. Raskob, interviewed by Samuel Crowther, under the title "Everybody Ought to Be Rich" (*Ladies Home Journal*, August, 1929) said, "The way to wealth is to get into the profit end of wealth production in this country" and made it clear that the profit end, as he called it, was to be found in "good common stocks" which will give a man eighty thousand dollars in twenty years if he saves fifteen dollars a month. Rising above the level of the salesman and becoming a statesman, Mr. Raskob blamed inequalities in the distribution of wealth to the "lack of systematic investment and also the lack of even moderately sensible investment" on the part of the men who can save fifteen dollars a month.

The accolade from advertising was impressive, for advertising writers weigh the value of every word and will use no symbol which is not notably effective in universal magic. Four days before the crash the makers of Chesterfield cigarettes varied one of their slogans to read, "What a whale of a difference a few points make."

The blessings of the presidency came, as we have noted, when Mr. Coolidge saw no reason to worry over brokers' loans; those of Mr. Hoover were not so explicit. In silence, he assented.

For the Church, James Cannon, Jr., Bishop in the Methodist Episcopal Church of the South; to be sure, his approval was not without bias, as he had been in the market himself. Nevertheless, the Fundamentalist Bishop said: "Gambling in the Stock Market is not different from gambling in other business transactions. The purchase and quick resale of shares is not any more gambling than the purchase and quick resale of lots. . . . The amount of margin upon which a man trades does not determine the gambling element. A man can buy stock for a small cash payment . . . and there is no reason to call him a gambler because he sells the stock shortly after at a profit." The Bishop added that he had never "loved money for its own sake" but cared for it as an instrument of service.

From the racketeers came the highest tribute; they bombed Chicago brokers who had demanded more margin. The act brought stock speculation into the select company of the best American industries.

I have used the word "panic" in the accepted sense for the event of October, 1929, but I consider it misleading. There was a panic in America, running from 1926 and becoming a rout in the six months *before* the market break, which was an inconsiderable item in the whole. Using again the most shocking terms, I put it that *the boom was our panic,* and am willing to defend that position.

I call it panic to be afraid to sell at a profit, lest an additional profit be lost. I have met, in the past three years, perhaps half a dozen men and women who did sell in time, and most of them have been frank enough to confess their reluctance; they knew financiers of the first order and resisted pressure to sell which these few wise ones put upon them. They spent weeks or months following the upward swing of stocks they no longer owned, regretfully scribbling figures on scratch pads, estimating what they had lost by selling at a hundred points more than they had paid. These rare fortunate ones mark the panic of the others. It was panic, not greed. Some of them had risen from a salary of ten thousand a year to profits of a hundred thousand, to assured incomes as great as they ever expected earnings to be. But the panic which keeps people at roulette tables, the insidious propaganda against quitting a winner, the fear of being taunted by those who held on, all worked together. It became not only a point of pride, but a civic duty, not to sell, as if there were ever a buyer without a seller. "Put it away and forget about it" was supposed to add the dignity of investment to pure speculation; few put it away and none forgot about it. In the end, it did not matter, as the crash was no respecter of good intentions. The investors went down with the gamblers.

America in 1928, and the first months of 1929, was a mob, a little maddened by the sight of sudden wealth, its hysteria concealed because it was making money, which is the normal thing to do in America. The responsible leaders, the statesmen and the financiers and industrialists, were paralyzed, precisely as the British Government was paralyzed in July and August of 1914. The situations are almost parallels. In each case, a disaster threatened; in each case, authority refused to check the force of events lest the very movement of checking should bring on catastrophe. The memoirs of Grey of Fallodon match the apologies made for Coolidge and Hoover. There was the chance that if Britain announced its adhesion to France, Germany might not have gone to war; yet if the announcement were made, Britain would have to go to war, should Germany persist. There was a chance that if the warnings of the Federal Reserve, and the more specific warnings of the industrial records, were accepted by the Government and a check put to speculation, the break in Wall Street could have been averted; yet if the warning were issued, it might bring on the very calamity it intended to avoid. That is the argument. Behind it lies the awful symptom of panic — indecision. The individual lacked courage to withdraw from the market, because the financial mob might hoot; the Government lacked courage to tell the truth and continued to inflate public optimism like a small boy who is afraid to stop blowing up a balloon. The America of eccentrics, of individuals with strength of character enough not to want to make too much money, disappeared in these years, engulfed in a mob.

CHAPTER FOUR

AROUND THE CORNER

BETWEEN the Wall Street break and the campaign of 1932 the years divide roughly into two parts and an interlude; first comes the effort to do nothing, then the effort to do everything. In the first period the object was to keep or restore wages, stock prices, dividends, commerce and industry to the levels of 1929; in the interlude we named what had actually been going on: deflation; in the second period, counter-inflation set in. Other divisions have been made. According to Mr. Hoover, the first period running to the middle of 1931 is the time in which we absorbed the shock and started on the road to recovery; the second, from the middle of 1931 to the creation of the Reconstruction Finance Corporation, is the time when the disasters of Europe brought a second misery upon us and prevented us from continuing on our natural American way of prosperity. In this position, the President has considerably more support from economists than he usually enjoys; ranging from the experts employed by banks to Sir Arthur Salter, these economists insist that the crash of 1929 was in the natural cycle of *industrial* depressions, a storm which rose to a hurricane, which we should, however, have weathered if the *financial* cyclone hadn't arrived from Europe the very moment we were lifting our heads.

Two items in the classic explanation are implied in this view: that the industrial depression was inevitable but not serious, since we were coming out of it in less time than we had come out of the minor depressions of the past; and that we had nothing whatever to do with the financial collapse in Europe. Neither has been proved; for the moment they can be left in the air; they will return in due time.

In the first period the general promise (still implying that nothing serious had happened) was that the country would be all right if

wages were kept up;

railroads and utilities continued their programs of construction;

public works were started on a fairly large scale;

and certain mild financial aid were given to investors and to farmers, the first through expansion of credit, the second to support of commodity prices by the Farm Board.

We had had a little shock, it was good for us, we were taking it up, the President and the great industries were preparing a cushion for the few unfortunates who might suffer, and prosperity was around the corner.[1]

It is difficult to recapture the tone of the first half-year after the crash. I think that under the strain of three years of worry, we have forgotten that we ourselves lived in December, 1929, and March, 1930; we have created another population for those days, so that we can say to ourselves that if "they" had been resourceful, energetic, and courageous, they could have prevented the miseries which later fell upon us. That "they" should have gone on living, more or less calmly, more or less comfortably, when the obvious duty before them was to confront the facts of the situation and prevent the downfall of the

---

[1] It isn't possible to find the exact date on which the corner myth began, nor to say exactly when it was received with jeers instead of cheers; as Vice President Curtis arrived at the conclusion that prosperity was around the corner in November of 1930, I judge that phrase was commonly accepted by the beginning of that year, was certainly in public favor when Mr. Hoover made his sixty-day proclamation in March, and had been rejected by early autumn.

social and industrial system, mystifies us and makes us vaguely resentful; vaguely, because in the backs of our minds float the images of ourselves in that time. For ourselves we make excuses; we were not told, we were ordered to do business as usual. So "they" turn into our leaders and we have a scapegoat at last.

What our leaders were doing will shortly appear. What we ourselves were doing is remarkable enough. When Mr. Frederick Allen and Mr. Mark Sullivan come to write the record of those years, they will have strange material. The plan of this book compels me to omit the hysteria over the tombstone of a priest in Malden, Massachusetts, just as later I shall have to omit the brutality and horror of the Lindbergh kidnaping, because I cannot be sure that these, or similar events, would not have taken place in times of prosperity; a link can be made, but it is not strong enough. I limit myself, therefore, to the circumstances of life which illuminated our crisis. That almost the entire population of the United States seemed at one time to cast all care, all interest in life, aside at 7 P.M., in order to listen to the resuscitated minstrel-show conversation of Amos 'n' Andy is purely a social commentary; that during the year after an unparalleled financial disaster had come upon the country, when unemployment and bread lines began to be noted even in the loyal press — that then Amos 'n' Andy should receive $100,000 a year for radio work and a guarantee of $350,000 for a single talking picture, tells us something about the way we were preparing to go through with our difficulties. At the end of two years a measurable change, for the worse, in public taste appears; but I cannot believe that the feebly scatological jokes of Chic Sale continued to be popular in 1930 because the American people wanted to "get away from it all."

In fact, the most popular subject for joking at the end of 1929 was the market itself and particularly suicides caused by the panic.[2] Hotel clerks, in these jokes, asked if rooms were wanted for sleeping or for jumping, and Eddie Cantor told of two men who jumped hand in hand — they had held a joint account. (Later the word "flumped" was suggested for those border-line cases in which any doubt existed as to intention or accident.) People were advised to buy stock in gas companies and in those manufacturing red ink; the brokers' common phrase about "carrying you" was turned into a reference to pallbearers. Mr. Cantor made a neat sum with a little book of most of these jokes, called "Caught Short." It was not very funny.

Next to the tale of suicides came the tales of gallantry, a little trying when those who had lived meagerly on six thousand a year were asked to admire the men and women who, without whimpering, had adjusted their lives to an income which fell from a hundred thousand to fifty thousand. Suicide and despair on one side, courage and a high heart on the other, were the extreme and exceptional cases; most people in the market were stunned, recovered, went to work if they could find work, and lived for long on the highly spiced and not nourishing emotional food of vain regrets. They had bought at 60 ¼, held until it went to 143, and sold; but they had reinvested at 147 ½ because it was bound to go up and had been sold out at 133; if they had . . . if they hadn't . . . in brief, they were cleaned out. To them were left two consolations, one false, one real. The false one, emotionally speaking, was that they had never had real profits, only paper profits. It was like telling a man that his memories were mistaken and his childhood had really been unhappy; or that the money with which

[2] The suicide rate went up in 1929, but the increase "was not as marked as might have been expected", according to Doctor Frederick L. Hoffman, of the Prudential Insurance Company. The rise was from 17.5 per 100,000 in 1928 to 18 per 100,000 in 1929. After another rise in 1930, in the desperately hard year of 1931, the acceleration in the suicide rate was less marked.

he had lived like a duke for ten years had been declared counterfeit. The argument about paper profits never persuaded
any one but a banker, and even bankers understood it better
in respect to other people's money than to their own.

The true consolation was nothing specific; under the eddies
of disappointment and remorse flowed a powerful current of
excitement; people had an intensified feeling of the dramatic,
the swift changes, the reversals of fortune, the unexpected and
unpredictable in their daily lives. They were more aware of
themselves, at least superficially; they lived with a galvanic
energy. It was like the war — a disaster, but a precious one.

When they had to return to the commonplaces of existence,
things weren't too bad. In the savings banks lay twenty-eight
billion dollars; the American people were insured for and could
borrow on one hundred and three billions; on March 15 following the crash, about two and a half million people began
paying their income tax to the Federal Government and reported that their total income had been nearly twenty-five billion dollars; they reported also that their speculative gains had
been two and a quarter billions and their losses less than three
quarters of a billion; the balance seemed favorable enough.
More encouraging still, the "big babies" of the market refused
to concede defeat: before the echoes of the crash were silent,
in the middle of November, 1929, General Motors declared an
extra dividend of thirty cents and as if to show that radio had
been guiltless in the entire business, Radio Corporation showed
third-quarter earnings in 1929 of nearly nine million dollars
in comparison with a million and a half in the preceding quarter; an insurance company with headquarters in Canada
bought common stocks, and Aviation Corporation, with a surplus of twenty million, announced that it was doing the same.
The governors of the Stock Exchange took steps to prevent the
creation of a bear pool, the amount of brokers' loans showed a
reduction, the rediscount rate went down (indicating easy

money) and the Government of the United States weighed in with a promise to reduce the income tax by one per cent. Encouraged, the railroads of the country promised an expenditure of one billion dollars, the American Telephone and Telegraph Company alone estimated that it would spend over half a billion; utility companies, perhaps smarting under the criticism which made them a scapegoat of overinflation, expected to spend eight hundred and fifty million dollars. All these were basic projects, not the light-minded gambling of the Stock Exchange on which the price of seats dropped to $350,000 (a loss of $144,000). And perhaps the most gallant sign of our quick recovery, our completed convalescence, was that by the end of November, a month or so after the great crash, a new stock offering was made to the public which was invited to buy ten million dollars' worth of Federal Neon. The offer was made by Charles V. Bob and Company.[3]

This was not the prosperity Mr. Hoover had promised the American people, nor which the American people had, in effect, promised to Mr. Hoover; but, all things considered, it was good and many people may have thought that Mr. William Randolph Hearst, whose papers had been so friendly to Mr. Coolidge and so opposed to Mr. Smith, was merely being cantankerous when he called upon the President to make a reassuring utterance (an invitation to disaster which the President did not accept for several months) and "to assemble the banking and financial leaders of the nation and insist that they coöperate with the Government in reviving confidence and restoring normal prices." The emphasis on finance was, however, Mr. Hearst's only mistake; with his singular journalistic gift he had sent out his call at the very moment the President

---

[3] Mr. Bob's later career showed the same dash, but resulted in too many lawsuits. A mountain was named for him by Rear Admiral Byrd, whose Antarctic explorations Mr. Bob helped to finance before the prosecutions began.

was summoning a conference of commercial and industrial giants; at the end of November they came together. They were distinguished and important men; they were the rulers of industry in America; and except for Mr. Ford and Julius Rosenwald, not one of them had ever been able to stir the emotions of the country or any part of it. The conference, however, was guided by Mr. Hoover to purely industrial decisions; the tone was serious, not solemn; the President recognized no significant recession in business and what he wished was merely to create an atmosphere of confidence instead of an atmosphere of doubt and apprehension. The results of that meeting were important because they seemed to fulfill exactly the requirements for prosperity laid down by those in authority. (The coincidence was not remarkable; the same people who made the conditions prepared to answer them.) Thus from employers came a serious promise not to reduce wage rates; in return, labor promised not to fight for higher wages; in the struggle between capital and labor, a truce was called, for the common good. In return for cheaper credit and lower income tax, industry promised to go ahead with programs of expansion. And the general sense of well-being spread so that cities and government departments were all prepared to spend nobly and well.

In all this Mr. Ford was recalcitrant. Instead of keeping wages at the current level, he insisted on raising wages, and if his announcement was spectacular, his reasoning was sound. In fact, Mr. Ford made in 1929 one of the few statements which bear reading in 1932, analyzed the depression which others insisted had not yet come into being, and provided a solution for our difficulties toward which economists were groping two years later. As the head man of large-scale production, he spoke with authority when he said that "American production has come to equal and even surpass, not our people's power to consume, but their power to purchase." This was clairvoyance, for it recognized the necessities of the consumers' market; and

Mr. Ford's solution, also based on his own experience, was to reduce prices to the level of actual value and to raise the general wage level. It is an industrialist's, not an economist's answer to Mr. Dennis's question, "Is there any reason why we may not find a way to earn all we can produce?"

It is hardly a secret that this conference was a failure. Either it did not ask the right questions, or it did, and answered them in the wrong way. The reduction in income tax was nullified when a deficit was found in the national accounts; the spending of utilities and railroads and governments was haphazard, belated and insufficient; cheaper credit did not lead to investment; and six months after the conference, wages were being slashed and wage earners were protesting. Nothing succeeded; yet the conference as a whole could hardly have taken any other course. It could not have announced that the stockmarket panic had torn the whole fabric of industry and that, in consequence, wages would be lowered, against the protests of striking men; that no investment should be made; that motor manufacturers should stop bringing out new models; that railroads should try to get along with their old equipment. Between the duty of formulating a thorough program of reconstruction and the duty of preserving some public faith in the ordinary habits of life, the President's conference chose the second. The misfortune was that the President and his associates seemed really to think that the first was not imperative, that they couldn't offer their little program as a stop-gap and proceed further with an analysis of American industry, to the fundamentals. Or it may be put this way: that the Conference wished to create confidence and did not know that confidence, being a real thing, cannot be kept alive by unrealities.

The most conspicuous of the unrealities was the question of wages. As a restorative, the "maintenance of the wage scale" could mean very little, for it carried with it no guarantee of employment. It was a practical political maneuver, meant to assure the American Federation of Labor that the high level of wages won during and after the war would not be disturbed; it was a "talking point" in "selling confidence" to the American people, but like the talking points of cars and radios and orange juice, it was meant to last only so long as its worthlessness was not discovered. A wage scale of $16.50 a day for plasterers could not be easily sacrificed by the American Federation of Labor; on the other hand, it could not be paid if no plastering was done. The idea that labor would be kept contented by admiring a high-level shadow, without the substance of jobs, was not a good one. The agreement not to cut wages did not apply to salaries, which were promptly slashed, and by the middle of the next year actual wages were cut ten per cent. in the motor industries; a struggle continued to keep them up, ending in the noble defeat of President Farrell of the United States Steel Company, who felt deeply his obligation to stick by the agreement. But discharge of workers was not even so long delayed. By the end of March all the phenomena of acute unemployment were visible. The first demonstration (ascribed, perhaps with accuracy, to Communists) had taken place before the White House; soup kitchens opened in Milwaukee; the bread line became familiar in the East, the free-meal counter of the Little Church Around the Corner reopened after twenty-three years and fed one thousand a day, while the Young Men's Christian Association on the Bowery gave soup and bread to ten times as many; community chests, which had been oversubscribed in the last months of 1929, were being exhausted and less formally organized charity was helpless. Mr. Heywood Broun, more practical than most statesmen, reiterated his appeal, "Give a job till June." The Federal Government was without accurate data on unemployment; when Secretary of Labor Davis blunderingly said what every one felt to be the truth, that "there is distressing unemployment", estimating the number of workless at three millions, he was compelled to retract, in order to fall in with the ideas of the President, and said that unemployment in March, 1930, exceeded that of March, 1929, by only one and a quarter millions.[4]

The President announced that thirty-six of the forty-eight States showed only seasonal unemployment; that the low point had been passed in January and "since that time employment has been steadily increasing." He took pleasure in comparing the present difficulties with those of 1907 and 1920; and in his first and most disastrous essay in prophecy, said, "All the evidences indicate that the worst effects of the crash upon employment will have passed during the next 60 days." This set May 7th as a rendezvous for the reappearance of prosperity.

The figures upon which the President made his promise were offered by the Bureau of Labor Statistics, which found that employment had risen one tenth of one per cent. in February; the survey on which this almost invisible figure was based was known to be inadequate; Senator Wagner, who had introduced bills for the creation of a fact-finding agency and for the relief of unemployment, insisted that the Department of Labor's figures were wrong; and within the next two years scandalous misuse of statistics and harsh disciplinary action against those who would not let officials tamper with figures, gave the American public reason to believe that their Government was deliberately misleading them. Every three months or so new figures for unemployment crept into the press and into the public mind; it was always a million or so more than the official figure. The three millions which slipped out of Secretary Davis's mouth became five by the middle of the year; during 1931 people spoke of eight and nine million unemployed; by campaign time in 1932 the fact, or estimate, that twelve million people who wanted to work could find no work to do was

[4] As there may have been two million men out of work in March, 1929, the difference lies not so much in fact as in phrasing.

so generally accepted that it ceased to have the power and impact of reality; it was a statistic, like any other. By that time, however, one reality had displaced one falsehood: the economic term, unemployed, was almost universally used instead of the loose, half-moral term of opprobrium: "the idle." Only headline writers, compelled to brevity, still fell into the trick of confusing those who could not find work with those who would not work if they could.

The reason the agreement came to nothing rose slowly to the surface: the Conference had considered unemployment in a vacuum and had imagined a vain thing, that men could be employed on nothing, creating nothing. Except for public works, no new jobs were suggested; the theory was that men were to go on making shoes, suits, tables, ball bearings, and all the other commodities which people used; and continue making cosmetics, digestive tablets, trick cigarette lighters, and all the other commodities which people were badgered into buying — although too many of these commodities existed and the money to pay for them did not exist. If the workers could have been paid for twelve months without producing anything, the situation would have been changed; but they had to produce unwanted and unsalable goods before they could afford to buy even a small portion of the product. Manufacturers, taking inventories, comparing orders, observing the plight of the farmer, hearing about bread lines, and scanning in particular their own sales reports, refused to be taken in by this strange economic reasoning. They cut down production and, not being permitted at first to cut down the wage rate, diminished wages by the natural process of employing fewer men. It was pointed out to them that by so doing they were enlisting in the service of the vicious spiral, for the more men they discharged, the less buying power remained in the country. Their reply was that they had the choice between discharging men or going into bankruptcy.

I do not think that the American business mind showed, during this quarter year, its finest qualities, or that business proved as adaptable and courageous as it had believed itself. Yet it would be unfair to disparage an entire profession. There was, for instance, Mr. James A. Bohannon, President of the Peerless Motor Company, who proposed a simple plan for ending the depression in his own industry. It was to sell cars to those whose living depended upon cars, assuming that this benevolent circle would counteract the vicious spiral, and like a pebble in a pond, spread until public buying began. As men on the Ford belt and terrified holders of agencies and windshield salesmen and the half million operators of filling stations and garages were in precisely the same position as the other breadwinners of America, nothing substantial came of the plan.

In January, Professor Irving Fisher broke, at last, from his tradition of optimism and declared that "the United States is headed toward a period of business depression", but he did not wish to alarm his hearers, and gave it as his opinion that this depression would probably start "within the next two years." By the first of May every barometer of business showed dirty weather ahead; steel, car loadings, reports of earnings in the first quarter, employment, foreign trade, railroad income, prices of commodities, raw materials, and farm products — no matter to what chart one turned, the line continued to drop. Even the recovery of the Stock Market had not held up. Yet the first week in May was the time appointed by the President for the worst to be over (that is, sixty days after the announcement in March). He had seen other of his hopes fade. In April he was gratified by the income tax returns and was happy because "the unfavorable developments of last fall did not affect individual incomes to the extent feared." He justified the reduction in taxes and looked forward to closing the year with a comfortable surplus—not an extravagant hope for the country traditionally the richest on earth. Yet in a few weeks he was compelled to warn Congress of an expected deficit of thirty millions. In the meantime he had said that the problems of government could not be solved "without the fundamental engineers' approach to truth." With the records and all their indications before him, in May, Mr. Hoover said:

"While the crash only took place six months ago, I am convinced we have now passed the worst and with continued unity of effort we shall rapidly recover. . . . We have undertaken to stabilize economic forces. Our joint undertaking has succeeded to a remarkable degree. We have succeeded in maintaining confidence and courage. . . . The acceleration of construction programs has been successful beyond our hopes."

The terms used are moderate enough, yet I believe this statement began the long estrangement between the President and the people which was a disaster for both. The prophecy of March may have been a pious hope; the declaration of May was uninformed and ill-judged; unfortunately it appeared to be deliberately misleading. For the President, it should be noted that the *Business Week,* wholly without partisanship, goes far toward justifying optimism in 1930 when, in a review of the year, it says "the general level of business volume returned nearly to normal by July." But business volume was only a superficial indicator; below the surface was a serious contraction of credit which held us down until a scramble for gold and the collapse of Europe brought the final blow. According to the exceptionally sane and critical authority of the *Business Week,* "there was only a moderate recession of business in the first six months of 1930. The depression really began in the middle of the year." This justifies Mr. Hoover, and at the same time shows that the depression began within two months after he had suggested it was ending.

The degree of justification is important in any criticism of the President's ability; and it is unfair to him to check his

THE BOSTON HERALD

WEDNESDAY MORNING, JANUARY 1, 1930

CONFIDENCE IS KEYNOTE OF NEW YEAR

Leader of Investment Bankers Has No Fears for Normal Prosperity

Callaway Says We Are Now Well Along in Period Of Readjustment

CREDIT IS SOUNDER THAN FOR FEW YEARS

Hysteria Is Explained by Level Thinking as Reason of Boom Ends

Finds Hysteria Over

NEW ENGLAND'S BUSINESS NEVER MORE HEALTHY

Railfield Proctor Reports Notable Gains During Year Just Past

NET GAIN WAS MADE IN NEW ENTERPRISES

President Farrell of U. S. Steel Expects Early Substantial Gains

By EDISON B. SMITH

Secretary Lamont Says General Business Is on Sound and Stable Basis

Reviews Trade Year

Reached Higher Levels in 1929 Than Was Ever Before Attained

PROGRESS WAS NOT RESULT OF "BOOM"

Its Substantial Character Was Demonstrated in Autumn Break

BONDS RETURN TO FAVOR AS STOCKS BREAK

Sharp Reversal of Downward Price Trend in Senior Securities

CREDIT SITUATION IS STILL IMPORTANT

General Electric Head Predicts Good Year, With Steady Employment

statements only in the light of later events. It can be said that he believed the worst was over and the corner turned and many respected observers were far more optimistic than he. On the other side is the psychological effect of the President's reassurances. He felt that an eight per cent. decline in business below the level of 1925–1929 was no cause for alarm; but the evidence of men's eyes was against him in the next few months and nothing could have restored their faith in their leaders more than a frank confession of error after the redoubled crash of the second half of the year. No confession was made, and those who recalled the prophecies and assurances of the President must have believed that he was too proud to admit that he had been wrong or unwilling to confess that the machinery he had set in motion was inadequate.

The President was convinced that recovery was on its way and in the months which followed turned to other matters, chiefly the problem of disarmament. In order to end "the uncertainties in the business world" he signed the Hawley-Smoot tariff bill, against the violent protests of business men, financiers, and tariff experts, and against his own feeling that the bill was full of imperfections. For a year and a half the threat of a new tariff had frightened or over-cheered business men; the President had urged Congress to hurry; he had said, a week before final passage, that he had still an open mind; in the end he capitulated because he felt that a veto would have meant confusion worse confounded. People were glad it was over, but the President had not won back the enthusiasm of the masses; he had, in fact, held few communications with them. For nearly a year — until the middle of 1931 — he was the head of the country, but had abdicated as the leader of the people.

During that year he was on the defensive, rejecting the dole, vetoing the first bonus bill, struggling against financial schemes he considered dangerous, and defending with bitterness the "rugged individualism" which he believed to be the American system. He stood in the American mind as a complete negative. He became a sad joke for second-rate entertainers: the Hoover Flag was pockets turned inside out, and a comedian, hearing that business was going up would ask, "Is Hoover dead?" He was to make a spectacular return as a statesman and as a popular leader, but for a long time he did nothing important to govern or alter the course of the depression.[5]

By the middle of 1930 the country knew that it was in an industrial depression; it knew little of the causes; it was beginning to suspect that its leaders, in industry and politics, had been stupid. By the end of June it knew, also, that the President would neither lead nor be led. There was nothing to be done and the country sat back and waited. The summer months are a lull in the excitement of the crisis.

[5] In Mr. Coolidge's blanket approval of the Republican Administration, from which I have already quoted, the triumphs of Mr. Hoover are summarized, and the lapse of activity between the beginning of 1930 and the middle of 1931 is quite clear. Mr. Coolidge notes that Mr. Hoover "secured the adoption of a plan to put wage earners on part time" as one of the early achievements, but in the middle of 1932 the same object was still the special care of an *ad hoc* committee. The President did forbid virtually all immigration, preventing the admission of about 150,000 foreigners. The construction program and the maintenance of the wage scale are also mentioned, and belong to the first months after the crash. The relief program is, of course, an admission that the employment program was unsuccessful. It is not a positive act. The Farm Board had "pegged" and bought and held wheat by March, 1930, and was begging farmers not to plant. Its further activities varied, but were variants of an already established policy. If the dubious acceptance of the Hawley-Smoot tariff bill be added to this list, Mr. Coolidge's record of Mr. Hoover's leadership in the crisis, up to the time of the Moratorium, is completed, and almost all of it belongs to the first six months. During the campaign, much was naturally made of Mr. Hoover's record, the sum of which was really impressive, but showed the same lapse: the important things were done in the first few months of the depression and after the middle of 1931.

CHAPTER FIVE

WALKING BACKWARDS

THE shock and excitement of the greatest crash in the world were over; the assurances of authority were beginning to be questioned; dividends were still high,[1] and savings kept business going briskly; the prompt gathering of forces under the President's guidance hadn't been as effective as one was asked to believe, but they had "cushioned" the fall; and misery, joblessness, and discontent had not yet come to the pitch of affecting the whole nation; they affected only the miserable, the jobless and the discontented. In the lull between this phase of the depression and the more acute one to follow, certain habits of mind became fixed, and they had their effect, in turn, on the hopes and desperations of the next year.

It is natural to smile at the people of 1930 who thought that *they* had troubles! They had not yet experienced hunger marches and the cry for bonus payments; they were still unconscious of the power which gold was to exert in the later days of the crisis; they hardly mentioned deflation; inflation and reflation and counter-deflation were still terms safe in the textbooks on economics; the mania for Five Year plans had not yet come upon them and Bishop Manning could pray for godless Russia without referring to dumping or to Dnieprostroy. The hunt for a scapegoat hadn't proceeded beyond Wall Street; hoarding was not yet denounced by the President; Europe as partner in our distress and as villain of the second

[1] Higher actually than in 1929.

act of the piece was not yet known — Europe was only a participant in the Naval Disarmament Conference, even the question of War Debts dropping a few points in the chart of public interest. The Wickersham Commission was at work and still respected, the *Literary Digest* conducted its vast poll on Prohibition, but those who wanted wine wanted a little wine for their stomach's sake, and those who wanted beer still asked for it as a human right, and not as a source of revenue. Prices were lowered a little and there was a flurry of excitement over books at one dollar; yet more passports were issued than in the previous year and *Fortune,* a magazine devoted to exploiting the grandeur and beauties, as well as the truths, of industry, got thirty thousand subscribers at ten dollars a year. If Prosperity wasn't, Deflation surely was still around the corner, for while wheat prices went down, flour stayed up. A "know-nothing" in politics, destined to notoriety, Alfalfa Bill Murray, ran for governor of Oklahoma on a platform promising high taxes on large incomes, especially on the gross incomes of large corporations — an echo of 1912; he promised rain, also, to a country which was soon to experience a drought; but he hardly thought it necessary to come to grips with the economic problems of the depression. Not precisely a "know-nothing", but representing the average economic man, ex-President Coolidge began in July his year as a syndicated press writer with a survey of conditions:

"We need more faith in ourselves. Largely because of some decline in trade we have set about finding fault with nearly everybody and nearly everything. Yet our government, our physical properties and our industries have changed very little from a year or two ago, when people were fairly content." He did not say that "a year or two ago" brought us back to the days of Calvin Coolidge and he did not say that the very little change in industry meant the enforced idleness of millions of men. He suggested a practical improvement: "It will help somewhat to increase public and private construction. But the principal consuming power is in the people who have work. Unless they buy of the other fellow, he cannot buy of them. If those who have the means would pay all their retail merchandise bills and in addition purchase what they need and can afford, a healthy commerce would quickly be created." His customary ideas on thrift and frugality being thus set aside for the common good, the ex-President returned to New England with an admonition: "No one who has money now can afford to defer settling his accounts." [2] It is interesting to note that the good New Englander, an ex-President, the American man whom American men thought typical, should be one of the first to counsel the surrender of an American principle under pressure of economic need. Thrift is not only an economic issue of the Protestant Reformation; under the name of "savings" it had been considered for generations as the very foundation of capitalism. Nothing is commoner than the defense of the capitalist system which begins with the statement that capital represents self-denial, non-spending, and is the saved-up earnings of the wise and the farsighted. Merely to buy because one has the power to buy had been for generations the mark of the wastrel and the spendthrift. Mr. Coolidge, if one is to judge by his own actions, meant that we were to buy shrewdly and in moderation; but he had announced a new principle and abandoned an old foundation. The newspapers with their campaigns, Buy Now, and the department stores

[2] Mr. Coolidge's place as commentator on events was taken, in 1931, by Walter Lippmann, notably in the *Herald Tribune*. Mr. Lippmann had been editor of the *World*, a paper distinguished for critical liberalism; he was incapable of giving the solid industrialists who read him the kind of comfort they had received from Mr. Coolidge; yet they read him eagerly and accepted his judgments. Moreover, Mr. Lippmann is constantly aware of the interplay of economics and statesmanship; his popularity is one of many phenomena in the same field: the interest in economic problems which, in 1932, displaced almost all other subjects as table-talk.

who echoed it to their own advantage, were not so scrupulous.

It happens that Mr. Coolidge was quite hard-headed and realistic in his approach to the problem. He would probably have rejected the thought that new systems of production and new methods of salesmanship had knocked the law of supply and demand into a cocked hat; but he seemed to be aware of the new economics of capitalism which created demand and in which a steady and steadily growing demand, even to the point of extravagance, was essential to prosperity. We were turning from the economics of scarcity to the economics of plenty (to use the terms of the Douglasite "heresy") and it was a pleasant irony that he should be chosen to lead.

A year later we shall find dozens of abandoned principles, faiths, and ideals littering the road. In the middle of 1930 Americans were still preoccupied with what had gone before. By keeping them from confronting the present and the future, the leaders of the people had forced them to focus on the past. The President had spoken of "one good old word — work"; he had implied that as no grave complications had developed, the country would *return* to normal; people would *go back* to their jobs; (as late as the end of 1931 the President spoke of "*restoring* the old job" in preference to making a new job); stock prices would *go back* to their old levels; and on the radio the Lucky Strike hour began with a "signature"; "Happy Days are Here Again." The whole future of America was thrown into a *recapture* of things past; we were asked to *re*peat, *re*store, *re*cover — as if we could revoke the days of the crash and relive our boom times again.

In the years between 1929 and 1932, Karl Marx effectually displaced Sigmund Freud, and it would be foolish, although it might be amusing, to discuss the depression strictly in the terms of psychoanalysis. Yet at this point the language of the analysts is particularly appropriate because it corresponds to the common experience of mankind. The habit of looking back, the desire to live in the past and to re-create the past, is a symptom of infantilism — more specifically, of a lack of power or will to grapple with the present. In the dream as analyzed by the Freudians, the desire to creep back into the womb (corresponding to the return to savagery and the escape from civilization) marks a nervous and mental disorder, a desire to flee from the obligations of maturity.

The Administration and the governors of thought were saying that except we become as little children we should not enter the heaven of prosperity; prosperity, in short, was something which would *happen* to us again, not something we had to create ourselves. I do not imagine that Mr. Hoover consulted Mr. Schwab and agreed with him to form a conspiracy to weaken the will of the American people; for one reason, I do not think either Mr. Hoover or Mr. Schwab, and the thousands in power whom they represent, were either informed or Macchiavellian enough to do this. It was because they themselves did not wish to face the future that they persuaded the majority of us to look backward, and because they had no great work to which they could put their hand that they spoke of prosperity as a gift or as a force of nature, no less certain to return than Halley's Comet or to-morrow's sun. They could hardly have known that they were paralyzing the will of the American people and, by compelling us to avert our faces from actuality, were draining off our moral power.

The effects were noticeable even in the common language of the day. People hardly had begun to ask when the depression would end; they did not ask how it would end. They wanted to know merely when prosperity would return. The trick of setting a date was an unfortunate one, because it had all the quality of superstition and black magic. Lovers waiting on street corners say, — After four green cars have passed, she will come; children believe that if they blow all the feathers off a thistle, the weather will be fair for to-morrow's picnic.

Such devices may make waiting bearable, but they aren't particularly appropriate when waiting itself takes the place of action. For a people given to action, and not to contemplation, setting a date for good news from Heaven was out of place; it was not likely that the American people would become, in a few months, Orientally calm and spend their days in the contemplation of their navels. They had passed through two periods of excited action in a generation — the war and the great boom — and both had been more or less common enterprises of the nation. The third — recovery from the evils engendered by the other two — found them without a call to action.

They seemed to think for half a year in 1930 that prosperity would be brought back in the sack of Santa Claus. As a Democrat, Senator Copeland of New York refused to train with the optimists, but with regret he knew "as sure as fate, that by 1932 the chimneys will be smoking, the farmers will be getting good crops that will bring them good prices, and Mr. Hoover will be reëlected." Mr. Alexander Legge, Chairman of the Federal Farm Board, was sure in August that wheat had hit its lowest level; Colonel Leonard Porter Ayres announced in *Collier's* that "this is the last phase of the depression" and his prophecy came just before Labor Day when a Bull Market was promised and when, in fact, a bullish attitude did develop. Roger Babson recommended the purchase of good stocks and T. B. Macauley, of the Canadian Sun Life Assurance Company, supposed to be the largest holder of common stocks in the world, declared that by the end of 1930 stocks would have regained seventy per cent. of their losses and by 1932 at the latest would have attained their 1929 peak. Heaven was 1929, and to Heaven we should return, "by 1932 at the latest."

The psychological effects of these promises of return were beginning to be so marked that Chairman Fess, of the Republican National Committee, was moved to protest, saying, "Some leading Republicans are beginning to believe there is some concerted effort on foot to use the Stock Market as a method of discrediting the Administration. Every time an Administration official gives out an optimistic statement about business conditions, the market immediately drops. Even when the slightest bit of improvement is proclaimed, the market always seems to respond with lower quotations." The statement stands as the Republican Party's unique contribution toward national merriment.

The moment at which we are pausing is the time of equilibrium between the end of the first phase and the beginning of the second; with the last quarter of 1930 we come into full economic depression, during which an "American policy" was elaborated to take the place of the discredited explanation of the crash. That period, extending roughly from Mr. Hoover's King's Mountain Speech to his declaration of a Moratorium, is marked by a vast increase in unemployment and — a new and important factor — an acute and widespread consciousness of unemployment; by wage cutting (signifying that the fundamentals of the first plans for recovery were insufficiently understood); by the threat of a dole; and by the general attitude which is called "deflation."

The American people, lulled to sleep by promises and fairy tales, were willing to dream themselves back to prosperity, and when they stirred in their sleep, were still reaching for a phantom; but when they woke, the reality, annoying because it did not correspond to the dream, was still tolerable. Yet each successive disappointment staled the story of good times coming; each promise unfulfilled was an injection of scepticism counteracting the narcotics under which the patient was supposed to sleep. Still without reality to measure or work to do, people gave way to a waking dream and the scenic background of this waking dream is interesting. For fifteen years the malcontent in America had looked to Russia in which the enthusiastic destruction of the old system was slowly being formalized into the creation of a new one. The Five Year Plan of national economy was arriving at the point of criticism and publicity just as the American people became aware of the failure of their own system; Russia in 1930 was, in actuality, a boom country, the spectacular reappearance in the post-war world of pre-war America, with millions of acres, boundless minerals, and the spirit of the pioneer. Two men turned to the Soviets: the workman who heard that there was no unemployment in Russia and the intellectual who found in Communism a faith bolstered by an economic theory which had not yet been disproved. That both were discovering in Russia the America they had lost did not occur to them.

I shall return to the Russian phase of the American daydream a little later; it strode ("with giant steps") into the foreground in 1931. At this moment — 1930 — it is more significant that even Russia, presenting a process of industrialization and an economic problem, was not sufficiently remote to satisfy the American longing to escape from his problems. A setting more exotic, an interest which could not be associated with our own preoccupations, were necessary and they were found in Old Mexico. It is not true that the entire intelligent, or literate, population of the United States became passionately interested in the festivals and potteries of Mexico; but Mexico had a vogue which, begun by painters and writers (who usually escape earlier than day laborers from their problems) gave the reading public a new center of interest; Mexico was in the newspapers and then in books; in mural decorations and in plays; it was in the air and people were interested. It isn't necessary to overemphasize the point, and if the point is accepted, it should be taken with reference to another phenomenon which was remarked before the crash: the vast migrations of Americans to Florida and to California. The tin-can

tourist and the middle-aged plumber or shopkeeper who for-
sook his habitation and his job, and went south for an easy old
age, were new figures in American life, a little disturbing because in the very act of proving that business made one prosperous, they suggested that business was not the appointed end
of life. A considerable number of Americans were refusing to
die in harness and boom days and new forms of insurance permitted them to escape; the depression lifted the chafing harness
from their shoulders, but without money physical escape was
impossible. So they traveled in their minds.

The rich could still go to the South Sea Islands; the intellectuals went to Mexico; the poor went to the movies. The
enormous popularity of pictures which were, in effect, trave-
logues with melodramatic plots, sounds again the same tone.
"Trader Horn" had, to be sure, captivated an injudicious reading public before the crash; after, it found its appropriate end
in the films and enchanted the masses. The movies in America
may take the place of a religion as "opiate for the people";
but they represent definite aspirations and unconscious desires,
and in the depression three or four types have been most effective: the sentimental (as always); the smart comedy of in-
fidelity among the rich; the gangster epic (rude manners, brutality, and action — contempt of authority, the theme of the
bowl of cherries and the raspberry, and the desire for work);
and the exotic melodrama (savagery and escape).

The stage, with its more intellectual and limited audience, is
not as illuminating. Satire flourished, and sentiment. The plays
of 1930 were often in the spirit of 1910 or 1920. The year
before the depression had brought success to the sentimental
realism of "Street Scene" and the harsh galvanic movement of
"The Front Page"; "June Moon", in 1930, was precisely in the
spirit of the earlier plays of George S. Kaufman and was based
on an old story by Ring Lardner; the social conscience made
itself felt in two prison plays; the Pulitzer Prize went to "The

Green Pastures", but I cannot believe that the Heaven of Marc Connolly and Roark Bradford was sought as an escape from industrial depression or that it would have been less popular three years earlier; the vulgar production of "Lysistrata" gave pleasure because it was bawdy — a constant factor in the theater, not an economic phenomenon. It was only toward the end of 1931 and in the next season that the appearance of political satire in musical shows — playing to far greater audiences than the legitimate theater — showed anything like a change in the public temper. The lovely "Face the Music" and the hard-driven insults in "Of Thee I Sing" surprised and pleased the public, the latter to such an extent that the book and lyrics received the Pulitzer Prize which gave the accolade of propriety to a vicious attack on the shabbiness and stupidity of politics in America.

The religious commentary on the crash had naturally driven in the single lesson that the race for wealth was not run along the highroad to Heaven, a correct interpretation, in moral terms, of the economist's criticism of the profit system; the pulpit had hoped and even predicted that men would turn to God when they discovered the vanity of economic wishes; this turn is not remarkable in the first year,[3] at least, although it is

[3] The churches gained, but their gain was a loss. In 1928, over a million new communicants of all the churches were registered; in the great boom year, when people were preoccupied with material benefits, the number fell to 242,748; and in the first year of depression, when the vanity of wealth and business had been exposed, and men were to turn to higher things, the number fell again to 88,350. The Baptist, the Lutheran, and the Protestant Episcopal Churches showed gains; from the Methodist Episcopal Church, nearly 50,000 followers fell away and the Presbyterians and Unitarians also showed net losses. A Lutheran churchman said, "If the churches are losing ground, the reason and the remedy can be found in part in an analysis of the message they are proclaiming to the world; an age of doubt and question, of depression and lawlessness, demands from the pulpits of the land a clear and ringing statement — 'We should fear and love God.'"

possible that some people went to church because they could no longer afford to run their cars out to the country club to play golf. The lunatic fringe of faith, the seers and fortune tellers, were rather discredited by the crash; no profound mysticism was accepted. The Sunday supplement sociologists foresaw deeper feeling for home life (vulgarly translated into the benefits of giving up an apartment on Riverside Drive and going home at night); and of course the joys of a good book. Figures are not available. No doubt many men who had always wanted or thought they wanted, to read Kant or reread Dickens, now found time to do these things; whether they did them or enjoyed any other fruits of enforced intellectual life, I do not know. Of all these advantages of the depression only one certain thing can be said: that no one ever proposed to continue the depression in order to continue its benefits.

America did not want to enjoy a simple life in the wreckage of a rich one; if the change had worked equally at every level, if all the cars had been put up at the same time and all the night clubs closed and all the farmers cut down their crops and all the factories laid off all their men — then living grimly might have been less offensive to the private social sense of every individual. But it was absurd to spend the night reading in a modern game room with eight tables for backgammon; there wasn't much satisfaction in studying the stars while the lights of movie houses and night clubs still bloomed; and the intellectual life was not stimulating after a few years of good times. The crash did not make a clean cut between the past and the present; even prosperity overlapped and new enterprises were begun. To escape, it was necessary to escape entirely.

That is why Russia, already clouded with rumors of Fords, efficiency, and engineers, was not satisfactory, and Mexico, although nearer in space, seemed more remote in time and more enchanting. It had never entered into the industrial system and it had a religion; the rationalists (like Stuart Chase) wrote of the holidays, the fiestas, and the satisfactions of handicrafts-manship; the mystics, of the plumed serpent and the old religion of the Aztecs. Russia had a purpose in life; life in Mexico was pleasant without purpose or plan. Few bathtubs and no radios in the mountain villages, reported the American outriders, and the two symbols of American civilization and of American salesmanship were promptly cast away as contemptible. A religion existed to bind people together — and seemed profoundly enviable to the disjected Americanos; and work existed without factories — since the American factories were closing, the prospect was almost too good to be true. Mexico lay beside us, still unexhausted by thousands of multiple plows and mechanical tractors; plains and mountains were still to be explored and crossed; although it lay to the south, it was as good as the West again. It was a dream conquest for a nation which had ceased to conquer and been instructed to dream.

When the new phase of interest in Russia took the foreground at the end of 1931, it banished the Mexican dream and all the South Sea Islands reveries which went with it. The idea of revolution, slowly dissociating itself from the idea of the Union of Socialist Soviet Republics, supplied romance and escape; but the Russian plan itself became a practical solution, with many others, of our problems.

There were other, more immediate solutions and already they show traces of what was to become a dominant habit of mind. The plans made at the end of 1929 were expansive: great public works, large investment in plant and equipment, municipal projects — all on a large scale. In April of the next year work on national highways was suggested. But from the middle of the year the tide is turning back. For all the admonitions to "spend till it hurts", America gave signs of splitting into small, self-contained communities. There was the Live-at-Home movement in North Carolina, in which farmers and shop-keepers and factory owners combined for mutual support, try-ing to cut down to the minimum commerce with other States. Later the conflict between the States came into the open; public works were to be constructed only of material found within the State; men were to be employed only if they proved resi-dence; and workmen were asked to refuse to use materials bought outside the state line. The mutual dependence of the States was denied or discounted and if boycotts had been per-missible, they would have been put into force.[4]

Another practical way of fighting the depression was the building of homes. A year later it appeared as "Housing", ap-proved by nearly all economists as the great, and forgotten, ladder industry for which America had been looking. In the early stages it had the approval of President Hoover, who wished to provide credit for home building as easy as credit was for buying motor cars; he thus foreshadowed the campaign against the motor car which the home-building industry under-took in a few months. It was true that mortgages were being foreclosed and homes were being lost; but the manufacturers of houses (which could be ordered by mail from Sears, Roe-buck, and which, in the subsequent deflation, found them-selves photographed in the chic magazines of country life) were enthusiasts for the new idea, and with them stood the makers of brass and copper pipe, of furnaces, glass, lumber, electrical installations, and the like. What none of them seemed to know at the time was that credit was contracting and that money was not available to start the wheel rolling.

These were signs of returning to little America, to a provin-

[4] In 1932 Pennsylvania and New Jersey were for a few days virtu-ally blockading each other in respect to commercial trucks, the ques-tion being whether the licenses of one State should be good in the other.

cial and domestic way of living.[5] The regression was even more notable in Pittsburgh, the city of steel and mother of heavy machinery, in which an energetic construction program was put into work with the preference given to hand labor whereever possible.[6] (It reminds one of the French objection to labor-saving machinery, — that if a piece of work can be made to do for six men, there is no advantage in doing it with two men.) But old habits die hard. The Lions' Clubs promulgated a Confidence-in-Business Week, and in Virginia a thousand business men carried three dummies, named Depression, Pessimism, and Mis-Fortune, and after an oration delivered by the Governor of the State, these were lynched, coffined, and cast into the sea.

It has been my experience that the antics of sophisticated men and women lack the heartiness, but share the fatuity, of Mr. Babbitt's little sports. To complete the picture of the lynching, I note that toward the end of the year Miss Fannie Hurst, and Messrs. Louis Bromfield and Condé Nast announced they would ask a fee of fifteen dollars from every individual wishing to see their houses or their persons. This was in aid of starving actors. As I find no report of the money so earned, and as the integrity of these three is beyond question, I must con-

[5] Note that at the end of the jazz age and the beginning of the depression, the most popular characters are all simple, sweet, and quiet. Lindbergh was without question the most popular of all men in America — he was, for instance, *hors concours* in the lists made up by advertising agencies when they hoped to get endorsements — which, however, they did not get from him. He was an adventurous spirit and a pioneer, a man of the 1830's more than of the 1930's, with only the mechanical mastery to mark the passage of a century. Rudy Vallee was the precise counterpart of the young man in a straw hat who sang sentimental songs in front of dissolving views at amusement parks in 1900. Amos 'n' Andy were the interlocutor and end man of minstrel shows revived, using the technique of the comic strip for their continued story.

[6] Minneapolis also turned its back on the pride of American industry and, reverting to picks and shovels, kept 10,000 men at work on a public improvement program, without labor-saving machinery.

CONFIDENCE : 1931

*"Old Man Depression" Was Lynched as Part of the Ceremonies
Opening a New Subway in New York City*

clude that the American people suddenly lost its appetite for curiosities.

A number of people, dependent on brisk trade for their profits, wished that news of unemployment and all other signs of distress were minimized and slipped into the back pages of the newspapers. Later they had their wishes, when distress was no longer news. The argument also was heard that appeals for charity do more harm than good, as they make the country self-conscious of depression.

This self-consciousness was a new factor; its coming had been delayed, and it was not allowed to grow steadily into a mature view of the crisis; yet if America pulls through, this awareness which our leaders so feared will have the credit. It made nonsense of all the promises and predictions the country had heard and distilled corrosive acid into the syrup of confidence. Because in the end we became actively aware of a fact, a grim and dangerous reality, we were able to see where the real struggle lay.

Our enlightenment came slowly. During the last two months of 1930 we were fighting against unemployment as a local ailment and filling local community chests to give immediate relief. In Detroit a method was developed which other cities studied and followed: complete registration of the unemployed, promises of part-time jobs from the great motor-car manufacturers, and rotation of jobs; Milwaukee tried to find three days' work per week for some ten thousand men; Muskegon started a campaign to "spend-a-million-a-week"; everywhere householders were urged to clean up, paint, and repair; New York City cleaned its parks (and the police collected and distributed food, part of which was contributed by patrolmen themselves); against two and a half million dollars raised by the beginning of December in New York, Chicago showed a respectable million dollars for relief; States issued bonds for building roads and cities for smaller projects; for the unemployed, football games were played; the apple vender had become a fixed element in the street scene of many cities,[7] and tangerines were added to their stock — in Elizabeth, New Jersey, men sold celery; [8] comparatively mild weather in the East was a doubtful blessing, as many unemployed hoped for snowfall and the high municipal pay for cleaning the streets; in Kansas City a psychological necessity was recognized, any occupation, even such superfluous labors as "guarding public works" was considered good, so long as the men were "doing something."

The cities were dealing with a real situation, they were driven by human misery. And misery outran all efforts to help. In seven weeks the intelligently conceived plan of Detroit had had the following results: of eighty-six thousand unemployed who registered, eleven thousand had been set to work; two million dollars had been spent; and the number of unemployed had risen to ninety thousand. The figures varied with the cities; but the single typical instance suggests that the enormous outpouring of emotion and the solid thinking and planning which went into local enterprises were not enough.

We had come to the narrow place and faking was impossible. The meaning and the extent of the disaster were not yet clear; precisely because we had been told that no disaster had occurred, the shock was great; yet the activity into which we plunged and the occasional sighting of the actual conditions were tonic to the American system. The foolish pride in the biggest bull market and in the biggest slump gave way to the elation which men feel when they know they are seeing things as they are;

[7] Apple-selling, it was said, was the invention of an official of an association of growers, who won a large prize for this distinguished service to his industry.

[8] For many of these items I wish to make specific acknowledgment to *Time,* whose editorial eye for the curious is as bright as its general views are complete and sound. It has served both as almanac and summary of the past three years, and I think that later historians of the time will find it as indispensable as I have.

the feeling that they can stand the gaff is one which men enjoy. That is one reason for the sense of living more intensely and more fully in the presence of hardship and tragedy. Our destiny was still obscure, but we were beginning to know that we would have to fight for it. So, stirring out of slumber, brushing illusion out of our eyes, but clinging to our faith in the traditions of our government, we entered the second winter of the depression.

CHAPTER SIX

STRANGE INTERLUDE

THE newspaper record of 1930 might be found a complete verification of the facts and circumstances set down in the preceding pages; but any one with a strong visual memory would say that I had omitted the most striking of all the phenomena of that year; and justifiably. For *the* phenomenon of 1930 was miniature golf and, although it was not important, it touched on so many facets of American life in the first year of the depression, that I have chosen to deal with it separately. Through the summer months, a million and a half people spent half a million dollars a day on some thirty-five thousand courses in a game which had hardly been known a year ago and which turned rapidly into an industry considered, by hasty observers, a proper ladder on which America might rise again to prosperity.

The game was the invention of Garnet Carter, who owned a popular hotel on Lookout Mountain, near Chattanooga. An enthusiast for golf, he built a miniature course near the hotel, intending it for children; but adults took it over and Mr. Carter discovered that the plaything was actually bringing patrons to the hotel who preferred the little course to the expensive, full-size course he already possessed. He promptly leased vacant lots in Chattanooga and built more courses; as they prospered, he followed the usual course of American business and organized the Fairyland Manufacturing Company. Patent rights on the imitation greens, developed from cotton-seed hulls by Thomas M. Fairborn [1] several years earlier, were acquired, and the company went into business on a large scale. Mr. Carter himself took out patents for the hollow-log hazard which was one of the distinguishing marks of the little courses. They had eighteen holes, could be built on any lot sixty by one hundred and twenty feet or larger, and the greens and hazards sold for two thousand dollars; another thousand had to be invested for lighting, fences and other fixtures. More elaborate courses sold for as much as eight thousand dollars; the fees were twenty-five or thirty-five cents during the day, fifty cents at night. By November of 1930 the Department of Commerce estimated that the total investment in pony golf was about one hundred and thirty-five million dollars. If the Department's estimate on green fees is accurate, the receipts in a good year would run to one hundred and fifty million dollars.

Commercially, miniature golf was an ideal "proposition." A bright, rococo spot along grim highways, a touch of color given to what had been an unsightly vacant lot, it had the first quality of attracting attention; it was amusing to look at and satisfied the curious urban eye and the more curious urban impulse to stand and watch. The watchers were fascinated and drawn into the course; the fee was small; and the number of people who could play at one time was large; the turnover was rapid, for a single game took only a short time, although it satisfied, in that short time, many desires, including the impulse toward exhibitionism and the equally strong, but not so neatly labelled, impulse to make a public fool of one's self. [2] Admiration for a smart stunt made the business of Tom Thumb golf seem a perfect expression of American

[1] "In Our Times", volume iv, Mark Sullivan notes that Frederick W. Taylor, father of scientific management, experimented with synthetic "greens" years ago.

[2] It also gave point and destination to the meaningless Sunday ride in the car.

ingenuity, finding its way in the midst of hardships; the hankering for the game itself went back to the days when golf was all country club and riches, and the small courses somehow associated the player with great business executives who were popularly supposed to conduct important negotiations between shots (although this notion ran counter to the paralyzing pronouncements on the psychology of the major game). The shots themselves could be played trickily — the old American love for manipulating a mechanism had ample play, and the hazards grew more and more complicated and amusing. They began by being imitations of traps and water and sand; they became lighthouses (the light disappearing for a moment when the proper shot was made) or the Grand Canyon ("see the United States with a putter"); in Los Angeles a live bear had been taught to catch balls and was chained in a course as a hazard, the proper trick being to play so as to avoid him; elsewhere in California the courses were elaborated to include stucco caddie houses, drinking fountains on the fairways, and garden statuary; a slow-speed motor was added to the equipment and the hazards moved: windmills, swinging bridges, rotating cups and tenpins and dragon's mouths; elaboration in the opposite direction reduced the courses to the dimensions of a card table. The game went indoors and in Massachusetts a course combined all eighteen holes in one, the obstacles and hazards being hinged and movable, so that after each shot the arrangements were changed and the hazards appeared in new combinations. Sound-effects were added, in the home of the talkies, and barnyard animals opened their mouths to receive the ball, emitting appropriate noises. Among the barnacles attached to the game was the simpler "bucket of balls", "you drive, we chase", appealing to the major golfer. A boy, flatteringly far at the end of an open field, stood ready to retrieve whatever the enthusiast hit. Architects for miniature courses appeared and, soon, course professionals.

Everybody played. The lunch hour was reduced to fifteen minutes to make time for nine holes; chorus girls played on the two open-all-night courses behind the Roxy Theater in New York, which had twenty-eight hundred patrons in twenty-four hours; men working half time in the furniture factories of Grand Rapids played two or three games a day, unaware of spending ten per cent. of their wages; at Manhasset, Long Island, Mrs. Graham Fair Vanderbilt had a private course; in Los Angeles, Mary Pickford owned the most expensive public course. The spectacle of young men and women in evening clothes playing until three or four in the morning offended the residents of Edgewater Beach, who sued the proprietor of an hotel there; in the decision, which favored the complainants, the judge declared that "playing on a miniature golf course is not golf . . . but disorderly conduct." To satisfy the wants of brokers and bankers, an entire floor of a building in Maiden Lane, directly opposite the Federal Reserve Bank, was transformed into a course "arranged to give one the impression of . . . playing at some attractive country club" through the use of a new process which changed twelve columns in the rear of the room "into the semblance of oak trees." Allan Hoover, son of the President, played on a course constructed by United States Marines at Orange, Virginia; and Aldermanic President (later Mayor) Joseph V. McKee moved to check the growth of the courses in order to "insure full protection of the health and peace of the people of our city." Cities were licensing the courses for a fee of one to fifty dollars, but in one city in Florida the license cost a thousand dollars and was paid without demur. The course in Chicago on which Amos 'n' Andy played, with their wives, took in $1500 weekly — its expenses were $175. In the

South, Jim Crow courses were established; in New Jersey a single county entertained five hundred courses; on Long Island they were spaced one to every three blocks along certain highways; a department store advertised "tiny clothes for tiny golf." On elaborate courses the proprietor supplied straw sandals to be worn over the players' shoes. At Palm Beach the opening of the first course was reported as a social event. A national tournament was held at the fountainhead of the game (on its course every hole was named for a fairy tale) and won by players from Jacksonville, Florida, who had taken the wise precaution of coming four days early and playing the course steadily. Prizes in another championship match, in Chicago, totalled ten thousand dollars.

By the end of the year the estimated investment was far over a quarter of a billion dollars. In the *New York Times* a writer, perhaps sarcastic, suggested that miniature golf "gives some indication of replacing the movies as the nation's fifth industry." [3] In this investment and in the prosperity it brought many industries shared: power companies supplied light; copper supplied wiring; the National Pipe Products Company took over the original owners of the patents "to bolster up the sale of pipe"; bidding for desirable lots gave a spur to real estate; lumber manufacturers thought that they would sell fifty million dollars' worth of wood "before the game goes stale" (an example of exceptional caution — enthusiasts were signing leases to run five years); a special flood-light was produced and the manufacturer, prepared to make a thousand a year, sold his thousand in one month; the Armstrong Cork Company and the Ozite Rug Cushion Company both supplied special materials; Spalding reported five per cent. more business than in 1929 and gave the credit to miniature golf.

[3] The movies, I am informed, are not and never were the nation's fifth industry; but men in the movies liked to say so and there seemed to be a tacit agreement not to disillusion them.

MODERN ART : 1930

General View of the Miniature Golf Course Owned by Mary Pickford.   It cost over $50,000.
The Futuristic Trees Conceal Flood Lights

The churches and the theaters were both hard hit and both encouraged all protests against the game. At the same time, they compromised with the enemy: in Frederick, Maryland, the old Calvary Methodist Episcopal Church was turned into a course when a new church was dedicated; in Paterson, New Jersey, a church of the same denomination opened an eighteen-hole course to pay off the debt of the church and to build an addition; also in New Jersey a Catholic church opened a course in the basement of its auditorium. The Fox Theater Corporation determined to change twenty of its houses into courses; in Chicago negotiations "were completed for the installation of two courses in the Auditorium, one in the orchestra, one in the foyer — the stage being turned over to a hot-dog stand"; in East Orange and in New York unprofitable theaters were converted and in Los Angeles one theater installed a course on its mezzanine.

The game went to sea and presently assisted in the Americanization of Europe. The *Ile de France* had the honor of building the first seagoing course and the Dollar Line proposed a course on each of its world-circling vessels; when the Panama Mail Liner, *El Salvador*, arrived in San Francisco with the first sea-course to enter the port, the news was significant enough to be telegraphed to New York. In London the famous Kit Kat Club was a pioneer and the enterprising Underground put in two free courses for patrons waiting for trains. During a visit to Belgium the Prince of Wales spent most of his time, according to a report which is not worth verifying, on the course belonging to the Queen. An American company opened the first course in Paris; four operated in Peiping (two in the Old Imperial gardens).

The game had still to follow a few of the normal developments of American industry. In January, 1931, it appeared as a stock-market speculation, when 85,000 shares were offered at $16.25 a share; the net income for the first nine months of

1930 was set at $211,519. And a record was made: in a "marathon", a man played 146 hours without a stop. Finally, when a magazine devoted to the game (fifty cents per issue) had appeared, The Institute of Golf and Recreation was founded. Having reached the heights of steel and chemicals, miniature golf needed only one more proof that it was a great American industry — and the proof was not lacking: racketeers swarmed over the courses, demanding twenty-five dollars for "protection."

Six months later the game was dead.

CHAPTER SEVEN

FIRST DEFLATIONS

How much money we have in the bank, and how much it is worth; the price we pay for bread and bedspreads and mouth-wash; the number of days or hours we work and the length of the bread line; the occurrence of "wild children" in the West and the disappearance of yachts in the East; our health and kindliness of heart and our faith in human nature and economic law; the fluctuations of the charts for suicides, car loadings, and births — all these and many other things have been determined, to a certain extent, by the character and the social principles of one man, President Hoover. The degree to which he led the country or refused to be led by it; his eagerness to accept or reject facts; his domination over Congress and his compromises with Congress are all factors in the complicated problem of discovering what we are and how we became what we are. Later, when the review of events has been brought up to date, I shall put together a few incidents which may illuminate the temperament of the President; at the moment, I want to follow the development of some of his social and economic ideas, noting in advance that it is not a common thing for principles to have so much effect on American life as those of Mr. Hoover have had. Mr. Maynard Keynes has said that statesmen cannot turn over in their sleep without affecting the lives of every one of us in a thousand ways; certainly Mr. Hoover could not change his mind, during the past three years, without altering the tone and pace of daily life in America.

It should be remembered in favor of Mr. Hoover that he began his assertion of principles in October, 1930, before his party, and by implication his program, were defeated in the mid-term elections, and neither defeat, nor the clamor of his adversaries, nor the miseries of his people caused him for a moment to abandon his ideals. What the President said at King's Mountain in October was what every President in modern times is bound to say, what Emerson said, better, for all of them: "America means opportunity"; but Mr. Hoover had to convert his principles into definite standards by which actions could be measured. It would have been by far the easier way to abandon popular phrases and accomplish popular deeds; at the end of two years it is clear that the President deeply believed in the common words of flattery always given to America and was evolving out of them a philosophy of American life. He risked his popularity and his reëlection to stand by his beliefs. It was unfortunate that the actualities to which his beliefs correspond had vanished from America a generation before.

"The door of opportunity and the ladder to leadership should be free for every new generation," he said, and called this "the American system", rejecting the name of Capitalism because "under its ideals capital is but an instrument, not a master." The Government is conceived as an umpire between men engaged in a race for which they have been trained and in which "we strive to give them an equal start." And he ended with an echo of his campaign in 1928. At that time he said, "The present issue is the well-being and comfort and security of the American family and the American home. On that issue my party presents . . . the record of the growing comfort and security of the past seven years." With no such glowing record for the past two years to fall back on, the President still had impressive figures: "twice the number of homes owned . . . four times as much electricity . . . seven times as many automobiles . . . four times as many telephones and radio sets. . . ." The comparison was with less favored nations, not with ourselves under Coolidge, but it was not bad for hard times.

The speech seems amiable and negligible; but in the coming months the President had to face disagreeable facts, chief among them the slashing of wages and the outcry for relief of starving men and women and children. His principles forbade him to help and, jealous of the spiritual strength and purity of the American people, he fought for months against a hostile Congress. I have set an arbitrary limit to this phase of the depression, because with the Moratorium the American people began to be conscious of the dominant part taken in their drama by the figures of currency and credit which, having played havoc in Europe, were moving upon the domestic scene. But the principles laid down by Mr. Hoover carried on beyond the middle of June, 1931; they dictated the form and spirit of the entire program for reconstruction which was elaborated and, haltingly, set in motion a year later. The whole course of the depression in its central years was determined by Mr. Hoover's principles, acting upon those of his supporters and enemies, and at the end, compromising with them. The delays, the inadequacies, and the successes all come from the same source, a specific philosophy, or ideal, of what America's destiny should be, held, at a moment of crisis, by its chief executive.

What strikes us at once is that a scientifically trained mind was substituting a memory of the past for the facts of the present. Mr. Hoover spoke as if nothing seriously had changed in the span of his lifetime. Infinite opportunity was, in Mr. Hoover's childhood, the abstract ideal to which the boundless West was the corresponding earthly fact; yet the President clung to the ideal long after the West had been bounded and its capacity to absorb American energy was being exhausted.

He spoke as if he were addressing an agricultural community, not an industrial nation. He was doing what he had advised his people to do: he was looking backward. His own career was the traditional progress of the barefoot boy to the White House and, like many self-made men, he saw no reason to believe that the circumstances had changed. All that he had seen of mass labor abroad made him the more certain that the individual still had, in America, every chance for wealth and power. All that he had experienced in the year of depression, brought about by unchecked power, left him unconvinced that power without control might be a common danger.

In the campaign of 1932, Mr. Hoover was being praised, and not only by his supporters,[1] for having saved the financial structure of the country at the moment of its greatest peril (a moment so grave, said the President, that the Secretary of the Treasury at one time warned him the United States could remain only two weeks longer on the gold standard [2]). In that sense it might not be inappropriate to praise the President for having preserved the social structure of the country, confessing that the price, in misery and disaffection and corruption of morale, was high, but insisting that these are precisely the hardships through which a country must go to achieve its destiny. Nothing stands in the way of such an encomium, except, possibly, the future. If the American system, as conceived by Mr. Hoover, survives without significant change, if *private* capitalism pulls through and, without abrogating any of its fundamental privileges, reasserts itself as

[1] By Walter Lippmann, for instance: ". . . the gold standard and the general credit structure have been successfully defended. . . . For this result the President, Secretary Mills and Governor Meyer are entitled to great credit."

[2] This statement was instantly and emphatically denied by political opponents and by certain banking experts. Secretary Mills, without repeating the time limit of two weeks, insisted that the danger had been grave. The reference was to the last weeks in May, 1932.

the most satisfactory way of living yet invented by man, no praise for Mr. Hoover will be too high. He has been more seriously and more venomously criticized than any President since Lincoln; the attacks have been made by some of the most distinguished men of our time as well as by some of the meanest and lowest; the psychological situation of the country was peculiarly dangerous and his own position most unfortunate; yet he remained steadfast. If he succeeds — if America survives his success — he will rank as one of the greatest of statesmen.

The two lines of justifiable criticism are that he cannot succeed because the current of history has set against him and all he stands for; and that even if he succeeds, he will have saved a vicious system, a system ultimately doomed, at such cost in human life, and moral assurance, as no loyalty to principle can justify. Both these forms of opposition crystallized in the battle of the dole, the principal event of this period, and were implicit in the battle of the wage scale which came to an unhappy end at the same time. It is remarkable that most of those who opposed Mr. Hoover were, or seemed to be, unaware of the implications of their own actions and would have held themselves as stanch supporters of the American system as the President, if the question had been put to them. Nor were many of his followers aware of the meaning of success for their leader. Success, in practice, meant staying on the gold standard, preventing sudden inflation, keeping some part of industry and commerce going, and relying on private charity to keep alive, if in misery, those whom the system had temporarily to discard. Success for Mr. Hoover's principles, however, meant much more; as he drew his principles from the past, success meant a return to the past. (It was not remarkable that among the first suggestions made for improving our present condition and insuring our future prosperity was the old hope of the old guard: repeal of laws regulating combinations in trade; Mr. Hoover was not, however, quite rugged enough an individualist to accept the idea.) Success meant that the drift of the world toward some form of Socialism was not to affect America and that the drift of America toward State Capitalism was to be checked. It was, characteristically, in terms of standstill and return that the President's ideals presented themselves; success meant resistance, not movement.

In the actual order of events, the President faced first the problem of relief (the dole), then an acute aggravation of unemployment, and finally the problem of falling wages; but as his principles, and their effect on the future, are better seen in the political and philosophical quarrel over the dole, I leave it for the end. The other two, in any case, showed only a few changes from the past. Financiers had begun, a year after manufacturers had agreed not to cut wages, to see the desirability of escape; they knew that the price of commodities was going to go down, and that deflation was bound to set in; they wanted, and in Cleveland at a meeting of the American Bankers' Association, they openly said they wanted, industry to cut wages. (Inasmuch as they had financed industry and had to protect their loans, this concern for the welfare of industry was natural and could be easily translated into concern for the welfare of the country as a whole.) The influence of President Hoover was too strong; but in January the voice of the bankers was heard again, and Albert Henry Wiggin, head of Chase National, said, repudiating the economics of the boom, "It is not true that high wages make prosperity. Instead, prosperity makes high wages." And as he felt that the policy of keeping prices up had failed in a test of over a year, he thought "many industries may reasonably ask Labor to accept a moderate reduction of wages designed to reduce costs and to increase both employment and the buying power of Labor." Anxious for semi-official backing, so long as the Administration argued against wage cuts, bankers "bombarded" the Federal Commissioner of Labor Statistics for figures which would justify them. Many of the men who had taken the pledge in 1929 swore that they had remained faithful; but Walter C. Teagle, of Standard Oil, in New Jersey, went further, and explained much, when he said that his company had not reduced the wage rate, but had been compelled to put some of its workers on part time. The untrained reader of newspapers was still bewildered by reports that "wages had not been cut" or had been only slightly cut; he would have been puzzled by the figures showing that the wage scale had gone down three per cent., but earnings (which even the untrained suspected of being similar to wages) had gone down twenty per cent.

This meant that men were being thrown out of work. The number of unemployed is not so revealing here as the increase, for in estimating numbers, various systems were used and the habit crept in of not counting those "who had jobs but were not working", i.e., the "laid off" rather than the "fired." But the reluctant figures of government agencies indicated that in the nineteen largest cities of the country, unemployment had increased 149% in the nine months ending January, 1931. (The official estimate gave about two and a half millions in April, 1930, about six millions in January, 1931.) The new recruits included all those who had voluntarily given up their jobs, but no one assumed that they were numerous; the rest were men who, while wages were not being cut, were not receiving wages.

The President encouraged leaders of industry to employ more men and to employ men on part time; he brought to his aid in fighting unemployment distinguished organizers who discovered new work to be done and coördinated the agencies through which the unemployed could be reached; he believed firmly, then, in public works as a practical and psychological relief. At the same time his tendency to make small the misery of joblessness had a disastrous effect. In November he accepted the figure of three and a half millions unemployed and began a series of deductions ("a million in transit from one job to another" or unwilling to work; another half million out of work in communities so small that their poverty could be assuaged by friends and families; and so on) which left the actual unemployed at two million, representing at most eight hundred thousand families. About a year later the President spoke to newspaper correspondents and without giving them anything to quote expressed an official attitude which again belittled the seriousness of the crisis. His point was that people always thought six million men out of work meant thirty million men, women and children in misery, requiring the ministrations of charity; but the President gave assurance that savings (after two years of growing unemployment) would so reduce this figure that only four million men would be dependent. Genially he rebuked those who remembered only the millions out of work and looked always at the hole in the doughnut; he compared the figures of the current depression with those of crises in the past; he proved that America was better off than Europe. When he began to campaign for reelection he was surprised and hurt to discover that people thought him lacking in sympathy with the hungry and workless. He had vetoed the Wagner Bill for coördination between state and Federal employment agencies, although the bill embodied some of his own projects, on the practical ground that the new system could not be made to work for a year, but the Employment Service of the country was later reorganized so as to coöperate more earnestly with the States. The record of the Administration is not impressive; neither is the record of its critics. Except for the Wagner Bill, little suggesting immediate action was proposed by sound economists, visionaries or propagandists for panaceas, until the inflationary proposal for a five-billion prosperity loan became common property. The whole country seemed to surrender to unemployment, hoping that little local efforts would make the misfortune of others tolerable to themselves.

The parallel problem of wage cutting can be followed through the gallant figure of James A. Farrell, head of the United States Steel Corporation. In the summer of 1931 he had heard steel men say that wages must come down and had replied, "Oh, no, wages in the steel industry are not coming down; you can make up your mind to that fact. If you are going out to sell your goods and eliminate your profit and expect to get it out of the men in the mills, you are greatly mistaken." The steel mills as I saw them six months later were vast empty caverns lit by the occasional glory of a tapped furnace, inhabited by handfuls of men where there had been hundreds; it was impossible for Mr. Farrell to keep men at work when no work was to be done; but on his pledge that wages should not be cut, he was firm. At the beginning of summer Charles M. Schwab had propounded an ideal of justice to which Mr. Farrell could give assent: "In boom times our men have done the square thing by us. We have not had strikes or unreasonable demands to disturb us when markets were good, and in dull times we have not tried to take our loss of business out of the hide of the worker by reducing wages." But Mr. Farrell, looking away from his own company, had to confess that "we are living in a fool's paradise if we think that every steel manufacturer in the United States has maintained what is generally known as the current rate of wages. It has not been done. . . . I think it is a pretty cheap sort of business." [3]

[3] It was said that employers in some industries discharged expensive men and took on others who worked for less; this kept the "wage rate" of the discharged men intact.

At an appropriate moment this attitude of the steel kings proved helpful. Wages had been cut and, long after, the second half of the bargain was broken: strikes occurred in protest. The discomfort which always occurs when fact confronts a reiterated fiction was being felt; the lulling effect of keeping up wage rates while wages went down in sum was losing its potency, not only on those who bought milk and bread and meat with wages (and found the wage scale not negotiable at the grocer's), but on every one who had eyes and ears. At the beginning of August a Rhode Island Congressman attempted to bridge the gap by inquiring whether the Federal Government would do anything to stop wage-scale cuts. The Secretary of Commerce, Mr. Lamont, replied that corporations, in difficulties, had already cut salaries and dividends and had now but one alternative to shutting down altogether, which was cutting wages. He gave it as his opinion that it was *not* "the duty of the Government to interfere." A *démenti* from the Administration followed; its policy of "maintenance of wages", which was official language for maintenance of wage rates, had not been altered. Secretary Doak, on being asked what was going to be done to support this policy, asked in turn, "What *can* be done?" Appropriately at this moment United States Steel cut its dividend nearly in half, cut salaries, but did not cut wage rates; and Bethlehem, also lowering its dividend, held up the scale of wages. It was felt that by its resistance, Steel was encouraging others to postpone cuts; but the move was not universally imitated. In Colorado the Rockefeller mines cut wages twenty per cent., salaries in railroad offices and packing plants were "readjusted." The blow fell at the end of the third quarter of 1931; exhausted by its efforts, Steel openly cut wages, the chairman of the finance committee overruled Mr. Farrell, and "for the purpose of better meeting prevailing unsatisfactory conditions in the industry" the long fight was given over. The stock market bounded upward. At the beginning of the next year, Mr. Farrell resigned.

It had not occurred to Mr. Farrell or to Mr. Schwab that the contribution of faithful workers in good times entitled these workers to jobs in bad times; only rates of pay were held sacred, as long as they could be. Yet the conspicuous fight put up by Mr. Farrell, although it was a fight for a phantasm, was not without a good result. A connection had been established between wages and dividends. Because wages were confused with wage rates and because holders of stock — receivers of dividends — were often as numerous as wage earners,[4] the connection was still faulty, but it was being made clear. Former Secretary of War Newton Baker had said, discussing the particular unemployment which comes from improvement in technical methods, "The advantages and gains which come from machinery have no right to be all velvet to industry unless they are velvet to society. Industry has no right to take all the gain that comes from this rapid substitution of machine process for human hands without bearing a substantial part of the consequent dislocation of the human element which it causes." The American Federation of Labor which had voted against unemployment insurance as "a form of the dole" a few months earlier, found its lobbyist suggesting in January that industry should put aside part of its reserves for help to its men in time of enforced idleness; and, promptly to bring practice in line with theory, the General Tire and Rubber Company announced a dividend for labor as well as for capital. Half of a special dividend was to go into a fund to insure employment: "The fund will be used primarily to finance out-of-season sales. It will also provide money which may be

---

[4] U. S. Steel had 225,000 employees in 1929, and 168,000 stockholders; in 1931, when its employees had diminished, its stockholders numbered 233,000.

loaned to . . . employees who may be temporarily laid off.
. . . It is simply a matter of good business." More theorists
than practical men accepted the new principle, but it had, at
least, been uttered.[5]

The practical men were aware of difficulties. "The capitalistic system is on trial," said Thomas L. Chadbourne in public at about the time the Governor of the Bank of England
was privately filing for reference a prediction that "unless
drastic measures are taken to save it, the capitalist system
throughout the world will be wrecked within a year." To some
the word "wreck" was a simple thing, — the failure of dividends; to others the worst symptom would be lack of work.
In America, in 1930, the former was more influential: dividends, after the crash and in the first year of depression,
increased and wages went down.[6] Another item on the balance sheets was also protected, — surplus or reserve. The cut,
made by United States Steel in October was to save the corporation thirty million dollars a year; yet in two years (1930
and 1931) the corporate surplus of United States Steel had
been reduced by only thirteen million. It was to protect the reserve that Steel not only cut into, but finally stopped its dividends on common stock entirely; both dividends and wage
scales were abandoned in order to maintain a corporate existence. In spite of this, the deficit of United States Steel for the
first nine months of 1932 was $54,542,000 to which must be

---

[5] The bonus of more than a million and a half dollars given to
Eugene Grace, for the year 1929, by the Bethlehem Steel Corporation,
was much discussed in 1931, as it exceeded his average bonus of the
past five years by about fifty per cent. The bonus was considered as
a kind of special dividend and it shocked the public sense of propriety
that so much should have been paid.

[6] I borrow these rough figures from Morris Ernst's America's
Primer: "Dividends and interest payments increased to 8 billions of
dollars from 7½ in 1929. And meanwhile, wage payments which
amounted to 45 billion dollars in 1929, decreased to 35 billion in
1930."

added about $18,000,000 paid as dividends on preferred stock.

It is for the defender of capitalism or the Communist accuser to discover right and wrong in these figures. They have to be put down, one beside the other, to give them meaning, but I myself make no political deductions from them. I cannot see how or why employers should have kept not only their wage scale, but their wage list, undiminished when they had no market for their products; nor, under the system, was there any compulsion to pension the unemployed. The system did impose a single obligation: to pay dividends as long as possible; and those entitled to dividends were pleased to receive them even if payments drained strength and resistance out of their companies; there were even those who would have preferred to cut down surpluses in order to pay dividends; at that point corporations showed themselves as obstinate in self-defense as individuals.

They showed themselves apologetic also and the figures indicating cost of living helped them. Food and clothing were beginning to cost less; the wives of workmen knew it; rents, interests on loans and mortgages, insurance, and other fees, had not gone down so rapidly or had remained at their old level; but the purchasing power of the dollar was higher. According to the Department of Commerce, the cost of living had dropped some twenty per cent.; according to the National Industrial Conference Board, the dollar of 1923 and of 1929 was worth $1.16. But as money earnings were below normal, the gain on the dollar proved deceptive and was, according to experts, actually a loss in purchasing power. Over a long period of years the same thing was true: "between 1925 and 1931 the cost of living of the American workman had declined fifteen per cent., while the total amount paid out in wages by manufacturing industries had dropped forty per cent." [7]

[7] Lawrence Dennis, "Is Capitalism Doomed?", after figures from the Commissioner of Labor Statistics.

Few of us live on statistics and percentages. The working people of America knew that they were getting less money with which to pay bills and that only some of the things they bought were coming down in price. They knew also that many of their friends were no longer able to count on getting any money whatever as the reward of labor. The remorseless process had set in: extravagances were forbidden; savings were exhausted, the car was sold; a cheaper house was rented; families doubled up; money was borrowed on insurance; the insurance policy lapsed. The downward stages were well known; social service workers could tell almost to a day when each would be observed. So far nothing had been discovered to reverse the wheel.

The great struggle of principle did not, however, concern the lives of the men and women who were reduced to penury by unemployment. These millions, living in every State of the Union, visible to every man who walked the streets or rode along the highway, dropped out of sight and first place was reserved for a comparatively small number of farmers, living obscurely in the Southwest, who had the misfortune, during the summer, of a drought and the good fortune to be raised, in winter, to the eminence of an economic and philosophical issue. Their own share in the battle was small. Buffeted by an unkind fate, they rose once when, at the beginning of January, 1931, some five hundred farmers and their wives, hungry in spite of the efforts of the Red Cross, took their shotguns and invaded the little town of England, Arkansas. Law-abiding Americans to the last, they gave the Red Cross a chance to feed them, but the Red Cross was inadequate; thereupon they went to the stores, threatening to take what they needed, protesting that they were not beggars. The storekeepers doled out food to them; no actual violence took place. A year later it was reported that the same farmers, blessed with good crops, were sending what they could spare to less favored communities. For the rest, the hungry, the emaciated children, the dying cows and mules, the fruitless lands of Arkansas must be forgotten. The Congressmen and the Cabinet members and the President spoke often of Arkansas; but their quarrel was above the misfortune of individuals; it embraced a principle.

The Secretary of Agriculture had called the drought the worst in our history and the President had recommended that Congress appropriate twenty-five million dollars for relief of the suffering area. Congress, accustomed to higher figures, showed preference for a bill authorizing the expenditure of sixty million dollars, out of which food for human beings could be bought as well as food for beasts of burden. Irritated by carelessness about money and by schemes for relief which he considered unsound, the President denounced the Congress, asserting that the sums he had recommended were the maximum possible without raising taxes, and that "prosperity cannot be restored by raids on the public treasury." He accused his enemies of "playing politics at the expense of human misery." He was specifically replying to Senator Walsh of Massachusetts who had formulated the opposing philosophy when he said, "There are worse misfortunes than heavy taxes. One is the failure of the Government to remove the specter of starvation and misery and idleness and unrest." The President's open rebuke — it was issued directly to the press — almost broke up the entente which, at the instance of the victorious Democrats, the two parties had made, in a pledge to bury partisan differences and not to obstruct legislation for the recovery of the nation; it alienated, for a time, the leaders of the President's own party who informed him by telephone that they considered his statement indefensible and could not cooperate with him unless he consulted them. And it brought the problem of human relief into sharp focus; had the President chosen another way of showing displeasure, the subject might have lain dormant for a year.

The issue was drawn between the House, which insisted that supplying food would be a dole, and the Senate, which held to its intention to "put a man on a basis of equality with his mule." As Christmas approached Senator Borah cried, "For God's sake, get something done to feed the people who are hungry", and the two houses compromised on a bill for forty-five million dollars for feed and seed, but no food — unless food could be slipped in under the term "other such purposes incident to crop production." This may have been the intent of the legislators, but later events indicated that they had not persuaded the President.

At this point the Red Cross enters; it was approaching its fiftieth anniversary in America and stood without reservation or rival as the first American institution; the President of the United States was, by a tradition of which all citizens approved, its honorable head; its functions were so plain, its support from the whole people so heartfelt, that no way had ever been found to challenge its irreproachable integrity. Before a month was out the Red Cross had lost its standing and its power and had become, in the eyes of many unhappy people, a political agency.

In the struggle over drought relief, the President had made it clear that the Red Cross would, out of its funds, feed and clothe the victims of the cruel act of God, and the Red Cross, which was already in action, assured the country that it could continue the work. On that basis, the passage of the relief bill could not alter or improve the situation, and the riot in Arkansas came to cast doubt, not on the willingness of the Red Cross, but on its capacity. The Senate, still wishing to appropriate money for food and clothing, called the chairman of the Red Cross, John Barton Payne, to give testimony. He appeared, a man who had followed the course of Mr. Hoover and Mr. Farrell, had risen from poverty to command; he remembered that he had gone to work as a youth and in his first year, in a little town in Virginia, had earned fifty dollars; he had become a lawyer in Chicago and gone on to Washington as counsel for and later chairman of the Shipping Board, as Director General of the Railroads, as a member of the Cabinet; four Presidents had been happy to honor him. He had done business with capitalists and believed in the capitalist system; he said, "If the wealth of the country were to be equally distributed it would quickly find its way back into the hands of the more capable", never doubting that the methods of the more capable were humane and Christian and correct. His statement to the Senate committee was in the nature of a financial report, but its implications were specific: the Red Cross, having spent only about one out of five million dollars available for relief, needed no direct appropriation from Congress. Senators replied that a ration costing $1.15 (even at the wholesale prices enjoyed by the Red Cross) was insufficient for a family of three for a month; they noted that banks were closed, credit unavailable. Three days after Judge Payne's testimony, he recommended to President Hoover an appeal for ten million dollars for drought relief.

This appeal — when four million dollars still rested in the reserve — seemed strange. Judge Payne had said he could carry on and nothing had occurred in the three intervening days; his own explanation was that suffering had increased in the past fortnight; the suspicion remained that the appeal for funds was meant to embarrass the Senators who insisted upon appropriating money from the Treasury. The President appointed a notable committee: Calvin Coolidge and Alfred E. Smith stood together; Capital and Labor and the Church combined; the Red Cross was again to be a universal mother, regardless of politics; an "acute emergency" existed. The Senate refused to coöperate and by discussing its bill to add twenty-five million to the ten million which the country would contribute, effectively stifled enthusiasm so that in the first week, usually most bountiful, only a little more than half a million dollars were subscribed. The *Nation* pointed to the thirty-eight-million-dollar fund of the Red Cross, to the four million unexpended of its relief appropriation, and declared itself "uneasy" about the finances of the organization. Flanked by the usual movie stars, but with his predecessor and his rival to give weight to his utterance, the President spoke over the radio: "It is unthinkable that any of our people should suffer from hunger or want," he said, making no distinction then between those who suffered from drought and those who suffered because the economic system had thrown them out of work. "It is to the heart of the nation that I am appealing to-night." Money came in a little more freely, but in the next week Judge Payne was again in politics when he refused blankly to allow the Red Cross to accept any appropriation Congress might make. To do so, he said, would be to violate the spirit of the Red Cross, which had always been supported by individual and voluntary contributions and might bring the Red Cross into rivalry with community chests in cities, where it did not wish to operate; he gave every assurance that with its reserves and the ten million now being raised, the Red Cross could satisfy every legitimate need. It appeared that no one was actually starving, even in Arkansas.

The President supported the Red Cross as warmly as the Red Cross supported the President. "This is not an issue," he said, "as to whether people shall go hungry and cold. It is a question as to whether the American people will maintain the spirit of charity and mutual self-help." Yet the President, on this single occasion, admitted the possibility of abandoning his principles; he said "if the time should ever come that the voluntary agencies of the country are unable to find resources with which to prevent hunger and suffering, I will ask the aid of every resource of the Federal Government." As this seemed to lower the argument to the level of statistics on misery, the Senate was stubborn. Senator Borah had already repudiated the belittling name of "dole." He had said that in feeding the victims of the Mississippi flood, or famine abroad, we had never been accused of giving doles. "We will either feed these people," he cried, "or we will stay here and tell the American people why we do not feed them." In the beginning of February, Congress in a sense did both. It fed, yet officially did not feed, the starving; it provided merely for "further agricultural rehabilitation", which corresponded to the "other . . . purposes incident to crop production" of the first relief bill. The word food was to be cut out of the bill; the money appropriated was to be loaned on proper security. And although Republicans, defending the White House, did not deny that you could not rehabilitate a farm with a dead farmer, the Republican House Leader repeated again and again, "It's not a dole . . . it's not a dole." Before the compromise bill was accepted, a request for interpretation was wired to Secretary of Agriculture Hyde, whose bureaus would do the actual business of relief. After communication with the President, the Secretary praised the Red Cross to the Senate, and confessed that "there could be no prohibition against the proceeds of such loans being used for food or other supplies." Food became legal, not the dole. For the money was to be loaned, not given; and the security demanded by the Federal Government was prohibitive; even for its approved purpose of seed and fertilizer, the Government had advanced money to only twenty-two out of fifty-five hundred farmers in one Arkansas county. Of the twenty million dollars appropriated, about three fourths was, however, loaned by the end of March to about one hundred thousand farmers; Arkansas took about one fourth of the total, four other southern States a million each, and twenty-three other States the remainder.

A few weeks later the depth of the President's feeling was revealed when he spoke to the Red Cross (which had raised its ten million dollars in the end) and said:

"If your officers had yielded" (to the demand that the Red Cross distribute freely, and not as loans, money appropriated by the Government) "it would have injured the spiritual responses of the American people. It would have been a step on the pathway of government doles. . . . We are dealing with the intangibles of life and ideals. . . . A voluntary deed is infinitely more precious to our national ideals and spirit than a thousandfold poured from the Treasury. . . . You have renewed and invigorated the spiritual life of the nation."

This was the principle: the Federal Government should never give directly to the people. The point was finely drawn, but there was a distinction and the President's clairvoyance was never more remarkable. He had foreseen in an argument over the relief of a State crippled by an act of God, a struggle which had eventually to come between those who chose to aid the unemployed by direct gifts of money or goods and those who preferred to aid them by the more distant processes of providing credit to industry, stability to banks, and work to do. If the President had yielded in the case of Arkansas and again on the bill for Federal relief, his hands would have been tied a year later, when a violent effort to force full payment of the bonus and a less spectacular, but even more significant, effort to provide for Federal relief came to him for decision. He had clearly seen the principle involved and considered it as a power of corruption; what he said about saving the spiritual forces of America he no doubt believed, but it was not so important as the affirmation of his belief in the proper functions of the Federal Government. For his faiths, he had fought stubbornly and even angrily; he had not yielded and on principle his victory was complete. The Federal Government had repelled all raiders and given away no dollar. It had put upon the States and smaller communities obligations which were proper to them if they were also to have Rights. The irony should have pleased him that those who most wanted to evade these obligations were Democrats, the natural defenders of State Rights. The Republican had reminded the country that it was a federation of forty-eight States, each with inalienable rights, for which each had to assume responsibilities and duties.

The President had spoken of raids on the Treasury; for the perfection of his attitude, he should have been more specific and more candid. Neither in the discussion I have just reviewed nor in the more energetic one which came in the next year, was one point made clear: that Federal relief, especially relief every week to millions of the unemployed and their families, would have to be paid out of taxes and that taxation would probably fall upon wealthy individuals and corporations. The experience of England was clear: an income tax rising to seventy-five per cent. on large incomes at one end, a small dole at the other. With the President's opposition to the dole runs his fellow feeling for great wealth; it would have been franker for him to expose the connection.

On the other hand, Mr. Hoover avoided in 1931 and again in 1932 the moral reproach which others flung at the poor and the distressed. Mr. Coolidge had spoken of "our chastening" through the depression and, disapproving of the policy of the Farm Board, had written, "It is better for every one in the end to let those who have made losses bear them than to try to shift them on to some one else. If we could have the courage to adopt this principle our recovery would be expedited. Price fixing, subsidies and government support will only produce unhealthy business."

"*Those who have made losses*" were, like the unemployed in

Mr. Hurley's phrase, to be left to "shift for themselves." The morality is the same as that which makes the depression a retributive act of divine justice for our stock speculation in 1929 — "we are all in it." The President never so insulted the injured of our depression.

I do not intend to follow the complicated and disastrous activities of the Federal Farm Board. Through various agencies the Federal Government which refused to provide food and clothing for industrial wreckage, and even for the same farmers, went into the business of buying and selling commodities, chiefly wheat; it appropriated vast sums of money to keep the price of wheat high; it tried hard to dictate to the wheat farmer and the cotton grower the exact acreage they should plant; at times it was a potent support, at others it seemed an active rival to the private farmer. The Government was definitely in business, as later it was to go into the banking business. For the protection of agriculture, state lines were erased from the map and the Government bought wheat from the individual; the Government was not frightened by the contact and the individual was not humiliated. Somewhere a lack of logic was to be noted.

The man who sat at his radio and listened to appeals for aid might have noted another discrepancy. The program started in New York, with an address by a national figure; from Los Angeles the voice of a nationally popular movie maker was heard and a few minutes later orchestras, known for their services to national advertisers, came smoothly in from Chicago and New York again; Charles A. Lindbergh spoke and when he had finished, a composition in honor of his flight was played a thousand miles from his microphone. Everything was national: the network, the individuals, and the millions who sat and listened. But the appeal was local. The Federal Government was denying the unity of the United States. A thoughtful listener might wonder whether all the chances and changes through which we had gone had not transformed the character of the country; whether the problems had not become too involved and interrelated for local solution; whether the radio was not the truer symbol of our national status than the President who denied unity in the very act of using it.

CHAPTER EIGHT

First Disillusions

SOME fifteen months after the break in Wall Street, the Senate of the United States requested one of its committees to collect and report "information regarding the seriousness of the depression." It was a subject upon which most of the Senators' constituents would have been glad to testify. Their information was ample.

The preceding chapter has dealt with acute misery, and from it I have omitted everything I could, so as not to give the record any appearance of political argument. In this period more people had to deny themselves, more went actually hungry, more wore mended clothes, more suffered intense discomfort; and far more than all these together, a vast number of Americans began to live in the shadow of uncertainty. They were slowly giving up the cherished illusion that prosperity would suddenly break upon their dark horizons; they counted themselves lucky if they got cuts in wages instead of facing closed factory doors; they lived from day to day in growing apprehension. The calm sunlit confidence of America was clouded, for the first time in a generation; the country began to look for a scapegoat and for a deliverer; it turned and sneered at some of its silliest, and most cherished, idols. No statistics exist for these changes in public feeling, yet no one who lived through the period escaped them. They came not as strong winds of doctrine, but as gusts and flaws. It was astounding to see so vital a problem as Unemployment disappear entirely from the headlines, as soon as a drive was completed or an argument in Congress ended, as if the subject were of no importance, its place taken by local scandal or quick enthusiasm for some panacea; it was revealing for an Easterner to travel into the Middle West and find the depression considered as a phase of the everlasting difficulties of agriculture; or for him to meet returning exiles from Hollywood who complained that the East was whining, while the Far West took it on the chin and was almost unaware that it had been assaulted. The depression weighed more heavily in some sections of the country; it bore down on the holders of Liberty Bonds less than on the owners of Radio stock; the difference between taking advantage of the fall in prices and suffering more, psychologically, because prices were falling, might depend on such a little thing as the date on which one had signed a lease or another had taken out insurance. The health of the country was good; the suicide rate went up, but the death rate declined; the marriage lines showed no startling variation; savings increased (perhaps the increase in dividends and the absence of stock-market speculation accounted for it); and many more people than ever before were stockholders in great corporations. The movies were preparing their gangster cycle just as the radio was quartering its golden hours; magazines, instead of advertising their tables of contents, advertised the abstract idea of courage to meet hard times, and the optimistic among business men put up billboards urging passers-by not to miss the boat — not to miss the rare opportunity to buy their portion of America at prices which every one believed to be absurdly low. Toward the end of this period a few charming circumstances were noted: the little Eugenie hat saved the feather industry from collapse; city streets began to be cluttered with cellophane; the Navy reported fewer desertions than usual; prices of good Scotch and champagne came down; and a movement, full of sympathetic magic, to draft Coolidge began a full year before convention time.

For its villains, the country turned first to old and trusted friends. Wall Street had given the spectacular *coup de grâce* to prosperity, and although Wall Street seemed diminished and enfeebled, Wall Street was probably guilty; if not as a whole (since "we were all in it"), it was guilty in precisely that quarter to which the public had not penetrated, the lair of the bears. A year later a Congressional investigation of market practices showed that there was a general feeling that selling short was somehow against the public conscience in time of stress; but at this time people only felt that "somebody" must have made, and must still be making, a profit; the market had dipped, fallen, swooped, and collapsed several times, but there had been a few rises and as each one failed, it seemed reasonable to accuse anonymous individuals of pushing prices down, to their own advantage. Because so many people had been in the market and because stockbrokers were the first and most conspicuous suicides, financiers in general escaped the odium which had been their share in other panics. It is my guess that a certain resentment against the market rose from a feeling that Wall Street should, in its miraculous way, have led us to recovery.

Another old friend was the Red peril. Taken up with enthusiasm by Representative Hamilton Fish, it was allowed to remain his exclusive property. Although embargoes were put on Russian lumber because it was cut and sawed by "convict labor", and were withdrawn for lack of evidence, or for other reasons; although the Soviets were accused of dumping wheat in order to destroy American agriculture and of counterfeiting American currency to weaken our credit, the people refused to believe that the nation which was spending hundreds of millions on American machinery and American engineers was spending even hundreds of thousands to support the feeble Communist party in America.

It argued a kind of clarity of mind for Americans to look

to themselves for the causes of the depression. Conspicuous bank failures might be caused by scoundrels, but the general enthusiastic disruption of an entire system had to be traced to general causes. The incompetent business man let it be known that fortunes were made by fools like himself, but only God can make a depression; [1] critics with less to defend found other, closer villains and although the literate population of the United States did not suddenly become economically clear-minded, certain respectful attitudes were abandoned and the feeling that everything had not been for the best in 1929 was developed. Capitalism was on trial not before those who had gained most and failed to consolidate their gains, but before those who had suffered. Naturally they attacked first the industries and the habits of industry which had been most successful: the motor car, the radio, the great banks, and high-pressure salesmanship. The manufacturers of cars prepared their annual models and held their annual show; they gave out and advertised their stupendous figures: five million men employed; consumption of more than three quarters of the rubber and gasoline used in the country, of more than half the plate glass and the upholstery leather; of a quarter of the lead and more than that of the aluminum; and of more than one tenth of such basic materials as iron, steel, copper, and hard wood. These were joyful figures when cars were selling; when they were not, they meant that the contracting motor-car industry was undermining the others exactly in proportion to its previous support. The logic was a little twisted, but people felt

[1] A plea ultimately rejected by the courts. It is to the credit of Mr. Paul G. Forthy, of Birmingham, Alabama, that he brought the fundamental question of the depression to a decision. Mr. Forthy, like many others, had signed a lease and agreed to pay a certain sum per month in rent. When he found himself unable to do this he left his habitation. Sued by his landlord, he declared the lease invalid because the depression was an act of God. Judge Arthur Jenkins of the same city handed down a negative decision.

that the motor car had become a peril; they felt that if it had used a little less of each of its materials, it might have used them a little longer. A year and more after the panic, dealers' showrooms were crowded with second-hand cars, with current models which would have to make room for the new ones; and as the best possible system of selling had already been used (installment payments and turning in of slightly worn cars) no new way of putting the cars on the roads was discovered. It was estimated that the industry was ready to manufacture two or three million cars more than the country could absorb, certainly more than it needed; and the effects of depression abroad and a high tariff at home had cut exports down by nearly half (domestic sales went down by a third).

Against the bankers, the great cry was that they had ceased to be bankers and become merchants of securities. Several books of sour reminiscences were issued by ex-salesmen and even ex-bankers, exposing the methods by which securities were pumped into a community, always with the support of a great bank taken for granted; the banks had actually formed subsidiary companies for these operations and worked within the flexible ethics of their profession. The position of the banker was perfectly expressed by Thomas W. Lamont, of Morgan and Company, who spoke as a seller of bonds, not as a banker, and said, "It is a very deplorable thing, but it is the general investing public upon which these declines in every kind of bond have chiefly fallen, rather than on the banks." The dignity of bonds was being wrecked; but the general public remembered that banks had actually been backing ordinary speculative stocks and fancied that the operation had not been entirely correct. The scandal of our foreign investments went far beyond graft, although the graft rose to fantastic sums, as when the son of a Peruvian president was paid nearly half a million dollars for helping promote a bond issue of one hundred million to his country. The general question was whether bankers had not collaborated with financing institutions to unload on American citizens some fifteen thousand million dollars of foreign bonds, a great part of which could not have been considered sound security. Part of that sum had gone to finance in Germany projects which were hardly self-liquidating; but as the financing houses passed the bonds on and took only large commissions, their worries ended before bankruptcy set in. It was even possible that by over-financing we had contributed to the wreck of Germany's credit.

Into these problems the average man made small investigation; but he knew that something was wrong and suspected that those who made a profit knew of the wrong in advance. Fairly convinced that Lee, Higginson had not exactly profited by the failure of its Kreuger enterprise, the man in the street absolved the old Boston firm of chicanery; what he thought of the firm's intelligence did not exactly increase his confidence in bankers generally. In the beginning of 1932 this feeling of distrust was reflected in an advertisement of the Central Hanover Bank and Trust Company which emphasized "Banking and Fiduciary Service — *exclusively*" and went on. "It does not sell securities, has no affiliated security companies and performs no functions which conflict with its specialized services." And the moral was driven home again at the bottom of the page: "No Securities For Sale."

A generation cradled in advertising had, at the same time, begun to make fun of advertising. The satire of the intellectuals had not been quite so fatal as reported; the more they burlesqued preposterous testimonials, the more the testimonials grew to be burlesques of themselves; satire had only indicated to the advertisers themselves that they were pushing their favorites too far.

A more notable change was in the social promise of the

advertisements. They had been cast for wealth and position; with the depression, socks and razors and collars were sold as aids in getting jobs. But when the hope of jobs began to be faint, and advertisers did not wish to stir in their prospective customers an attitude of scepticism, they turned to Love. Here they were on safe ground. The man who shaved only once a day was shown asleep, his wife looking upon him with disgust and horror; or he was shown rubbing a day's growth of stubble, while his wife was on the way home to mother. The delicacy of domestic life in America was as great as that of a Court of Love in the late Middle Ages and our high divorce rate was at last explained. In these advertisements, the male was always the guilty one; it was he who neglected mouth wash and garters and starched collars; on his stupidity, love was wrecked. Europeans who had been in the habit of saying that American women do not care for love (as American men know nothing of its beauties) must have been surprised by the emergence of Eros as the dominant in advertisements.

Another element in salesmanship, installment buying, rode the first storm well. One of the promises of those who opposed the system was that it would break down the moment money grew scarce; but it did not, and the large credit corporations made money. (The percentage of failure to pay rose, by about half, but the general business was enormous: more than half a billion dollars were spent through motor-car financing alone.)

These were familiar things, and one of the qualities of a good scapegoat is that it should not be too familiar; too much knowledge checked fear and hate both. At the beginning of 1931, the Senate's committee on banking and currency gave at least a name, and suggested a personality, for America's devil: the Federal Reserve System and the governor of its Board. The argument was that speculation had spiraled to dizzy heights because money was freely available to speculators and that the Federal Reserve was precisely the organ for controlling the flow of money. The Federal Reserve Bank in New York had desired to check speculation by making money cost more; Washington had limited itself to vague warnings which sounded like outworn moral maxims and were in every case washed over by waves of optimistic predictions from equal authorities. The governor of the New York bank declared that the rediscount rate (the check on speculation) had been raised too late and too little (to six per cent. from five, on August 8, 1929); Albert Henry Wiggin and Owen D. Young agreed, Mr. Young handsomely confessing that he was as much to blame as any one (in his capacity as director of the New York Bank). Governor Harrison of the same bank added another item: "bootleg loans." They are mysterious to the layman who firmly believes that the rate of interest is unalterably fixed at six per cent. for every purpose, except loans the layman himself has to make. He does not know about loans representing huge sums of money lying in banks to the credit of manufacturers, corporations, and individuals; they were loaned "on call", that is, on a day-to-day basis; and the rate of interest varied with the demand. A speculator, having exhausted his credit at a bank, got further credit when heavy depositors offered fresh money at call rates; and these rates rose as high as twenty per cent. Obviously, to pay twenty per cent. for money, one must make a large profit quickly. (Part of the huge surpluses of commercial and industrial companies came not from earnings, but from interest on call loans.) From the outside came a further criticism: that it was unreasonable to expect Federal Reserve banks to check speculation when they were directed by bankers whose chief interest was to encourage speculation. Mr. Wiggin was not in favor of banks lending money on unlisted securities, but the subsidiaries through which banks sold securities were generally defended; Mr. Young, who wished to prevent call money coming from corporations, disagreed with these bankers, particularly as the selling organizations were not subject to the same scrutiny as the banks themselves.

The Federal Reserve System had been created to stabilize the banking business and to control currency; in the popular mind it was supposed to prevent bank failures and panics. It had not prevented the panic and although it had reduced bank failures — five out of every six banks which failed were not in the System — its judgment or its powers were seen to be faulty; it might do as a scapegoat for a time. The country was getting "warm" in the game of finding the real villain, hardly a personal devil, but one which combined all the best features of all the others: it was familiar and mysterious at once, dangerous and desirable. At the end of 1930, Viscount d'Abernon had said, "This depression is the stupidest and the most gratuitous in history", and declared that all the requisites for recovery were at hand "except monetary wisdom." And pointing, impolitely, he added, "The situation could be remedied within a month by joint action of the principal gold-using countries through the taking of necessary steps by the central banks." The sacred name of Gold had been mentioned.

The scapegoat still escaped us; the search for a savior was even less encouraging. We did not know whether to tinker with or scrap our system of living; nor, if we tinkered, whether to diminish or expand, deflate or inflate; nor if we scrapped, whether to go Communist or Fascist. Our leaders differed and, what was worse, gave us no sure direction. Mr. Andrew Mellon, doubly the exponent of capitalism through his private and his public careers, argued almost in the words of Karl Marx that capitalism is subject to epidemics of overproduction and deduced from this condition the categorical imperative that "the standard of living which obtains [in America] must be

maintained at all costs." To him the cure for the ills of capitalism was more capitalistic enterprise: "the ultimate solution
of the world's difficulties would seem to lie in the possibility
of building up a higher standard." (In grosser terms, finding
new backward countries to exploit, a new area of low resistance
to high-pressure salesmanship, a new body of consumers to
whom credit could be given.)

Another suggestion was that profit could be made even under
adverse conditions. The Austin Company, engineers and builders, known for their work in creating an entire city in Russia,
advertised "a revolutionary development" which reduced the
investment in a manufacturing plant by twenty per cent. to
forty per cent., delayed obsolescence in machinery and, controlling conditions in a factory properly planned to economize
on light and labor, promised "profitable operation, even while
running at fractional capacity." Revolutionary this was, to
promoters who believed that one must run always at full capacity and that the moment capacity was reached, another
factory must be built in order to arrive at greater capacity.
Practical also, but held back by infinite complications in real
estate law and taxes and mortgages, was the plan to make
housing a ladder industry; each half year of the depression
found more and more people certain that housing was the
cure; H. G. Wells embodied the proposal in his voluminous
story of the Work, Wealth, and Happiness of Mankind; the
President gave the idea his heartfelt blessing and manufacturers
of all the materials which go into the American house were
banding together to fight the motor car, making a new house
as desirable as a car had been. (Houses lacked the attractive
qualities of motor cars: they could not be moved from place
to place, they could not be turned in at the end of a year,
and they could not be thrown away.) Public works were still
considered useful, although the President's own figures showed
that at the end of August, 1931, only seven tenths of one

per cent. of the unemployed had found jobs on Federal building projects (some forty thousand men). The large-scale Prosperity Loan, vaguely spoken of for six months, was made definite by William Randolph Hearst in June and became an issue of great importance long before its value as inflation was recognized, and was attacked eventually for being as "un-American" as the dole or the bonus.

Each industry had a suggestion; the railroads were agreed that higher rates would start business going; the farmers, badgered from Washington to cease farming (reduce acreage, destroy produce) were persuaded that Federal protection of prices would restore prosperity; a very rich man rebuked his fellows for laying up their yachts and swore he would keep his in commission because spending a hundred thousand dollars would "thaw out" a million in credit. But all these practical schemes appeared too visionary, and it was left for the scheme of the greatest of all visionaries, the Russian Communists, to persuade so many practical men that the President of the United States felt moved to denounce them.

The Five Year Plan of the Soviets was heard of in 1930, but insufficiently understood, and those who had most to learn from it assumed that it was largely a work of propaganda. At the beginning of 1931 "social planning and control" was put down as the basis of a Third Party by John Dewey, who had been in Russia when the Plan was germinating. Doctor Harry Emerson Fosdick accepted the phrase and, speaking from the pulpit of the "Rockefeller Church", said it was the alternative to violent Communism. Norman Thomas, a few months later, considered the lack of plan one of the gravest defects of the American system: "Employers have not been able to forecast the market . . . or prevent recurring depression. . . . This planless, wasteful profit system gives us a new type of misery: poverty and unemployment in the midst of potential

plenty." Meanwhile Russia was moving "with giant strides
. . . toward Lenin's aims" (industrialization, electrification,
mechanization) without attracting the attention of any but
radicals and intellectuals (the latter as prone as the first great
American intellectual, Henry Adams, to go down on their
knees before a dynamo). Then two things occurred: the first,
coming to a country with five million jobless men, was the
news that there was no unemployment in Russia; the second
was a small book, intended for beginning readers in Russia,
called "New Russia's Primer." It exploited the interest evoked
by earlier books; distributed by the Book of the Month Club
and gaining impetus with every enthusiastic review, the little
book was first an excellent piece of propaganda for Russia (as
the emergent nation more than as the Communist experiment),
then a bold attack on America, and finally an exposition of
the art or method of Planning. Within a few months the
magazines were full of articles on plans for America, the words
"Five Year Plan" became common enough to be seen in jokes
and to be heard from the stage, and several books like "New
Russia's Primer" were issued, not so much in praise of Russia
as in dispraise of America.

The enthusiasm for planning in America stirred liberals more
than radicals; if planning could save America from Communism, the Communists would as soon have none of it.
The liberals hoped to import a Communist invention, savior
of the Russian system, without importing any other part of
the system. That is to say, we were passionate for a plan, but
we dissociated it from the moral fervor which underlies the
Plan in Russia. Communism as a religion, we rejected. Planning
was for us an economic solution; basically it seemed to har-
monize the two elements which, at odds, had ruined America:
production and consumption. In an advertisement of the Graybar Electric Company the problem had been stated even without reference to the Russian experiment:

"We can . . . endeavor to control the delicate interplay between production and consumption. Or we can let matters take their own sweet course.

"We can try to keep our reserves of supply materials down to fighting trim. Or we can pile up huge and wasteful stocks each in our own little storerooms. . . .

"We can watch out for the germ of overproduction before it becomes malignant. . . . Or we can continue blissfully to ignore the early stages of the disease.

"All this is nothing but mere abstract economics." [2]

Yet I think the emotional factor was even more important. Planning appealed to us as a principle of unity in a world which was falling apart, a principle of growth in a country which, we feared, was merely growing old. Patriotism had held us together; pioneering had given us a common adventure; prosperity had let us share experiences and given us pride. Now nothing bound us; we had lost an old faith and gained no new one; if we had known of an enemy outside our own frontier, we might have become marching men, rejoicing in companionship, but we could not even join in a parade, because we had nothing to celebrate. We had lost faith and friendliness and here was a system which would force us to coöperate again. We knew that we were not a unified, harmonious, happy country and got more proof of it on every side. I have already mentioned the breaking up of the unity implied in the name of our country, when States attempted to live in isolation. We were unable to uphold a unified principle of Prohibition. In industry our two greatest forces were hostile,

[2] The advertisement was for Graybar as a distributing agency, the distributor appearing as a regulator of, and bridge between, producer and consumer.

motors forcing down the price of steel, steel trying to hold its prices against motors; the campaign undertaken by the housing industries which I have alluded to was a serious effort to break down the dominance of the motor car; in more familiar fields, the tobacco manufacturers attacked the makers of candy ("Reach for a Lucky instead" — the final words "of a sweet" were omitted after a violent quarrel) and the advertisers of Listerine seemed to go out of their way to belittle eggs. Some, at least, of the veterans of the Great War were dividing off from the citizenry as a whole, demanding special privileges; a deep economic division began to appear: our *rentier* class, those who derived most of their income from fixed rates (mortgage holders and holders of certain bonds) were hostile to those who drew their money in variable salaries and wages — the deflationists against the inflationists. It was to the advantage of some people that others should go to the wall. We were hardly one people, with one problem.

I have said that the contrast between our unemployment and the virtual assurance of work in Russia was the prime reason of our interest in the Five Year Plan; that interest, in itself, was a shock to old established beliefs. That any other country could be "better off" than ourselves had been unthinkable; that it should be servile, ignorant, and, according to our leaders, economically unrighteous Russia, was unbearable. This was the immediate, day-to-day, economic surface; beneath it lay another and more serious *malaise*. For four and a half centuries we had been The New World, imagining ourselves to be the leaders in political thought, the foremost of democracies in a world which was obviously becoming all democratic after our model; the sneers of Europe were symptoms of its malady of old age, and the flattery of Europe, in a century of revolutions, ending in the Great War, was more important, because after each violent event, converts to our cause were registered. We held ourselves the creative center of the world, nothing less. We were changing, growing, progressing, and leading. It was bad enough that we should be suddenly thrown back by an economic depression; but we could still believe that we had the future in our hands until we saw the eyes of the world turn from us toward the East. Russia, larger than the United States, as rich and varied in resources, suddenly developed a violent creative energy to which we knew only two parallels in history: in the Renaissance and in our own country. We who had broken the great tradition and made the great experiment saw our tradition flouted and a new and perilous experiment made by others. We who had been mocked for too much energy knew that the center of dynamic power had been shifted from us to the one rival we had never taken seriously. Napoleon had said that a century after his death the world would be dominated by America or by Russia; but we had never admitted an alternative. We had barely arrived at dominance, our political position was still challenged although our financial authority was accepted; and Russia arrived to take over the mysterious power which an ideal, passionately pursued, always gives to a nation. Russia was creating a new world; we were, like Great Britain, perhaps, falling back.

It had been the good fortune of the United States never to know what it means to be a country of the second order of importance. When we were making our awkward beginnings, Europe was in turmoil; while we were exploring our country, desperately concerned with our own affairs, we kept out of competition and almost out of contact with Europe. Our first entry on the international scene was a spectacular success, for we destroyed the power of one of the oldest of European nations. In our own opinion we acquitted ourselves well in the great European sport of making war; we had colonies, dependents, and economic vassals; we had learned all the tricks of financing and were adepts in the patter of peaceful penetration; our overlordship over South America had been questioned only by South America. In 1918 we had dictated peace to Europe (we thought) and proved our superiority by rejecting the peace ourselves, that simple action wrecking the League of Nations, to reëmphasize the dependence of the world system upon our whims and ambitions. In 1919 we were obviously destined to command; in the next ten years we Americanized the world to such an extent as to make ourselves thoroughly feared and disliked; but our sense of lordship was not diminished. We looked upon the two systems of dictatorship in Europe as aberrations, temporary shiftings of power before our methods would be found superior. And then, with a moral fervor we had lost and a faith in the very technique which had led us into the swamps, Russia arrived to shove us aside, not as the leader of the world, but as the center of the world's interest.

It was a consolation to know that Russia was importing men and methods from us. The three giant strides could be summed up as Americanization; but we knew that Russia was not importing the capitalist system, only its advantages. She had the strength and the courage to experiment, to build, to move masses of men from one post to another, to cut working days down to five or extend them to seven; the fabric of life which was so stiff and worn and dirty in our hands was new and flexible in hers. "Why," asked Mr. Stuart Chase, "should Russia have all the fun of making a new world?" The economic arguments against the Five Year Plan were cold consolation; the repeated assurance that planning fatally involved a corresponding loss in liberty meant little to those whose only liberty was to be worried by harassed employers or to be harassed themselves by the fear of never getting another job. At some distant time the necessity to repair and rebuild the dam at Dnieprostroy might mark the beginning of the

end for a system which used capital without enjoying capitalism; for the moment, the world belonged to Russia.

The doldrums into which we sank in the middle of 1931
showed us that the wind of a common purpose had been taken
out of our sails. Unable to rearrange our lives on the Russian
plan, we fell back on the dreariest of economic explanations:
the theory of cycles. The trained economist may mean by the
theory of cycles anything from the grim determinist (and
brilliantly prophetic) analysis of Marx to the idea that an
occasional economic blood-letting (in which the weak bleed
to death) is desirable. The layman takes the theory of cycles
as part of the black magic of business. I have heard it said that
depressions must occur every twenty-seven years, or in years
with the number three or seven (the latter is an obscure
throwback to the seven lean kine in the dream of Pharaoh) or
at other intervals bearing some mystic relation to each other.
The Marxist analysis is that "modern bourgeois society with
its relations of production, of exchange and of property, a
society that has conjured up such gigantic means of production and exchange, is like the sorcerer who is no longer able
to control the powers of the nether world whom he has
called up by his spells. For many a decade past the history of
industry and commerce is but the history of the revolt of
modern productive forces against modern conditions of production. . . ." (That is, against the property relations upon
which the rule of the bourgeoisie depends.) "It is enough to
mention the commercial crises that by their periodical return
put on its trial, each time more threateningly, the existence of
the entire bourgeois society. In these crises a great part not
only of the existing products, but also of the previously created
productive forces, are periodically destroyed. In these crises
there breaks out an epidemic of overproduction. . . . Industry
and commerce seem to be destroyed; and why? Because there

is too much civilization, too much means of subsistence, too much industry, too much commerce. The productive forces at the disposal of society no longer tend to further the development of the conditions of bourgeois property; on the contrary, they have become too powerful for these conditions, by which they are fettered, and so soon as they overcome these fetters, they bring disorder into the whole of bourgeois society. . . . The conditions of bourgeois society are too narrow to comprise the wealth created by them.[3] And how does the bourgeoisie get over these crises? On the one hand by enforced destruction of a mass of productive forces; on the other by the conquest of new markets, and by the more thorough exploitation of the old ones. That is to say, by paving the way for more extensive and more destructive crises and by diminishing the means whereby crises are prevented."

It is a pity that Karl Marx was a propagandist and a prophet as well as a critic; and that Americans, disliking his propaganda and hoping he was a bad prophet, have never given him the attention he deserves as a critic. The translation above — a bad one, I fear, because it makes such hard reading — is from the Communist Manifesto which should be read not as the foundation of Soviet Russia, but as a criticism of American capitalism. When Marx says that modern productive forces periodically rebel against the conditions of production, he is saying precisely what the engineers and technologists of to-day are saying — and the Manifesto is ninety years old. We stumble over such phrases as "the development of the conditions of bourgeois property", not accepting Marx's terms or ideas; but he is saying in this sentence that the time comes when our factories and our shops become too skillful, mastering their technique too completely to care about the community as a whole. The intelligent half of America's great producers, the

[3] Is this Marxist for a failure of buying power?

heads of corporations, the bankers, and the economists, have been saying the same thing, in other words, during the past three years. It is one of the prime stupidities of Capitalism that it neglected Marx as a critic, because it had seemingly discredited him as a prophet. (Note, however, the prophecy at the very end of the paragraph above and compare it with the course of events in America after 1890.)

The Marxian theory of cycles is respectable because it is conditional: the periods of depression must come *if* the capitalist system continues to produce as it now does. The theory as it generally appears is not respectable because it omits the condition; not only the capitalist system, but its defects and extravagances are taken as eternal factors, and the theory of cycles simply means that every seven or twenty-seven years we must suffer. It is the hardest and bitterest version of infant damnation since Jonathan Edwards preached; it assumes that if a machine is built to produce fifty times as much as its predecessor, nothing can be done to keep it working only one fiftieth as long; it exiles the will from the common affairs of mankind. It does not even frankly say that the wrong-headedness of human beings is responsible; it draws the curtain of determinism between the victim and the guilty. It is an excellent theory for those who thrive on depressions.

It is a bad theory for those who have to go through them with any kind of courage. The theory of cycles was properly exploited in the spring of 1931 because America felt that the worst could not yet be over, since nothing decisive had been done, and nothing could be done. In effect the theory of cycles was a psychological return to the know-nothingism of the early days after the panic, the abandonment of criticism and of action, the spread of lethargy — since what had come was inevitable and would, by the healing processes of time, wear off. That the depression was world-wide, and much advertised in that way, was another excuse for doing little and thinking less. We walked with "exaggerated caution" (we were told) and confidence and credit had to be "thawed out." The best thing we could do would be to wait (destroying a few crops here and there, planting less) until we had exhausted the stocks of goods on the merchant's shelves and the raw material in the factory storerooms. Then — automatically because we had to live — industry and business would resume. These two gods — industry and business — were conceived as abstract forces, independent of our will.

Stocks were low in June, 1931, and were to go lower; but the morale of Americans had descended as low as it would go for at least a year and a half. Unpleasant things and dire things were to happen, but after June the Americans began to resist. Until then they had looked with the dumb appeal of a rather stupid dog to their leaders and their leaders had openly refused to lead. At Valley Forge, Mr. Hoover repudiated his own opportunities, referring with contempt to the "specious claim that hired representatives of a hundred million people can do better than the people themselves in thinking and planning their daily lives." Later he rejected, on economic grounds, the suggestion of a five-billion-dollar loan and, apparently unaware that the choice might ultimately lie between inflation and a planned equilibrium, went on to reject the popular idea of Planning in these words:

"Many citizens insist we produce an advance 'plan' for the future development of the United States. I presume the 'plan' idea is an infection from the slogan 'Five Year Plan' through which Russia is struggling to redeem herself from ten years of starvation and misery. I am able to propose an American plan to you. We plan to take care of twenty million increase in population in the next twenty years. We plan to build for them four million new and better homes and . . . thousands of factories; to increase the capacity of our railways; to add thousands of miles of highways and waterways; to install twenty-five million electrical horse power; to grow twenty per cent. more farm products. We plan to provide new parks, schools, colleges, and churches. We plan more leisure for men and women. . . . We plan to secure a greater diffusion of wealth, a decrease in poverty and a great reduction in crime. . . . We should have full faith . . . in those mighty resources, those intellectual and spiritual forces which have impelled this Nation to a success never known in history. . . . Under the guidance of Divine Providence they will return to us a greater and more wholesome prosperity than we have ever known."

Within a week the President was to make himself the intellectual and spiritual leader of the nation. It would appear that in this speech he wished to announce the intellectual and spiritual bankruptcy of himself and of his people, so that he could start with a clean slate. His plan was, essentially, to remain planless; the promises were only more and more of the same things — the things we had enjoyed in the past and which had brought us into the malady of the depression. The President was still looking back to the Golden Age of Calvin Coolidge for our future and asking his people to look back. Seven days later their eyes were across the sea and the depression had entered a new and more inspiring phase.

CHAPTER NINE

A NEW HIGH

ON the 20th of June, 1931, the United States made its third dramatic entrance on the international scene in fifteen years; our declaration of war in 1917 and the descent of Woodrow Wilson on European shores to make the peace were events forecast and prepared for; the Moratorium proposed by Mr. Hoover was, to most people, sudden and spectacular. From the day of the announcement, international finance became the new quantity in all the equations of the depression, an X which could be figured to infinity. In a sense, this appearance of Gold, delayed and mystifying as it was, could be taken as an act of justice. It was on the basis of the two and a half billion dollars in gold enriching us between 1914 and 1929 that we had built up the monstrous (or magnificent) credit which created the special kind of prosperity we enjoyed until the crash came; much of this gold had come from Europe, some of it in payments to us, some of it as investment or as deposit with the strongest and safest country on earth. We had not stopped to think that for every dollar we gained, some country in Europe was losing not only a dollar, but ten to fifteen times as much in credit; nor did we know that this meant a breakdown in the machinery for keeping factories running and distributing their product. We knew only that we liked to have a great gold reserve because it made us "rich." We did not know that our wealth meant to Europe a fall in the prices of commodities which, to experts, signified ruin. We did not know that the accumulation of gold which we never saw and hardly heard of was causing difficulties abroad between those who had borrowed and those who had lent; and that with the wage earner on one side and the receivers of income on the other, virtually every European was being affected in the simplest and most universal way.

The facts of the European situation came to us slowly; in spite of millions of cabled words a week, we knew little of the economic and financial complications abroad; we were going through a period of intense interest in ourselves during the boom and worry about ourselves in the depression. When the President moved to aid Europe, we took the plan to be a simple remission of debt, a temporary relief during which Europe could restore its forces. The intricacies of central banking and the mysteries of gold remained foreign to us. To a great extent they still are; and in this brief survey of the events before and after Mr. Hoover's announcement, I shall limit myself to those elements which actively touched on America and affected the emotions of the American people about their own problems. It would take another book to describe the events in Europe which took place simultaneously with those recorded here; and the mystery of Money I have to leave to more expert, and more clairvoyant, minds to explain.

The general assumptions about Europe were these: that France was the dominant nation and was wealthy, especially in gold; that Germany was fundamentally bankrupt (or pretended to be), but was living extremely well on borrowed money, and that her international standing had been assured by the Young Plan; that Great Britain had had no prosperity for ten years; that Italy's steadiness in finance concealed difficulties which Mussolini would eventually overcome; and that the other nations of Europe, Russia and Scandinavia excepted, revolved about these principal powers.

About international finance, the general assumption was

Section
1

"All the News That's
Fit to Print."

The New York Times.

LATE CITY EDITION

Section
1

VOL. LXXX... No. 26,811.

NEW YORK, SUNDAY, JUNE 21, 1931.

Copyright 1931, by The New York Times Company.

TEN CENTS

HOOVER PROPOSES YEAR'S WAR DEBT SUSPENSION WITH MORATORIUM FOR GERMANY ON REPARATIONS; EUROPEAN CAPITALS HOPEFUL; STOCKS RISE HERE

CITY STIFLES AT 93, YEAR'S HOTTEST DAY; WAVE NATION-WIDE

Firms at Leipzig Fair Favor
Ending Tariffs, Survey Shows

Heat Opens Parks to Sleepers
at Six Baths and Score of
Fountains Are Reported.

POPE DENIES ACCORD, DENOUNCING FASCIST; STATUS AGAIN ACUTE

Surplice Attack Charges Rome
With Spying, Persecutions
and Continual Menaces.

SEES FALSE IDEAS ABROAD

MOVE CHEERS ALL GERMANY

Hoover Hurries to Camp
To Escape Capital's Heat

STOCKS EXPERIENCE 'BOOM'

But Rises Up to 15 Points Are
Nearly All Lost When Curb
on Credit Is Ordered.

DRAIN OF GOLD CONTINUES

Text of the President's Statement Proposing Suspension of Debts

He Emphasizes That He Does Not Approve Cancellation of Obligations to Us and Says That No Nation Has Proposed Such a Course.

CONTINGENT ON CONGRESS

Plan of President Also Is
Linked to World Arms
Reduction.

HE PUTS ISSUE TO ALLIES

Purpose Is to Give Coming Year
to Economic Recovery of
the World, He Says.

DAWES AND YOUNG FOR STEP

Senate and House Leaders, Diplomats and Treasury Experts
Give Aid to Proposition.

BRITAIN LIKENS MOVE STOCKS SPURT HERE TO OUR ENTRY IN WAR ON AID TO GERMANY

Statesman Says Hoover Effort
to Avert Economic Disaster Was
Seen as Inevitable.

Up 3 to 11 Points In Biggest
Upswing in 19 Months on
News of Hoover Move.

FOILS KIDNAPPING OF W. A. FLAGG'S SON

Young Daughter of Broker
Screams and Chases Man
Till He Drops Infant.

MAID STUNNED BY A BLOW

BANKERS TO APPEAL, KRESEL UP TUESDAY

Bank of U. S. Counsel to Plead
to Indictment When Three Convicted Men Are Sentenced.

POLLOCK VINDICATION SEEN

Marcus and Singers Spend
Night in Tombs
Near Gangster's Cell.

that all of Europe was, compared to ourselves, poor, but that all of Europe was accustomed to being poor. Remission of war debts, rejected as a moral obligation, might be a good thing for increasing foreign trade; but it could not be essential to the prosperity of Europe because it represented so small a portion of the expenditures of all the European governments.

We did not know that Austria was approaching complete bankruptcy and was being saved by loans from Great Britain; we could not understand, if we had known, how Great Britain, in the midst of her stringency, could borrow money from France to lend to Austria; the connection between international politics and finance was always obscure to us, and we did not know that Germany, forced by internal dissensions, was preparing an arrangement with Austria, that France would oppose it, and that consequently France would refuse to join England in supporting Austria; that Austria would go down and France would begin withdrawing money from the Bank of England; that Germany would be left without support; and that a great separation would be made between the money Germany owed to private citizens of foreign countries and the money she owed to foreign governments. We had heard, indeed, that money was international and thought that the great banks coöperated; we did not know that the unity of Europe might be based as much on mutual hostility as on mutual advantage, and that Austria might pull England down, but England, going down, might send France up on the international seesaw.

The moment Austria collapsed, Germany was doomed and England was threatened. In each of these countries, Americans had investments; more than half a billion dollars in Great Britain, more than a billion in Germany, in stocks and bond issues. We had further investments in countries affiliated with these; and beyond our investment we had an interest to see that nations enjoying more or less the same system as ourselves, politically and economically, should not go down. To save Germany from bankruptcy was to fortify an emplacement against Bolshevism; to help England was to help a conservative capitalist State, threatened with socialism; merely preserving our investments and our customers were minor advantages compared with these.

No taint of smugness or hypocrisy spoiled the announcement of the Moratorium; the advantage to the United States was stressed. The President allowed a touch of drama in the way the news was given to the newspapermen of Washington, calling them suddenly, keeping them waiting, and handing them the most important item of news on a Saturday afternoon with instructions to hold it until the Sunday-morning papers, preventing the issue of extras. Yet the wording was calm and unemotional; it was an economic document carrying domestic and international provisos:

"The American Government proposes the postponement during one year of all payments on intergovernmental debts, reparations and relief debts, both principal and interest, of course, not including obligations of governments held by private parties. Subject to confirmation by Congress, the American Government will postpone all payments . . . conditional on like postponement . . . of all payments on intergovernmental debts owing the important creditor powers."

The President's covering statement was a little warmer:

"The purpose of this action is to give the forthcoming year to the economic recovery of the world and to help free the recuperative forces already in motion in the United States from retarding influences from abroad. The world-wide Depression has affected the countries of Europe more severely than our own. . . . These and other difficulties abroad diminish buying power for our exports and in a measure are the cause of our continued unemployment and continued lower prices to our farmers. . . .

"The essence of this proposition is to give time to permit debtor governments to recover their national prosperity. I am suggesting to the American people that they be wise creditors and good neighbors. . . ."

The Moratorium was received with enthusiasm at home and abroad; Mr. Hoover came closer than he had ever been to the position of Woodrow Wilson at the end of the war, when he was hailed as the savior of the world. Criticism at home scattered its shots, Mr. Hearst alone coming to the one possibly important point, that the Moratorium favored the bankers and the large investor over the people as a whole, since it gave precedence to private debts and postponed and, he suspected, made it simple to cancel public ones. This, a point in economics, had meaning; the rumors that the President had been forced into making the move, and that it was inspired by members of his Cabinet, were trivial. The further criticism, that the Moratorium was belated, had some bearing; but politically, the later the move came, the more certain it was to be acceptable to the American people; it was like Wilson's declaration of war — the people had to be persuaded that the President had exhausted every possibility and had been driven to it as reluctantly as themselves. We had grown so used to the plight of Europe, and so indifferent to it, that the President had to wait until a desperate move was justified. He made it and the process by which Central Europe, and its backer, England, were being starved of credit, seemed definitely arrested.

There followed one of those negotiations which are familiar to Europe and dishearten the good American. The proposal had come to us with provisos and conditions, but it seemed unthinkable that any one should reject it; and, in fact, the approval of Europe was prompt and almost unanimous. But at the end of a week we knew that France would not accept. Fortified by his first strong draught of popular approval, the President fought for the integrity of his plan and fought for instant action, time and the psychological effect of universal agreement being essential to success. The French made counterproposals; they were offended, it was learned, because the President had handed to them an accomplished fact, instead of a tentative scheme; they had not been consulted; and they did not wish to suspend German payments to themselves under the Young Plan. (They calculated that the per capita sacrifice was greater for the French than for Americans.) In New York, stocks rose, as the Moratorium favored the great bankers and the private owners of German securities; the bankers carried Germany through the period of negotiations by lending her more money; the French continued to make concessions and create delays with their demands. The international telephone, fruitful instrument of misunderstandings, was busy between Paris and Washington; neither of the heads of the two governments spoke the other's language; the French Senate gave approval to its Cabinet and denounced the "apparent levity with which the American Government regarded signed contracts" [1] and it was not until the 6th of July that the French signed the accord which put the Moratorium into action. In those weeks gold had fled from Germany as from a pesthole and even after the French signed, they insisted that they had agreed only to a principle; to maintain freedom of action, they transferred to London the amount of gold they would have to pay if the Moratorium did not go into effect; and as Germany staggered closer and closer to the pit of complete bankruptcy and political anarchy, the French made stricter terms for the security and peace of Europe as the French interpreted these ends. A conference in London was

[1] This was not an allusion to the contracts under which France promised to pay certain debts to the frivolous Americans.

remarkable only for the deepening of British uneasiness about their own condition, and it was not until the middle of August that the foreign creditors of Germany agreed to continue a credit to her of over a billion dollars and Germany could assume that her position among the nations had been made regular. In the meantime some of her greatest banks had closed, others had been forced to refuse payment of more than ten per cent. of deposits on demand, and the entire financial system had been irreparably shaken.

In August the Bank of England borrowed one hundred and twenty-five million dollars from the Federal Reserve Bank and the same amount from the Bank of France. In the same month, the Labor Government fell, pushed, it was said, by American financiers who refused to extend loans unless the English dole were reduced and other domestic economies made; when a Coalition Government was formed to meet these demands and to keep England on the gold standard, private bankers in America and France gave it a loan of four hundred million dollars; a month later the gold standard was abandoned.

CHAPTER TEN

DISASTER

THE day the Moratorium was announced was the first happy day in America in a year and a half; morally, for the qualities of pride and hope and confidence, it is the high point in three years. At last the newspapers had something to throw across their front pages; a word forgotten since August, 1914, became the talisman of prosperity; the flaccid will, the torpor of the intellect, and the grave lowering of the spirit from which we had suffered were put aside, as promptly as darkness is put aside by light. We saw an action begun and were invited to share in putting it through. It was an action on the international scale; it was generous and at the same time wise; and the desperate need of the American people was shown by the cry of gratitude which rose from them; gratitude and relief that something — anything — had been done was as marked as approval of the Moratorium itself. About its effectiveness they could only hope and pray; what gave them hope was that they were again being led.

The President was acting in the absence of Congress and had phrased the announcement so that it could not fail to appeal to the American people: it was that thing dearest to their hearts: a "business proposition" with a strong overlay of idealism. The emotional elements were all favorable: the Moratorium saved, in the first instance, Germany, so that we were forgiving our enemies; it helped Europe, so we were heaping coals of fire on those who had called us Uncle Shylock; it

meant surrendering immediate money and cleared us of the
bad name of dollar chasers; it postponed, and took out of political action, the problem of war debts, offering to the can-
cellationists a great hope and to the strict collectors enough
security. By including the other creditor nations in the enterprise, the Moratorium reëstablished the harmony and good
feeling of the war and at the same time seemed to lay forever
the ghosts of old wrongs and hatred. The world was again
united, again stood firm, and again America led. This was the
international side. At home an even greater change had occurred: the President, who had seemed for a year to be fighting
against the people, was once more on their side, leading them
in the direction which they had unconsciously wished to go.
He had done what all great leaders do; he had expressed the
will of a whole nation when the nation itself did not know its
will. Unity, purpose, and the will to action were combined.

For a time we enjoyed the tonic effect of the cold water
which France threw over our enthusiasm; since we had for
several years been doubtful of the goodwill of the French in
European affairs, their refusal to coöperate in an enterprise
which the rest of the world had taken to its heart even added
to our pleasure, for we had an enemy and a struggle, as well
as an ideal and a purpose. We had never been able to see eye
to eye with the French since the end of the war, and at this
moment it seemed to us that our former friend was deliberately
spiting us, even at the risk of ruin for herself. All that France
gave up, for the space of a year, was a hundred million dollars;
we were surrendering two and a half times as much. Italy with
its rocky finances, England with its desperate need, were willing to stand their share; France, with all her wealth, refused.
We dramatized the motive as a deliberate effort to destroy
Germany and we were determined not to let France have her
way. We were not convinced that Germany should not have
a second pocket battleship, and although we were not enthusi-

asts for Hitler, we assumed that the best way to crush Hitlerism was to help Germany to prosper and not to dictate to her the names and numbers and motives of the political parties she should allow to exist within her own borders. We could see no reason why two countries as close as Germany and Austria should not have a customs union. Later, when France was making the terms of an actual loan to Germany, it seemed right enough that she should demand economies, as we had suggested economies to England; but the other requirements and the willful delays in setting the Moratorium in operation seemed to us full of bad will and mean motives.

It had not occurred to us that we should fail and the feeling that we were failing caused us a profound uneasiness. The President said that "economic relief (for Germany) means the swinging of men's minds from fear to confidence, the swinging of nations from the apprehension of disorder and governmental collapse to hope." But as the weeks went on and the condition of Germany grew more and more perilous, we began to feel that Germany was swinging at the end of a rope, the other end being in the hands of the French. They had had the last word, in practice; we, on paper. The Moratorium, our birthday cake to the world, had grown stale on the way because France had the power to delay it; that it was delivered at all was due not so much to our insistence as to the indulgence of the French. We had known, since 1918, that we were babies at diplomacy in comparison with the descendants of Richelieu and Talleyrand; we could even take moral pride in our simplicity. That our two great powers — moral and material — should both be defeated by another nation was, however, not to be explained by finesse in statecraft. Indeed, as we looked over the negotiations, we saw little guile in the French moves; they had been direct as our own. We had proposed and the French had flatly rejected our proposal; the compromise was more favorable to them than to us.

The Treaty of Versailles had been, in many ways, a diplomatic defeat for the United States and we had made Europe pay for it by refusing to join the League; the Treaty was, in any case, primarily a European affair. The single American element, the League itself, we had forced upon an obstinate and sceptical France. The Moratorium was different; it was our own invention; and like the White Knight, we had been pitched headlong off our horse.

It was our high horse of national pride and we did not recover from the fall for many months. In my opinion, the discovery that we had been defeated by the French marks one of the three unhappy phases of the depression. The others are, first, our disillusion when we found that the official explanation of the depression was false, and second, when we found that the Army of the United States could be used, by official order, against ex-soldiers. In the first our economic faith was touched; in the last the strain had brought many of us to breaking point and we recognized the symptoms of hysteria. Both were domestic, both could be remedied; but the victory of the French, coming after an international struggle, was a crushing defeat for us.

We became aware of it first during the negotiations themselves; from Paris and London and Washington we learned that we were not having our own way. Even after France signed, she withheld from us any satisfaction, by insisting that she had accepted only the principal and had held out for her interest. More convincing was the news from Germany; in the middle of July, the President himself had to confess that the Moratorium had not brought any relief and that if Germany was to be saved, private bankers would have to protect their loans by lending again or Europe would have to save the country she had so nearly destroyed; the American Government, in any case, had no authority to help. The upturn of stocks was a deception; and the continuing German crisis checked whatever tendency there might have been toward brisker business in the early autumn. We could not fool ourselves into believing that we had accomplished anything; we could only believe that things would have been worse if we had not tried.

Why had we failed? Obviously because we were not strong enough to overbear France; even with the support of England, we were not strong enough. We knew that we had more gold than France; so we were compelled to look for another factor, which could only be a kind of steadiness, a stability. France, then, was in a better position than ourselves, had more confidence, and was not threatened as we were. Out of this new and unpleasant thought rose the fears which dogged us through the next winter, although we were not conscious of the reason until the weekly reports of shipments of gold to France gave up tangible evidence of our weakness and a direct pointer to the cause. At the time, we knew only that we had been overborne and could only believe that our predicament, bad as it seemed to us, was infinitely worse in the eyes of others — and in reality. It would have been worse if, let us say, Mexico had gained a diplomatic victory over us in some Pan-American dispute; but it was bad enough.

Whatever consolation we found in the fact that we were still powerful enough to help Great Britain was again taken from us when our help proved insufficient; we withstood the second shock of Europe, the abandonment of the gold standard in England, but again it seemed to us, perhaps unreasonably, that England had gone off because France had let her down. Willing as we had been to let any nation dominate Europe, it did not please us to know that the first nation in Europe was, in all disputes between us, the first nation in the world. Russia had taken precedence of us in excitement, in faith, and in experimentation; now France elbowed us out of her way in direct combat between us. Our noble idealism

THE BOSTON HERALD **EXTRA!**

TWO CENTS

MONDAY MORNING, SEPTEMBER 21, 1931—TWENTY-FOUR PAGES

BRITAIN DROPS GOLD STANDARD

American Security Markets to Be Open Today for Business

Wall Street Considers Effect on U. S. Will Be Limited

N.Y. BANKERS APPROVE MEASURES BY BRITAIN

Now Look for Inflation of The Pound—Credits Here Payable in Gold

STIMULATION OF TRADE DUE IN OPINION OF FINANCIAL MEN

(Special Dispatch to The Herald)

NEW YORK, Sept. 20.—American security markets will not be closed...

British Pilot in Crisis

England Checks Drain on Reserve—Exchanges Close Today

BANKS TO REMAIN OPEN; PARLIAMENT WILL ACT

Discount Rate Put Up to 6 Per Cent.—No Panic— "Business as Usual"

SUSPENSION TO BE TEMPORARY; POUND MAY BE REVALORIZED

(By the Associated Press)

British Cabinet's Statement

Not Alarmed

LONDON, Sept. 20 (AP)—The text of the British cabinet's statement announcing suspension of the gold standard is as follows:

Boston Comment on Crisis

CHINA DEMANDS JAPAN'S TROOPS QUIT MANCHURIA

Wang Says Steps Will Be Taken to Appeal to the League of Nations

TOKIO PREPARES CASE FOR GENEVA

(By the Associated Press)

ROY A. YOUNG
Governor of Federal Reserve Bank, Boston.

BONUS AND BEER WAR THREATENS TO SPLIT LEGION

Stormy Sessions Expected As Convention Opens At Detroit Today

---

LARGE BAY STATE DELEGATIONS ARRIVE

ATTY. T.L. WALSH SHOUSE URGES DIES SUDDENLY WINE AND BEER

Senator's Brother a Leader   Chieftain of Democrats

J. RAMSAY MacDONALD
Prime minister.

OTTAWA, ONT., Sept. 20 (AP)—R. B. Bennett, prime minister...

had been soured, our purpose frustrated; for the first time we turned away from Europe not with indifference, but with humiliation.

This was a sad end to the high hopes of June. Yet the country had gained one thing which could not be taken away: we had learned that we need not collapse ignominiously under our difficulties, doing nothing, waiting for the healing processes of time. We discovered that things could be done if the intelligence and the will to do them were forthcoming. At last we could hope that the worst was over, because we had experienced the tonic effect of action. Since the will to act had asserted itself, it might do so again. We had set our hand to the most intricate and difficult job of all, the post-war affairs of Europe; we might have been successful if our hand had not been paralyzed by outsiders. But at least we could believe that we might proceed to our own adversity with considerable courage.

CHAPTER ELEVEN

SECOND DEFLATIONS

FROM the moment the word Moratorium was uttered, the United States passed into a new phase, in which the actual forces of the depression were at last recognized. It was the recognition that was important; instead of fumbling with dull and doubtful tools, we turned to the actual mechanism by which the prosperity of the world had been ruined and by which it might be restored. A month or so after England left the gold standard, gold began to leave the United States, flowing into the Bank of France; a month later the drain was serious; it subsided, then rose again, and, following roughly the course of legislation proposed or passed, came twice to menacing figures until, by the third week in June, 1932, when the tide turned, we had shipped to Europe nearly a billion and a quarter dollars, over three quarters of a billion going to France, and had seen the French reserve rise from about half our own virtually to equality.[1] As each bill for taxes, public works, payment of bonus, and relief to the unemployed was discussed, the effect on our gold reserve was watched; at the end of May, when a wearying Congress was still debating budgetary economies and the sales tax, while the Bonus Army camped outside its doors, it was known that nearly a quarter of a billion dollars had been withdrawn in the preceding thirty days alone. With the defeat of the bonus and the apparent

[1] Per capita, the French supply of gold was greater than ours at the end of 1932.

balancing of the budget, the outgo ended and money began
again to enter the port of New York. We had passed through
a flight from the dollar; it meant that we had lost, for a time,
the confidence of France and, in the end, had resisted several
deliberate, but irresponsible efforts to ruin our credit.[2] This
was not headline news until the worst was over; it was only a
constant threat under which we lived.

If human beings were entirely governed by economic law
and if all the citizens of a country lived under the same economic pressure, the dominant factor, the flight of gold, would
have compelled us to form a single army on the defensive. That
simplification did not occur and the remarkable thing about
the period from September, 1931, to June, 1932, is that months
of it were given over to a struggle between two hostile principles, X and Y, and that in the complexities of politics, the
two principles took up residence not only in the same party, but
often in the same individual.[3] The first had gone into action

---

[2] October, 1931, was one of the bad months, and in October, Lord
Rothermere began pounding the dollar in his newspapers, particularly the *Daily Mail*, of London. He advised, in headlines, "Sell Dollar
and Franc Securities" and hinted that America would go off the gold
standard. Similar suggestions occurred in France, and, in May, 1932,
all over Europe.

[3] I use the symbols X and Y, instead of the specific terms, Deflation
and Inflation, because the elaborate mystery thrown about these
names has made them virtually meaningless to the average reader.
I do not propose, however, to make the following pages look like a
textbook in algebra; the terms will be used after they have been explained. The common reader knew in 1931 that the two principles
were in opposition, but he did not easily learn that choosing one or
the other was a matter of the gravest importance to him, and was left
to assume that because deflation had set in "automatically" (that is,
without the exercise of human will or understanding) after the crash,
inflation would also set in at its appointed time. That his comfort,
his home, his wage, and his mortgage were all affected by the duration
of the deflationary period was a little secret. The unified field theories
of Einstein might have been under discussion; they were equally obscure and, so far as any one knew, equally a matter of indifference.

as soon as the market voided its excesses; the effort to stop it
(keeping "wages" up, public works, lowering taxes, etc.) had
failed; the question now was whether it had gone far enough
or too far or only halfway; and if it had gone far enough,
whether it was not time to try the other. Thus we see a desperate effort to cut down salaries and stop extravagance and
balance budgets, and, at the same time, the process of pumping
money into the business system. In the end it was clear that
Y had won, and the new dispute was on the proper and just
way to use it; as to which, the only principle made clear in
Congress was that each party wished to use it in the way
chosen, for various reasons, by the party leaders.

"Some of the weaker," said a professor of biology, "according to the law of Nature, will naturally die under the stress
of the times. Others will not propagate their kind. The strong
and hardy will survive and reproduce. Thus the human race
will be strengthened." [4] This, the classic defense of war and
other man-made calamities (never applied to flood, drought,
or volcanic eruption), is, in effect, the defense of deflation.
Since the strengthening of the human race is part of the Divine
Plan, deflation must also be divinely guided and inspired. It
was, in any case, allowed to continue from 1929 to 1932 unchecked. That it inevitably squeezed the unfortunate and the
feeble to the wall was not one of the news items of the daily
press. The press had, however, to record the shifting of power
which deflation implies, from the man who mortgaged his
farm to the man who advanced the money; from the movie
company which financed itself in Wall Street to the bankers
who made the loans; from the owner of speculative stock to
the owner of Liberty Bonds; from the debtor, everywhere,
to the creditor.

This, the simplest fact about deflation, that it works against

[4] Edwin Grant Conklin, of Princeton, quoted in *Time*, February 8,
1932.

the man without secured income, in favor of the man to whom he pays interest on mortgage or loan, has been kept concealed or been obscured in the complex folds of the gold argument. The farmer who borrowed a thousand dollars in 1928 paid his interest by selling, let us say, a hundred bushels of wheat; in 1931 he had to sell perhaps a hundred and fifty bushels of wheat, had to work fifteen days instead of ten to plant and tend and reap enough to cover his debt. The holder of the mortgage, receiving sixty dollars, could buy in 1928 six hats; in 1931 he could buy eight. It is quite true that if the farmer made any profit, he could also buy more hats; but the burden of debt is so great that the farmer had to do without.

The salaried man who signed a lease for a house in 1929 might have paid one fifth of his salary in rent; the next year, he demanded a reduction because his salary had been cut ten per cent.; but the interest paid by the landlord to the bank or loan society had not been cut ten per cent. The landlord might economize on the services given free in the house, or postpone repairs, or take the loss himself; the salaried man couldn't work harder or, usually, get himself a supplementary job, to make up the ten per cent. But one of them had to do it; the holder of the mortgage was under no compulsion to cut his interest.

The Government of the United States, eager for every economy, has never suggested a reduction in the rate of interest on Liberty Loan and other bonds. (The Government of Great Britain has recently converted a vast amount of its debt into bonds bearing lower interest; but so long as our credit is maintained, the rate of interest must be kept up.) The result is that the buyer of Liberty Loans in the open market, three years ago, is now receiving the same rate of interest, but the actual amount he gets is worth more to him because it buys more shoes and food and theater tickets for him.

The moving-picture industry, inflating itself to keep pace

with its own advertisements, put itself finally into the hands of financiers; unable to pay its interest, it fell into the arms of the same financiers, a tricky and exigent mistress, calling bankers from lower Broadway to Hollywood, making them presidents and chairmen of boards. It is a more entertaining parallel to the bankruptcy of the farmer who has to turn over his acres to the local bank, remaining on the land perhaps as a tenant.

Confusion comes if one tries to make a clean cut between the beneficiaries and victims of deflation. The extremes are clear enough: on one side the neat, elderly little widow receiving a hundred and fifty dollars every month from her late husband's insurance company and five thousand a year from Liberty Bonds, with a few mortgages on good real estate and perhaps some bonds in solvent companies; on the other side, the man with no income and a job which used to pay him forty dollars a week for six days and now pays him twenty-two dollars for four days, out of which he has to pay as much for insurance, as much for interest on a loan or a mortgage, as much per month for the piano he bought in 1929, and other fixed charges, as he did when he got full pay. But a great many citizens are in both classes. A landlord rejoicing in a five-year lease signed in 1928 may worry over a mortgage he was forced to take out in 1930; he may have a few good bonds, a lot of stock which is not paying dividends, and no family — so that his savings on food are negligible. And the great banks which have taken over a moving-picture company may find that deflation which gave control has handed to them an expensive toy which can only pay for itself if deflation ends. "Another such victory," the bankers may say, "and we are lost."

What happens when deflation goes too far may be uncomfortable for the powerful, but the principle works long after the weak have suffered and collapsed: deflation not only gives more purchasing power to those who have untouched income;

it actually shifts power into the hands of the comparatively small number of people who control and lend money. The number is small, but the amount of the lending, in America, is colossal. I have used one estimate in another connection; Mr. W. E. Woodward uses two which do not coincide, but even the smaller figure is impressive. "Dean Donham," he says, "estimates the fixed obligations of the American Government and the American people at about two hundred billion dollars"; submitting this estimate to Carl Snyder, the great statistician of the Federal Reserve Bank, Mr. Woodward received an estimate "of all forms of indebtedness in the United States" of one hundred and fifty billion dollars, but this does not include certain sums which bring the total close to Donham's figure, even if the hundred billions in life-insurance policies are omitted. It is variously estimated that the total wealth of the United States is a little below or a little above this total of debt. On this debt we pay interest; and as the interest is compounded, we go under.

Theoretically there is no limit to deflation; it can go on so far that all securities, all mortgages, all loans become worthless by a universal bankruptcy disguised as a revolution or as complete devalorization of a country's currency — the disappearance, for example, of the old German mark and the old Russian ruble. But this is too far, because it sacrifices all the advantages — it pours out the baby with the bath and bankrupts the lender as well as the borrower. So when deflation has gone to a certain point, something must be done to check it. One plan is to stabilize at a certain level; another is to counter-deflate or perhaps, to inflate. As to the first, Mr. Woodward, seeing signs of an effort to consolidate the gains of deflation by making the conditions permanent, wrote, in March, 1932: [5]

"A price stabilization on the present level means that millions of people will lose their equities in their homes and farms;

[5] In "Money For Tomorrow" (Liveright).

that most of the real estate in the cities will have to be turned over to the holders of the mortgages; that many of the large corporations, especially the railroads, will be taken over by their bondholders; that the finances of the Federal, state, and municipal governments will fall into confusion and probably become unmanageable; that wages will go down and unemployment will increase. The total effect will be to turn the country over to its creditors."

Most economists believe that over-inflation caused the crash and the depression. (Mr. Woodward is not one of them, I suspect; he says that the only way to have counteracted the Wall Street smash was by keeping men at work and raising their wages enormously.) In order to get us back to earth, the gas had to be let out of the balloon; whether slashing the gasbag with a knife is as good a system as opening a regulator valve is doubtful. The process of deflation exaggerated itself; beginning at any point, it doubled back, so that lack of confidence caused hoarding and hoarding caused lack of confidence; or reduction in prices caused stoppage of manufactures and stoppage of manufactures, causing more unemployment, eliminated more potential buyers and forced prices down; or withdrawals of gold by France reduced the amount of credit which hastened on deflation which caused hysteria which brought about renewed hoarding. It had always been assumed that inflation was the more dangerous process because it reduplicated itself so rapidly; but our experience with deflation shows that when control is lacking, it is as easy to fall ten thousand feet as to jump ten.

As an expanding country, the United States has been inflationist almost all its life, but inflation has, fortunately, not always meant unsound money; of this our memories are vague, but we use the phrase "not worth a Continental" as the equivalent of "Confederate money" and we admire the curt definition, "The way to resume is to resume" (when we redeemed greenbacks at par). Our real inflation came from the gold fields of California and was justified by the growth of the country. Yet the word itself is a bogey and the very people who would gain most by it have been taught to fear it. At the same time a definite opposition to inflation exists; naturally, since every holder of a promise to pay will lose by inflation. In a sense it is a struggle between the living and the dead — only the dead are represented by their heirs, the holders of debts which are the symbols of credit we used up yesterday and last year and a generation ago. The man who wants a job now is prevented from working because his father worked in a factory built on borrowed money; or because he himself worked in such a factory ten years ago; or because his son fought in the war for which we are now paying. There isn't, obviously, enough gold to pay these debts; and the holders of promises to pay profit by keeping the amount of money (gold and paper and credit combined) low, rather than high.

I think it necessary to state these obvious things because in all the Congressional discussion about the bonus and the dole and the budget, it appeared that our legislators were animated by loyalty to some abstract economic principle. In effect, one side was holding the borrower to strict account and protecting the lender in an exceptional advantage; the other was not only trying to take away this advantage, but wanted to ease the way of the borrower. One side wanted us to face our past and pay what we had agreed to pay and a little more; the other wanted us to dissolve at least a part of the debt, so that we could borrow again for the future. There was, in all this, a definite conflict of principle; but the immediate interest was there also. I do not mean that Congressmen were urging the system which would profit them most individually; only that they spoke for men and women whose lives were to be changed by the issue of their debate, that some of them favored a small

class, some a large; or, at its best, that some of them believed
prosperity could come to the country only by favoring a small
class directly, the rest indirectly, while the others believed the
reverse.

That inflation tends to get out of hand may be taken for
granted. It has another disqualification: it affects us internationally. Inflation is genteel bankruptcy and the international
financier is troubled by it. He had seen its effects in Germany
when the mark fell so rapidly that bank notes issued in the
morning at, say two hundred thousand to the dollar were, according to report, called in by afternoon and surcharged in
red with a new figure, perhaps five hundred thousand, for the
five star final edition of currency. On the other hand, inflation
had been checked in France when the franc fell to about fifty
to the dollar and, by skillful management, the franc was
stabilized at about twenty-five, so that the country enjoyed
all the benefits of both inflation and deflation, and rose from
the process as the financial giant of Europe, a rival to America.
Obviously the French, watching our stumbling moves toward
inflation, did not think we should do as well and did not think
that if we succeeded, it would be to their advantage. The jobless worker, lacking the experience of the international financier, knew only that the moment Great Britain inflated, by the
drastic process of going off the gold standard, its industries had
at least a flurry of orders; he must have wondered whether our
loyalty to a standard which a great part of the world had re-
nounced wasn't a little quixotic and whether he, who had no
taste for tilting against windmills, wasn't paying the price for
the nobility of others.

He was, in fact, an unwilling sacrifice to a god he did not
worship. On the whole, he was a free-spending man; a great
argument against paying the bonus was that the money would
be foolishly spent (which was, in the circumstances, the best
thing that could be said for it; the more serious objection was
that it would be hoarded or used to pay up back debts, so that

only a small portion of it would go into circulation). Now he was told to spend and, at the same time, was told that neither the Government nor the great corporations were spending; they were economizing. Deflation meant simply that money was not being used, either because there wasn't enough of it or because people were afraid to use what there was. In September, 1931, the position was even worse: less and less money was available and the fear of using it was approaching panic. In addition to gold sent to France, and the large sums of money frozen in banks which had closed, about a billion dollars in gold and gold notes was being kept in vaults or private safes or in the historic American sock. Each of these dollars, deposited in a bank, could have been multiplied by ten in the issue of credit, so that ten thousand million dollars were being kept away from financing American business. To get this money back into use was counter-deflation without any of the ill repute of inflationary measures, and the President acted decisively; the slacker dollar was attacked, the hoarder was branded a traitor to his country, and at the end of a few weeks the President announced that hoarding was over and that instead of losing money to the public at the rate of one or two hundred million a week, the banks had gained twenty-four million dollars.[6] The real struggle against deflation was still to come.

[6] Actually the anti-hoarding campaign was not a great success. Mr. Garet Garrett (in the *Saturday Evening Post*, October 8, 1932) calls it flatly a failure, saying "only a small part of the enormous aggregate of money estimated to have gone into hiding had been returned to the banks" and this is corroborated by other observers. Mr. Garrett found in the Middle West "a very high proportion of cash sales in the field of high-priced products", the ratio of cash to installment buying being much higher than in 1928 and 1929.

It is generally believed by economists that the habit of saving bank notes instead of actual gold was a godsend to the country's financial standing. In New York one hoarder was found to have saved counterfeit notes. A notable anti-hoarder suggested to the *Herald Tribune* in that city that every one should deposit luck pieces and other gold coins, to create millions of dollars of credit.

Before expansion (or as it was timidly called, counter-deflation or reflation) appeared on any scale larger than that of the anti-hoarding campaign, industry went through several periods which it named "scraping bottom." [7] By the middle of 1931, cigarettes, which had held themselves "depression proof", were slipping and a ten-cent package (Paul Jones by name) was being called for, although it was never advertised, as the equal of the usual fifteen-cent brands. In the process of scraping, the greater industries began to look less like rowboats stuck in mud and more like great steamers being ripped by the sharp edges of coral reefs on which they were stranded. The predicament of the railroads was bad and was so advertised, particularly as the roads were appealing for a raise in rates; but the interconnection between railroad bonds and savings banks was too perilous to be stressed. The railroads knew it and the savings banks knew it; they knew that if the railroads failed to earn certain fixed amounts for two years in succession, the savings banks (notably of New York) would be compelled by law to sell those bonds within six months. Directors of trust funds would be drawn into the decline and insurance companies, with their vast commitments, might follow.

All the indices were unfavorable: the automotive industry, steel, building permits, amounts of dividends, car loadings. The last three months of the year were a profound disappointment; the Moratorium had done nothing to improve our domestic situation. Banks were failing and investigating committees were turning up evidence in municipal government and bond issues (especially for South American countries) which seriously undermined confidence. Except for the disappearance of optimistic statements from government officials, there was no sign of light in the sky. At this moment occurred one of the minor miracles of the depression: the problem of unemployment was solved.

[7] There was no "bottom" to scrape. See pages 320, 321.

I have to assume that it was solved because it disappeared from the minds of men, from the first pages of their newspapers, and, apparently, from the discussions of their leaders. For two years every economist and every politician had insisted that finding employment, and restoring men to jobs, were the essential problems of the depression; that everything else must be secondary. And then, after the wave of a hand and the utterance of a new magic word, unemployment vanished.

The magic word was "relief." Until the end of 1931, relief for unemployment included finding jobs; thereafter it meant relief from cold and hunger. Sporadic efforts occurred, the old campaigns were brightened with new names, but the principal business now was to treat the symptoms and let the disease take care of itself. The habit of two years could not of course be abandoned over night; a list of projected works was issued from Washington and the Employment Service of the United States had put some three hundred thousand men to work, whether for a day or a week or a year was not known (the number of unemployed was creeping up toward seven million); the three hundred thousand were to be added to the one hundred thousand men who might be employed by January 1, 1932, directly on Federal building; the President, as I have noted, also explained that if six million men were jobless, the situation was not as distressing as it seemed; it was from a conference with the President that bright newspapermen returned and, without quoting him, conveyed the suggestion that it might be a good thing to omit the word "unemployment" from the newspapers (whether to call the jobless our new "leisure class" or "the happy few" was not determined); Secretary Doak was working for a six-hour, five-day week, the intent being to give more men a little work to do; the number of unemployed, including many skilled men, strengthened the hands of employers who cut wages; the American Federation of Labor approved of dividing work, especially through a five-day week; in several Eastern States, strikes occurred.

The distinguished men who had been summoned by the President to deal with relief had, in truth, appointed a sub-committee to consider plans and suggestions for increasing employment; the subcommittee reported in favor of Resumption of Work. It also approved of White Collar Relief and Public Works. Private citizens were urged to take a sporting chance and buy ahead of their immediate requirements and industry was invited to buy instantly a portion of its annual needs in raw materials.

In the middle of February the problem of unemployment was again thrown back to the private citizen. In a great campaign, using all the tricks of wartime propaganda, the American Legion undertook to persuade a million employers each to take on one additional man; from the radio, from billboards, from bright boxes on newspaper pages, the campaign was encouraged and advertised; those who gave a job got a sign to put in the window, "We have enlisted", like the famous Red Cross sign of war days. The Bok Award, given annually to distinguished benefactors of Philadelphia (among them Leopold Stokowski and Connie Mack) went to "the Unknown Citizen", the money going to the unemployed; this caused some confusion of thought. By the middle of May, 1932, people were growing accustomed to the idea of ten million unemployed and the Brotherhoods (the combined railwaymen's unions) summed up the achievements of eight months of remedying or forgetting unemployment in the most serious words a President of the United States had had to hear from loyal labor in many years:

"Unless something is done to provide employment and relieve distress we cannot be responsible for the orderly operation of the railroads. We refuse to take the responsibility for the disorder which is sure to rise if conditions continue. . . . The unemployed citizens we represent will not accept starvation."

Starvation was the last thing from the President's thought. He had said again and again that no one should go cold or hungry. For months before the Brotherhoods called on him with their somber warning, he had planned to avoid the very thing they threatened. He had engaged in the second, by far the greater, battle of the dole.

It is reported of a Chinese philosopher that he wrote one of his greatest works while waiting for his luggage to be examined by customs officers; [8] the position of Mr. Hoover was a little different: he was compelled to write a philosophy while running for his life; his opponents were also making plans, but the responsibility was all the President's. In the midst of a disaster, he had not only to keep the business of the country going, a vast enterprise in itself, but to create a new social system, checking the rout, reforming his lines, and improvising an entirely new scheme of battle. The defenders of the President say that he was not to blame for the crisis and is to be praised for all he did to make tolerable its rigors; the better defense is that the President had to act without immediate orders from the people and without any way of referring back to the people; the American political system had isolated the President in a vacuum. Under the French or British system, the President could have come before Congress with his program and, suffering defeat, would have gone to the country; in six weeks of campaigning, the issue of the dole would have been thoroughly canvassed and the President or his opponents would have been returned to power *with a specific mandate*. As things stood, the Democratic Party held uncertain power in Congress out of

[8] Bertrand Russell, who tells the story, says the only reason for doubting it is that the book isn't long enough.

general discontent with the Administration, but the country had not voted on any of the principal planks in its legislative program. The outbursts of political wildness among the Democrats and the stubborn Bourbonism of the Republicans rise from the same source: neither party was directed by the people, neither had any fixed responsibility to the people. Instead the mandates came from the newspapers and the lobbyists; and responsibility was postponed a year, to the presidential campaign which might be fought on issues totally irrelevant to the economic crisis.

This lack of support was particularly trying to the President; conservative not only in temper, but by the very terms of his oath of office,[9] he had to resist all radical suggestions, even if only to delay them, so that he would never sacrifice the thing he knew for the untried and, in his opinion, unworthy. The President was not a great political thinker, but his principles can be discovered in the dynamics of his action; he was slow to start because he believed in letting established forces alone as long as possible; he resisted change because he knew that America is not essentially a revolutionary country and hoped that the interaction of radical and reactionary principles would create a smooth compromise. He was a believer in institutions and would not scrap one which was working badly, to establish a new one, because the interval between the end of the old and the perfection of the new could leave us without directing force. Against the wild men of Congress, he was a rock; but he was also a rock against the sane men when they did not share his principles.

Every step by which the question of the dole moved from the country to Congress, through Congress to the President, and back again, illuminates a mental and spiritual change

[9] ". . . preserve, protect, and defend the Constitution of the United States", with never a word about changing, improving, scrapping, or nullifying.

brought about by economic pressure. Before following these steps, we need one definition: the city or the State could give food and clothing and even money, in extreme cases, without violating the American principle of No Dole; it was only when the Federal Government did these things that the principle was in danger. On the other hand, there was no limit to the money which the Federal Government could advance to banks or industrial corporations. What the radical and the humanitarian made of this fine difference will presently appear; the one thing they did not mention is that, delicate as the distinction may appear and trivial in comparison with the issues of life and death, it has been fought over for a hundred and fifty years in America, as the reverse of the doctrine of State Rights *vs.* Federal Rights. Confusion only rose from finding the Republican Party, traditionally Federalist and Hamiltonian, refusing to take responsibility and throwing it back to the States, while the Jeffersonian and State Rights Democrats insisted upon the obligations of the central authority.

I have noted that a year after the crisis began, the American Federation of Labor rejected unemployment insurance as unAmerican. In the twelve months which followed, the lines were more closely drawn, with employers against direct relief, and the unorganized unemployed willing to receive it from any source. The opponents of the dole insisted that it was vitally necessary to maintain the American tradition of private charity, although the President's own appointees were telling him that in Boston at one time only five per cent. of direct relief came from private sources,[10] the rest from the city government; in Chicago the percentage was higher, but private contributions amounted to only half the sum spent; in Cleveland and Philadelphia and New York, the gifts of individuals were exhausted before half the year was over. Mr. Silas Strawn, President of the

[10] Reported by the National Association of Community Chests and Councils.

United States Chamber of Commerce, said, after these facts were published, "It would be deplorable if this country ever voted a dole. When we do that, we've hit the toboggan as a nation." The prospect did not embarrass Governor Gifford Pinchot of Pennsylvania, who wrote to the President asking for a special session of Congress to deal with unemployment and suggested appropriations for the relief of the needy; he was rebuked by Senator Reed, of his own State, but the powerful and ultra-conservative Reed Smoot said bluntly, "We should raise sufficient funds to feed the hungry, even if we have to issue bonds to do it." From Texas a wilder voice suggested a rump session of Congress to force the President's hand. The President replied by organizing, much earlier than in previous years, his committee of distinguished men, placing at the head Walter S. Gifford, of the American Telephone and Telegraph Company.

The division was clear: private relief, bolstered by municipal and state appropriations, against relief flowing from the Federal Treasury. The first question Mr. Gifford had to answer was inspired by the experience of the Red Cross six months earlier: would he accept and administer moneys voted for direct relief by Congress; he skillfully evaded the issue. At about the same time, Franklin D. Roosevelt, Governor of New York, and receptive to suggestions that he might lead his party against Hoover in 1932, sent a special message to the Legislature:

"Modern society . . . owes the definite obligation to prevent the starvation or dire want of any of its fellow men and women who try to maintain themselves but cannot. . . . To these unfortunate citizens aid must be extended by government — not as a matter of charity but as a matter of social duty. . . . Private charity will prove inadequate. . . . The State of New

York . . . must itself make available a large sum . . . to provide work . . . and where such work cannot be found, to
provide them with food . . . and with clothing and shelter. . . ."

The Governor had announced a social principle but he had
not accepted the dole. "Under no circumstances," ran his pro-
viso, "shall any actual money be paid in the form of a dole to
any unemployed or his family." Jobs were to be found and, jobs
wanting, food, fuel, clothes and shelter. Not money. This was
excellent political strategy, but Mr. Roosevelt was forced to
uncover the hidden joker in all discussions of the dole. The
money required was twenty million dollars; the Governor proposed that it be raised by an increase of fifty per cent. in State
Income Tax. There was neither guile nor exceptional financial
genius in this; the money probably could not have been raised in
any other way as well. All Mr. Roosevelt, and the State of New
York which did as he desired, had shown was the direct connection between *relief* (dole or not) and *taxes*, almost certain to be
income taxes. For months thereafter the discussion of the dole
went on with silence on this fundamental point, as if Congressmen were suddenly overcome with the vulgarity of talking
about money; and did not like to say that as you cannot tax the
poor in order to feed them, you must tax the rich. The whole
argument had, therefore, a tone of artificiality which marched
well with the intense desire of millions of people not to be made
aware of the physical suffering of millions of others. This was
called keeping the discussion on a high plane. On the lower plane
were the brutal facts of hunger and cold, of homelessness and
hopelessness.

The dole, under whatever name, had arrived in the foreground of the American mind; by September it appeared in an
advertisement of the Packard Motor Car Company in an attack

on hoarding: "A Dollar for Dole — or An Hour of Work?" was the alternative offered, the implication being that the man with ten thousand dollars to invest could do more good with it, and give himself profit, by putting it into motor cars or any productive activity, than by holding on to it until it was pinched from him, little by little, to support those whom his timidity kept in idleness. Organized labor was on the side of the manufacturers; again, as a year before, the American Federation of Labor rejected unemployment insurance (the more accurate name for the dole), but this time the vote was far from unanimous. The dole system was compared to slavery, under which employers guaranteed shelter, food and work; and President Green indicated the prime objection of organized labor when he said that insurance against unemployment could only come under a system which could compel men to take jobs whether they wished to or not — that is to say, it would destroy the power of the unions. The Federation voted to protect itself against Federal control of labor; it was against State Socialism and State Capitalism, both.[11]

We are still in the pre-Congressional period, the time of pressure without direct object, for no specific bill for Federal relief had even been seriously announced at this time. The President was being beforehand, trying to rally behind him all the people, to whom he addressed himself in earnest appeals, not so much defending his doctrine as asking them to put into the action their own principles. On the radio he said, "No governmental action, no economic doctrine, no economic plan or project can replace that God-imposed responsibility of the individual man and woman to their neighbors." In his message to Congress he established his principles without the slightest equivocation: "I am opposed to any direct or indirect government dole. Our people are providing against distress in true

[11] In October, 1932, the A.F. of L. was virtually committed to some form of unemployment insurance.

American fashion." The House of Representatives received the notification and promptly a few of its less influential members, from the South, began an attack on the Moratorium, which was to be ratified after the event, and coupled it with a demand for a dole. The oratory is not impressive, but it probably represents the thinking of the average man:

"President Hoover has given an outright dole to the railroads. He would give a dole to the building and loan associations. He would come to the aid of banks with frozen assets. He would help foreign countries. . . . To these interests he would give billions, but to starving American women and children he wouldn't give one red cent."

(And another): "You Republicans are willing to give a dole to the predatory interests, to the lords of industry, to international bankers. But when in the midst of this terrible panic we attempt legislation to help feed hungry millions, you accuse us of standing for the dole." [12]

So that one may judge that at the end of the year 1931, the question of the dole was still in the moral, not in the social stage. The old spiritual values (patriotic regard for the American system) were against it; the quick indignation of the people could be captured in its favor. With the beginning of the year it entered its serious stages when Senators LaFollette and Costigan offered bills, later combined, for direct Federal aid. Their first move was to outflank the President's repeated assurance that private benevolence could carry the burden of an unex-

[12] The aid of the Reconstruction Finance Corporation to the banks headed by Mr. Dawes, shortly after Mr. Dawes resigned from the directorship of the R.F.C. was a desperate and successful effort to save the financial system in Chicago; yet it was spectacular (the total sum given and promised was $80,000,000) and much was made of the contrast between this lavishness and the objection to aiding "the little fellow."

ampled public distress. Testimony was taken from directors of charities in Chicago and Philadelphia and New York, from the Federation of Labor, from Catholic bishops, from rabbis, and finally from the head of the Association of Community Chests; their detail varied with their experience; their common agreement was that the burden had grown too great. In Chicago they might carry on for three months; the community chests, hopeful of raising a hundred millions, needed four times as much; Toledo was in acute distress; the American Federation of Labor, having spent fifty millions, was nearing the end of its reserves; in New York, six per cent. of the jobless could count on getting help. A little later it was reported that one hundred and twenty-two cities had no relief appropriations whatever for 1932 and that of five hundred and twenty cities (with an aggregate population of nine million) over three hundred favored direct appropriations, but two hundred and fifteen, including the larger cities of the East, were opposed to it. In the middle of February two million men were reported "drifting" across the country, ineligible for any municipal or state support.

To ex-Governor Smith, the Administration seemed not to have escaped its own dilemma. Home relief, he said, is a dole, and "made work" is a dole in disguise. He proposed a bond issue, to coax out money hoarded "in sugar bowls, between the mattresses and in safe deposit boxes" and to put men to work on "necessary public works and buildings." (It is, of course, the Hearst prosperity loan, taken over by no great friend of Mr. Hearst.)

While the discussion went on, Wisconsin passed an unemployment insurance law. If it was not the dole in America, it was the first step toward the dole.

In the middle of February, Benjamin C. Marsh, secretary of the liberal People's Lobby in Washington, told a House committee that the Costigan-LaFollette bill "is designed merely to keep people from starving while we organize our economic system to prevent a revolution." This long view was too philosophical for Congress, which debated the issue as if it had no implications and was merely one of a series of party measures. Even the fervor of Senator Borah, whose eloquence was often moving, was affected by the atmosphere of unreality in which the whole discussion took place. One reason was that while the Senate debated, the House must eventually determine the appropriation; the Republican leader of the Senate could say that "some form of direct Federal Unemployment Relief appears inevitable", but was not impelled to frame a bill with his Democratic confreres. The level of the discussion can be gauged by an excerpt from the Congressional Record:

Mr. Borah: What is the difference on the individual recipient between levying a tax upon the people of a State to take care of the hungry through the operation of the State Legislature and levying a tax through the operation of the Federal Government to take care of them?

Mr. Fess: Just as much difference as the Federal Government differs from the State Government. . . .

Mr. Borah: Suppose the people were in actual hunger and the local authorities were unable to take care of them, does the Senator still say he would not appropriate money on the part of the Federal Government?

Mr. Fess: If the local authorities are not able to do so; but if the local authorities refuse to do it, that is a different thing.

Mr. Borah: Suppose then that the local authorities are not taking care of them, that they are actually suffering; would the Senator still refuse . . . ?

Mr. Fess: I would. I would insist upon the local authorities doing their duty. . . .

Mr. Borah: Of course, if the Senator says "able to do it", I suppose he would reduce the balance of the community to the same state of pauperization as the people who are in need.[13]

Mr. Fess: Then the Senator would loan to every human being who wants money?

Mr. Borah: I will venture to say that ninety per cent. of the people who are out of employment to-day would be perfectly willing to give the United States Government a guaranty that they will pay back every cent loaned. They abhor charity.

Mr. Fess: And the Senator would make the loan?

Mr. Borah: I would. I would feed them in any way practical.

Mr. Fess: There is where the Senator and I differ.

Mr. Borah: I would save human life.

The struggle went on, complicated by the fact that in the meantime the President had delivered to Congress a complete reconstruction program which assumed that no direct relief from the Treasury would be voted. As his opponents attempted to hold up this program, the supporters of the President met them on their own ground, by proving that States and cities were quite able to take care of their own. Thus Senator Bingham telegraphed to the governors of all the States, inquiring whether they had noticed any starvation in their communities; thirty-nine out of the first forty who replied had never heard of it; Governor Pinchot stood alone with his remark that "we

---

[13] It is a pity Senator Borah did not develop this idea. The community can take from the citizen in two ways: by social pressure in charity drives and by taxation. Chicago, New York and Philadelphia have long felt themselves at the limit of their taxing power. Whether the limit of charitable impulse has been reached is doubtful; it has not, in any case, kept up with the need. The only class which has been urged to save the needy by comparative pauperization is the working class, through spreading work which social service workers brutally call "spreading misery." Radical labor, at least, feels that this is one of many moves calculated to keep the power of labor low if and when prosperity begins to return to us.

know that starvation is widespread." [14] The *New Republic* said, in moderate terms, "actual starvation has little bearing" on the merits of the road-building bill which the Senator was trying to defeat. "There are millions of unemployed to-day who, while they still somehow find food for themselves, are nearing the end of their resources and are desperately in need of assistance." Mr. Hoover had often used the words "go hungry" as synonymous with "starving", but at intervals the strict definition was invoked, especially when statistics showed that very few people actually "died of starvation" in hospital reports. The question is abstract and unimportant.

Just as unemployment had been thrown back to the private citizen with the "Give-a-job" campaign, relief was thrown back with the emergence, in February, of the Block-Aiders. Originally tried out in Buffalo, this system of making the dwellers in each city block responsible for one destitute family living in that block, was received with enthusiasm in New York and some two hundred thousand workers were enrolled, each to go out and get a pledge of a small sum *per week* (the maximum was one dollar) from every man or woman who rejoiced in a job. Mr. Will Rogers said, "This is the most human thing I've ever heard of"; Commissioner Mulrooney offered the aid of the police; the *New York Times* said, "The block population is often not unlike a small town with wealth and modest means in close proximity. To bring them close together in a common interest is something worth while in itself." The amount collected in the Block-Aid campaign was not negligible, although the two million dollars of the first week could not be steadily matched and the collection of pledged contributions grew difficult; it was, however, the filtration of the collectors to the poorer levels of the city that was significant. In the major appeal for funds of the same year, eighteen million

[14] He was to suffer for it later, when the application of his State for relief through the R.F.C. was put aside and neglected.

dollars had been raised, but ninety per cent. of the total number of donors gave only one fifth of the total sum, leaving over fourteen million to be collected from the prosperous and generous ten per cent. The Block-Aid stamps were better distributed, at least a third going to households of comparatively small means.

This effort, and parallel ones in many cities, were intended for immediate relief of suffering; they had a sentimental interest which is important enough. Yet when they are taken as interludes in the great struggle of the dole, they seem to lack principle and adequate scope. They were bucket brigades fighting a skyscraper fire, just as the Give-a-Job Legionnaires were a sheriff's posse trying to defeat an army equipped with howitzers, aëroplanes, and gas. The reason is that they all tried to make individual kindness cope with a national calamity which had gone far beyond the point at which kindness, even of the noblest sort and highest degree, could function. Mr. Arthur Brisbane had said, "No nation can exist half starved and half fed", but he had not suggested that the half-fed could save the half-starved. The nation was, in fact, undergoing another division. There was an American system of charity based on the American system of prosperity; the effort to keep the charitable half, the peak of the pyramid, suspended in mid-air while the broad basic half, our national prosperity, had vanished, required Oriental magic not possessed by our leaders. The unreality I have noted in the debate in Congress, the impatience of those who were continually being asked to give, the sentimental unreality of treating New Yorkers as "neighbors", can all be traced back to this effort to keep half of our Siamese-twin principles alive while the other was dead. A prompt, dangerous surgical operation was needed.

The Red Cross, still bent on proving the superiority of God to man, continued to give aid when God-sent disasters occurred, but insisted that nation-wide unemployment in the midst of a universal depression was a local problem. It did not figure in the outcome of the Congressional debate, too much discredited to be attacked by one side or to be called on for aid by the other. The opponents in Congress needed only to wait for all other agencies to exhaust themselves, when they could resume their debate.

It was resumed in May and came to a strange end in July, when the President signed a relief bill. The important moves were:

A Democratic bill offered by Senator Robinson, endorsed in principle by ex-Governor Smith, Bernard Baruch, and Owen D. Young, the essential provisions being a bond issue floated by the Government, to lend three hundred million dollars to States and cities for immediate relief and two million dollars to them for "self-liquidating" projects, *i.e.*, toll bridges, tunnels, and such other works as would eventually pay themselves out.

The President's counter-proposal was that something of this sort be done, but that it be done through the Reconstruction Finance Corporation; the President wished to deal with States, not with cities; and to lend over a billion to industry for new production.

A bill sponsored by Speaker Garner, authorizing a vast building program.

The President then issued a statement: "We cannot squander ourselves into prosperity. . . . Such a program as the huge Federal loans for 'public works' is a fearful price to pay in putting a few thousand men temporarily at work." He followed this with an analysis of the Garner bill, declaring that "this is not unemployment relief. . . . It is the most gigantic pork barrel ever proposed to the American Congress. It is an unexampled raid on the public treasury."

The question of direct relief was, by this time, a tiny parasite on the body of reconstruction. The mayors of twenty-six large American cities met and, recounting the collapse of their best efforts, begged the President to change the charter of the Reconstruction Finance Corporation, so that it could lend to municipalities. They were gathered in Detroit and Mr. Ford told them that "the charity of our cities is the most barbarous thing in our system." Speaker Garner spoke of "mercy money."

The Senate passed the Wagner bill authorizing the Reconstruction Finance Corporation to lend three hundred million dollars to the States, at three per cent., with provisions for repayment. Senator Reed noted the day as the beginning of the decline and fall of America and, more practically, said that not one penny of the money would ever be repaid. The House passed Speaker Garner's bill, which included a hundred million dollars for direct relief.

Before the political conventions, the Senate and the House worked over their two bills; the points of difference did not touch the principle of relief. After Mr. Hoover had been renominated, and Mr. Roosevelt chosen to challenge, the compromise bill was passed; the President vetoed.

A week later another bill was prepared, passed, and accepted. The bill was so important in its extension of the Reconstruction Finance Corporation's powers, that the presence in it of an appropriation of three hundred million dollars to be lent to States for direct relief to the needy passed almost unnoticed.

For months it had seemed that the profoundest intellectual effort of American statesmen was to discover a new word for the dole, so that we might have the dole without the odium of the name. In the end we got the name, but forfeited everything of importance in the thing itself: the workers' weekly contribution which carries the English system outside the range of charity and the two further contributions, from employer and State, which make a complete circle of interest and responsibility. We created no alternative system, no permanent organization; having seen our Government muddle in the commodity market and in finance and in agriculture, we decided to make an experiment, — the Government in charity; for the way in which the item for relief was passed marked it definitely as a grudging benevolence. The only principle one can unearth is that when the Federal Government flings its small change to the people, the States have to scramble for it first. The incapacity of Congress and the Executive to deal with a social problem which has been so simplified that in Europe it is almost a matter of statistics, was demonstrated to perfection; both sides in the battle of the dole had passion, neither had principles. So in the end nothing was settled.

Except this: the American Government established no system by which it would have to feed from five to twenty-five million people forever after and dispose of one to five million workers, sending them to jobs, shifting them from place to place, creating a vast complicated labor exchange and a machinery of settling disputes. All that — the responsibility it acknowledges and the money it costs — was rejected. Perhaps three hundred million dollars was deliberately sacrificed, a small sum, to prevent the enormous increases in income taxes which a true dole would involve. There is a story in "More Merry-go-Round" which may be appropriate. Mr. Hoover, it runs, received from Secretary of War Hurley the suggestion that "eventually big incomes would have to be scaled down and small incomes up."

" 'Not if I can help it,' " remarked the President dryly.

And directly to the point is the summary of the entire agitation for the dole made by a famous industrial leader, a notorious receiver of bonuses, who remarked, "This winter the poor want to live on the capital of the rich; they won't get mine!"

CHAPTER TWELVE

Low Point: the Record

It took six months to break down the principle of unemployment insurance and substitute a haphazard loan of money; in those six months a vast reconstruction program was passed by Congress. In the campaign which followed, each side insisted that the other had attempted to block this program, each side assuming that its value to the country was already proved. The record is a simple one:

The President's Messages	Acts of Congress
Asked for ratification of the Moratorium.	Moratorium ratified.
Asked for Home Loan Banks for mortgage discount.	Home Loan Banks established.
Asked for creation of a Reconstruction Finance Corporation.	Reconstruction Finance Corporation created.
Asked for a balanced budget.	Budget theoretically [1] balanced.
Asked for creation of further credit.	Glass-Steagall bill passed.
Opposed bonus payments.	Bonus bill rejected.
Opposed general bond issue.	Bond issue rejected.
Opposed tariff revision.	Tariff not revised.
Opposed dole.	Compromise.
Opposed vast public works.	Compromise.
Opposed loans to private individuals.	Compromise.

[1] For the conflict between theory and practice, see page 277.

In the list above, the Glass-Steagall bill does not count as a triumph of the President; he approved of its object, but the method was a compromise with his adversaries. On the positive side, nevertheless, his batting average is near one thousand; on the negative side something over five hundred; considering that he had a hostile Congress, with the Democrats in control in the House, the record is impressive. It was made more impressive during the campaign when friends of Mr. Hoover gave to him sole credit for checking a variety of inflationary bills; but the President never had a chance to veto the Goldsborough bill, for example, which was an effort to inflate by fiat, making the dollar equal to the dollar of pre-boom times; the bill never reached him. His actual vetoes compelled Congress to omit from its relief bill an uncontrolled building program and to drop wide-open loans to individuals; to forego a great pension bill; and to leave the tariff alone. The President had accomplished what he set out to do: that is, inflate through banks, railroads, and trust and insurance companies, while a smaller dole was issued, as a loan, on homes and farms. The indirect method was preferred to the direct; for the small shopkeeper and the jobless man, nothing was done directly on the assumption that everything done for the others — the banks at the top and the farmers at the bottom of the heap — would benefit the millions in the middle.

A dictator, not buffeted about by political necessities, would have made clearer the motives of the Administration and would not have left himself exposed to the taunt that he favored the strong and the rich over the poor and uninfluential. He might have said, "There are two principles, two methods, of saving the country; one in accordance with our experience, the other untried and probably dangerous; the first assumes that we are predominantly an industrial nation and that industry is being checked at this moment by finance; we therefore loose the bands of finance, start industry going, and through jobs and wages, spread prosperity. This method can be put into action at once. The other would make us believe that unemployment, being a permanent problem, has to be relieved directly and that the plumber, the grocer, and the garage keeper can come to the Government for aid. Even if we agreed to this, we have not the machinery to go promptly to work. The purpose of both methods of action is the same: to start recovery. We have chosen the one in which we believe. We believe in the goodness of wealth, we believe that the wealth of a small number does, eventually, tend to the prosperity of the great number."

And if a dictator were in the anomalous position of seeking reëlection, he might well say, "Don't you see how much easier it would have been for me to scatter money over the land, to stir up a temporary and false prosperity, to play on your emotions, and capture your votes. I have taken the hard road because I know it is the only right road."

Yet even a dictator might have hesitated to tell all the truth. If the President's mind had been so supple that he could see the advantage of Mr. Garner's plans as well as his own, pressure was still on him to follow his plan because money flowing around the base of the pyramid would have to go uphill where, at the top, some banks and all the railroads were being parched. The collapse of a few great banks and the failure of the railroads to meet the requirements set by state banking officials would have meant complete collapse of the financial and industrial structure. Even the pooling of resources in the short-lived National Credit Corporation failed to save the banks; and the disaster of the railroads was becoming a matter of weeks when the President began pushing his program of relief.

The railroads went promptly to the Reconstruction Finance Corporation and were, in effect, saved. For the time, at least, the savings banks did not have to unload their securities on the market. Banks also crept into the protecting shadow of the

Government's great Home for the Fallen, and failures were checked. Seventy banks a week had failed just before the Reconstruction Finance Corporation was created; the number dropped to eight a week; at the end of February and the beginning of March, fifteen days passed with only one national bank failure. The top of the pyramid, which had threatened to float off like the island of Laputa in "Gulliver's Travels", was at last grappled to the mainland.

The next phenomenon, increase of general business through an increase of credit, did not occur so promptly. I will not go into the details of the financial expedients by which the Federal Reserve and the Reconstruction Finance Corporation interacted. The essence was that the Federal Reserve piled up a vast sum of money, in the form of credit available to banks, and that the Reconstruction Finance Corporation stood ready to lend banks money to tide them over difficulties; the banks which needed help went to the Reconstruction Finance Corporation, but the solvent banks did not go to the Federal Reserve to use the credit waiting for them. If this were purely a financial choice, it would have had no significance. It was, however, the very foundation of industrial recovery that the banks should lend money freely; for that, all the reconstruction program had been arranged. And the banks did not lend.

For a long time the banks hesitated because they could not know what Congress would do about taxation. A country of business men felt the necessity of balancing the budget, a business ideal; the country went back to its almost forgotten principle of living within its income, cutting down expenses and trying hard to raise necessary funds. To the bankers the thing that mattered was where the taxes would fall; if they fell on corporations and manufacturers, or were doubled for the upper brackets of the supertax, the effect on business might be evil. If Congress failed to cut expenses enough, the effect on foreign observers might be just as bad; if, instead of following the strict scheme, Congress proposed inflation of currency instead of expansion of credit, the banks which had loaned good money would get back bad money. In these uncertainties, the masters of money did a simple thing: they hoarded. Only for great banks the name was not considered dignified: they "remained in a highly liquid position." Moreover, they swore that no respectable requests were made; they could not lend on bad security nor for projects which were obviously doomed to failure. In brief, the unuttered criticism of the bankers had a curiously radical tone: the Government had gone about creating confidence by creating credit; but credit was of no use unless confidence came first. The financial structure of the country had been saved — and now had no enterprise worthy of financing, because the industrial structure was still unsteady.

The bankers' doubts about the Government were not unreasonable. Mr. Andrew Mellon, the greatest Secretary of the Treasury since Carter Glass, had guessed so badly on national income that a deficit appeared where a surplus had been promised, and further guesses, on the extent of the deficit and the probabilities of tax returns, were equally uncertain. In June, 1931, the United States had issued some bonds at the lowest interest rate since the war, and the mouths of brokers watered when they read that some six billion dollars had been offered by the people of the United States for a loan which ran to less than one billion. A few months later a second flotation showed that the enthusiasts for government bonds either had less money or didn't like their Government; they barely oversubscribed the loan. On one side the Administration seemed to favor the sales tax (long advocated by the Hearst papers) and on the other it was making gestures toward increased supertaxes, if the sales tax were not passed; a Republican representative talked like a socialist, saying that "the only class which reaped substantial profits from 1925 to 1929 consists of 14,700 individuals with net incomes above $100,000." It was impossible to tell whether the Administration was going to be sound or not, whether Mr. Hoover would defeat the wild men. The mishaps of the various government agencies dealing with farm products, especially wheat and cotton, were unsettling; when the Democrats got out of hand the good old cry of "Soak the Rich" was heard — or imputed; the President definitely came out for a sales tax; incorporated in separate proposals in both Houses, the sales tax after defeat in the House, against the will of a Democratic Speaker, was promptly rejected by the Senate, a rebuke to a Republican President. Private hoarding and withdrawals of gold went on during all this time and at the beginning of May the President solemnly warned the country that a serious hour had arrived. The hour lasted three long weeks, the low point being reached in the last days of May, and it was not until the end of the session that a revenue bill was passed and signed.

The President had to a remarkable degree imposed his will upon a Congress hostile in its majority and without great faith in him even in the minority, a Congress which on both sides played for political advantage, which let itself threaten the credit of the country by bringing in wild bills or by stubbornly opposing all change, and which, at the end, made many thoughtful people believe that in any emergency, the entire Congressional system was a danger to the republic. Looking over the record, it is clear that a number of the essential laws might have been enacted in two months, instead of in six; on closer examination the blame shifts a little, for it is also clear that the President might have made his compromises more promptly and more graciously. But in estimating the effectiveness of the President's program, the factor of time has to be considered: he proposed measures in December which were passed in March and May and July. He cannot be blamed if their effect was vitiated by tardiness.

Much of the important legislation was passed in the second half of the session; and from April to July there came to the ears of Congress, over the roaring and snarling of its own political oratory, a clamor first from the lobbies where petitions were presented, and later from the streets where the Bonus Army was encamped. Always a prey to organized pressure, Congress was peculiarly sensitive to the presence of ex-soldiers in Washington, and it needed the combined pressure of financiers, citizens, and the President to head off an abject surrender. Congress had surrendered once, only a year before, and asserted itself over the President's veto; it was not remarkable that the leaders of the veterans thought they had a good chance.

The American Government had issued to its ex-soldiers certain certificates, redeemable in 1945. The suggestion that these should be redeemed, partly or wholly, at once (instead of allowing a meager borrowing with the certificates as security) had been privately made in 1930; at the beginning of 1931, Mr. John Garner, then Democratic leader in the House, announced himself in favor of the plan, estimating that a billion dollars would be sufficient and that this sum, put into circulation, would have an instant effect on unemployment and general business. It was more a measure of inflation than a measure of justice, which Mr. Garner proposed. The American Legion had voted down the cash payment a few months before, but smaller groups of veterans had forced its hand and the executive committee of the Legion now gave its approval to the principle. Secretary Mellon appeared before a committee of the Senate, gave a total three times and a half greater than the estimate of Mr. Garner, and said the Treasury could not sell bonds to that amount except "on terms which it would be very hard to justify." (He might have added that sale of such bonds, necessarily backed by the Government, would have a bad effect on the sale of all other, non-governmental bonds.) The bankers of the country deplored the agitation, fearing that a bond issue would cause bank failures and "wreck all chance of economic recovery." Only Owen D. Young, opposing immediate payment, made a suggestion: that the holders of certificates be allowed to borrow up to half the face value instead of a little less than a quarter. The political complication was that the Democrats had proposed a bill which many Republicans favored and which would bring to its sponsors the vote of the soldiers in the next election; a Republican bill, embodying Mr. Young's ideas, was thereupon presented and was passed by both houses, although the President had announced that he would veto it; he did so and the bill was passed over the veto.

The Government held nearly a billion dollars in securities for the ultimate payment of the certificates and as applications for loans came in, these securities were sold for cash. In the first month after the bill was passed, more than a million veterans applied for loans to the sum of six hundred and thirty-eight million dollars. At the end of three months, the total had gone over a billion dollars (which happened to be the size of the deficit in the Treasury and, also, the sum generally supposed to be the annual profit of the bootleggers and racketeers of the country). The promised stimulation to business did not occur; the President was informed, and told the country, that more than half of the money borrowed by the veterans went to pay old bills for groceries, back rent, and overdue installments; about fifteen per cent. went to buy secondhand motor cars. The bonus payments had, in sum, added a quarter of a billion dollars to the deficit and had not helped business.

In September the Legion held its annual convention. Although he had previously refused an invitation to speak, the President suddenly decided that he must face the Legion directly; he took train to Detroit, told the Legionnaires that the country could not sacrifice its cash and its credit and its hopes of recovery merely to pay them now the rest of the money due in 1945. The argument was particularly effective when the President made it clear that he was asking no favor of the Legion: "You would not have the President of the United States plead with any citizen or any group of citizens for any course of action. I make no plea to you. But you would have your President point out the path of service in this nation. . . ." When the President had finished, great cries of "We want Beer" rang through the hall, but the Legion knew it would not demand full payment of the bonus.

To the President, the demands of the Legionnaires represented two thoroughly vicious principles, one social, the other economic; neither was unfamiliar in American history. The social principle was that an organized minority could demand special privileges for itself; the economic one was fiat money. The President was at work on a large program of reconstruction intended to prosper the entire country and, at the same time, he was fighting desperately to preserve the financial soundness of the nation. The Legionnaires served as conspicuous enemies of both these enterprises; rebuking them, the President rebuked all private ambitions and all unorthodox financing. The method and the tone of the rebuff were not, however, good politics. The President had scotched the snake, not killed it. Six months later, Legionnaires were presenting petitions for full payment; ten months later they were being driven out of Washington by the Army of the United States.[2]

---

[2] The argument in favor of the bonus was a mixed one. One element was the fact that the veterans needed the money, in which they did not differ from millions of non-veterans; another was that the country owed them the money, legally or morally, or both. That a debtor owes in 1932 the full sum he has promised to pay in 1945 is not true. The more complicated moral argument compares the low pay of American soldiers with the enormous profits of workers in shipyards and makers of munitions and speculators during the war.

Somewhere an appalling blunder had been committed, one of those blunders worse than crimes. In September the President had defeated the Legion, even if he had not persuaded them; by April the men of the Legion had repudiated the agreement their leaders had tacitly made; from that time they were in open warfare against the President. They found leaders in Congress willing enough to embarrass Mr. Hoover, but the critical moment, in my guess, came before the petitions ever reached Washington; it came when the President, having driven the Legion into a corner, left it there, to sulk and nurse its wounds, because it did not occur to him that angry, independent men could not be treated like slaves. It was one of the familiar criticisms of Mr. Hoover, made in books bordering on the obscene, that he had handled coolie labor and had never learned how to deal on terms of equality with men; in all his record as President, the episode of the Bonus Army alone seems to justify this criticism. It was not only that Mr. Hoover took his victory somberly; he seemed actually to resent the possibility of the Legion asking for full payment of the bonus after

It would have been a more effective argument if the Legion had not always been so enthusiastic for the war and if the bonus seekers had ever questioned the moral desirability of the war. The United States had, perhaps, called its soldiers heroes, but it had never promised to make its heroes a privileged class if they happened to survive their time in the trenches.

The financial arguments were that the country could pay and that payment would be a powerful stimulus to trade. The partial payment of the bonus gave no proof that the second assumption was right; the first implied one of two things: paying the bonus at the expense of some other enterprise or issuing fiat money. Traditional government economy was opposed to both.

The discussion of the bonus and of the Bonus Army which follows is based on the belief that demands for special privileges are common in American life and that demonstrations of force in favor of these demands are rare. The method by which the Administration met the demand and the demonstration is, psychologically, the most interesting factor.

he had vetoed the half-payment loans; as if there was a personal affront to him in the proposal. And worst of all, he so far misunderstood the character of the men with whom he was dealing that he left them without any fixed objective. They approved of the Moratorium, they cheered for a large navy, they cried for beer; but the one practical thing the President could have done — gathering the Legion around himself as the spearhead for an attack on the depression — he failed to do. Perhaps it was impossible; no one tried it. The Legionnaires ran wild because the President had not persuaded them to run in harness.

Warnings came to Washington with the beginning of the session of Congress, not clearly, because they had no label of the Legion and no title to represent the ex-soldiers. They came first as single spies, then in battalions: fourteen marchers, called Communists, paraded outside the White House in the rain, asking for food and lodging, directing their banners to Mr. Hoover: they were arrested and the next week sixteen hundred hunger marchers from the North and East and Middle West were asking for an unemployment insurance bill — and food. They were also called Communists on the principle that the Constitutional "right of the people peaceably to assemble and petition the Government for a redress of grievances" could only be exercised by enemies paid with Russian gold.[3] The next army was led by a Catholic priest from Pittsburgh; it came by truck and motor car across Pennsylvania, with the benediction of Governor Pinchot; it was fed by the army at Fort Myer; and a thousand men followed Father Cox to the steps of the Capitol, where the earlier petitioners had been turned away, and begged for "the God-given right to work." The President received Father Cox and told him that "we are

[3] In a sense this is so. The habit of meeting in protest has almost disappeared from American life, possibly because meetings have become merely a method of propaganda.

giving this question our undivided attention." Andrew Mellon paid for the repatriation of the marchers who returned home by train.

No one cared to see in these manifestations signs of anything more than the desire for publicity or an effort to capitalize hunger and discontent. They were a sign of something more important, which was neither political nor in the strict sense economic: men were drifting. The marchers who came to Washington were a few, but all over the country men were so little attached to any place, because their jobs had failed them, their homes been taken away, their families dispersed, that they were prepared to go anywhere. A new kind of mob was forming in America.[4]

The next marchers came in April, about a thousand ex-soldiers, bearing a petition which, they said, was signed by over two million Americans, all asking for immediate full payment of the bonus.[5] Their coming was against the presidential will. Enough members of the House had been reported in favor of the bill to alarm the President's advisers, who foresaw that an unrestrained public movement would overwhelm Congress; the President therefore gave a message to the press, alluding to the informal polls of the House.

"I am absolutely opposed to any such legislation," said the President, and "I do not believe any such legislation can become law. . . . The first duty of every citizen is to build up and sustain the credit of the Government. Such an action would irretrievably undermine it."

---

[4] I use the word mob, here, without any disrespect. It comes from the Latin adjective *mobile*, in its special sense of movable or easily stirred; it is the mobility of the hunger marches which should have warned Washington.

[5] Nearly two million five hundred thousand certificates had been pledged for loans by this time, for a total of a billion and a quarter dollars. To pay off the rest would take about two and a quarter billion dollars more.

The account I have ends with the words "That's all" after those I have just quoted. I do not know whether they were meant as dismissal of the newspapermen or were included in the statement as a dismissal of the approaching petitioners. The brusqueness of the statement is a symptom of that lack of understanding to which I referred before; the curt words at the end seem so dictatorial that I give them the benefit of the doubt.

The advocates of the bonus in the House were quick to assure the President that he erred; if the Reconstruction Finance Corporation could give millions to "the big boys" (bankers and railroad executives), millions could be found to go "to the little fellows in every nook and corner of the nation." That the bonus bill was straight inflation was never doubted; the intention of its sponsors was to pay the bonus by issue of unsecured notes, a return to fiat money in America. In May the President turned upon them and with all the weight of his authority, multiplied a thousand times by the march of events, for the flow of gold to Europe had become a grim and steady drain on the country, he wrote:

"The Government cannot be dictated to by organized minorities. . . . I know these actions do not reflect the will of the country and I refuse to believe that the will of the country is unable to reflect itself in legislation."

Submissively the House abandoned all bills for immediate payment of the bonus.

The problems presented by the bonus agitation were complicated and they are still controversial; so far as I know, there is only one point of universal agreement: that it would have been better for the country if the subject had never come up, and I am tracing here chiefly the defaults by which Congress and the President allowed it to become first a misfortune and then a national disgrace. The lost opportunity at Detroit might have been regained in Washington in May; it was missed again, not by the act of the House in dropping its legislation, but by the method. The President had virtually issued an ultimatum; the House accepted it in committee. A full-dress debate, painful and long-drawn as it must have been, and a whole vote of the House and the Senate, might have persuaded the ex-soldiers that their cause was hopeless; instead they felt that they had been blocked because the legislature and the executive of our government had been afraid to come into the open.

The calendar now favored the agitators. Enough men had slept in doorways and under bridges during the winter to await with eagerness the soft nights of late spring; early fruit and vegetables were ripening along the roads in the Middle West; and men who had hoped to get thirty days in the workhouse, to escape the rigors of cold and hunger, now were ready to move. They would have gone anywhere; merely to be going meant that they had a better chance to beg food or pilfer or, by supreme luck, get a job; nothing kept them moored to one spot and movement gave them a feeling they had lost for two years: companionship. A man out of work, separated from his family, rushing from place to place on the rumor of a job, feels that the hand of every man is against him; even when he stops looking he still feels himself an outcast of society and a rival to every other man who begs a dime or steals a ride. He resists the companionship of the professional tramp as long as he can, holding clear in his mind the distinction between them, the idle, and himself, the unemployed.

The march of the veterans on Washington needed only to start for it to gather recruits. It satisfied certain psychological needs: it gave aimless men an objective; it gave weak men an arduous job in which they were supported by their brothers; to chaos, it brought a kind of discipline; for meaningless tramping about, searching for what was not to be found, it gave the route march; men who had been accustomed to take orders from a boss, and missed the word of command, were put under some kind of discipline. Deepest perhaps of all its appeals, the bonus march spoke to the memory of the army and the war, the good old war which was even better than the good old job, the days of health, free fights, protection and excitement. The men who marched did not stop to consider that it was the war which had brought them low; they thought of the amazing freedom which makes military discipline so attractive,[6] freedom from responsibility and care, physical activity, and the great happiness of common work and easy companionship. Out of their little bundles they drew whatever was left to remind them of days in camp or in the trenches: a khaki cap, or canvas leggings, or the uncomfortable high-collared tunic. They wanted to be soldiers again, to march in an army.

They began on the Pacific Coast, wandering, slipping into freight yards and riding in box cars, presently regimented by their own military police — an astounding proof of the triumph of habit over passion. Only a few hundred were gathered when they reached East St. Louis and tried to take a freight train in mass formation. The Baltimore and Ohio Railroad refused to move the train; for a day and a night all eastward freight traffic from its yards was suspended. The marchers were as full of guile as soldiers usually are; they moved up the line, soaped the rails on an incline, and boarded the laboring train. The issue between the marchers and authority was clear and it was met as it was met again and again for weeks: the militia was called out, but the merchants of the town prevented a battle by providing food and transportation into the next State; from Indiana the marchers were transshipped to Ohio, and so, each time by the decree of an anxious governor, through West Virginia, Pennsylvania, and Maryland, to their

[6] The pacifists have never understood this.

objective, — the Capitol. They had become news and as the news spread, other detachments, from California and Utah and the South and the Middle West, were on their way to join the army. A commander appeared, Walter W. Waters, — he came to be known as "Hot Waters"; he was belligerent and lawless in speech — and the army, the Bonus Expeditionary Force, never seemed to resent his smart officer's boots. By the beginning of June, Waters was in command of about twenty-five hundred men, settled at Anacostia Park in tents, or in empty shops in the City of Washington. More were coming. They began to expect as their right the trucks which were to shift them across state borders; they were fed by merchants and municipalities who recognized the difference between hospitality and discretion. Their quarrels were chiefly with railroads; at Cleveland, for instance, nearly a thousand men held up freight traffic and other acts of minor violence occurred. They sang old war songs and shouted demands for their rights, but they were eminently patriotic and one group, from the South, began its crusade with daily prayer. Wives, sweethearts, and women on their own began to join the army. In Washington, Pelham Glassford, still in his first year as Chief of Police for the District, had been astute and kindly; he collected food, did not molest the encampment, and said little. He had run across some marchers outside of Washington and had noticed their banner — "Give us a bonus or give us a job." He knew at once that he would have a difficult affair on his hands.

While Hot Waters announced that he and his men were ready to stay in Washington "until 1945" in order to get cash payment for their certificates (1945 being the year full payment was due) General Glassford sat on the grass and listened. Long after the event, he told an interviewer for *Collier's:*

"I agreed, of course, with their determination to be law-abiding and orderly. . . . As I listened to this first group,

I suddenly realized that what was ahead of me was not a mere local police job. It was national. From all over the United States ex-soldiers were heading for Washington and what would be the result? I didn't know. Nobody knew. . . . I told the Commissioners that the few hundred men already in Washington were only the advance guard of what might turn out to be a huge army and I wanted to be told how they wanted it handled.[7] Imagine my surprise when it was suggested to me that I treat these men as indigents, pass them along to the Salvation Army or any other charity organization that would feed them, and then make them move on as rapidly as possible." [8]

General Glassford, remembering the tradition which, since Coxey's army, had permitted marchers to "come into the Capital, parade, petition Congress and remain in the city on a scheduled program", refused to carry out the order unless it was handed to him in writing. The baffled Commissioners backed down and General Glassford had his own way until "orders in writing were issued . . . which completely repudiated the policies which had been pursued."

[7] The rumor at the time was that a million men would concentrate on the Capitol.

[8] The City of Washington has lived in a belljar for generations; looking out, its inhabitants see dim shapes moving, but seem unaware of the forces which impel them; they are the inhabitants of the cave, in Plato's allegory. The peculiar economic basis of their lives made understanding of the plight of the rest of the country difficult for them, since a vast number are civil servants and are receiving salaries to which they had become accustomed while the power of their dollar was rising. The Bonus Army converging on Washington paid tribute to the American respect for law and legislators; yet it was a financial and economic problem they were bringing with them, and many observers wondered why they had not chosen to concentrate on the economic and financial capital of the country, New York, instead of on the political one. There must have been many motives; one certainly was that the men wished to confront their adversaries and to force Congress to say to their faces what had to be said; again they had the tradition of direct physical pressure. And it occurs to me that Mr. Hoover may have drawn the lightning to himself.

One of those policies was untiring friendliness; it worked so well that General Glassford is quite justified in saying that "I realized that they needed a supervising leader, and so without going through the formality of holding an election . . . I simply took the job over." [9] Another part was to discourage further invasions. It was said that certain Congressmen were actively instigating marches from their constituencies; General Glassford had the coöperation of the American Legion and the Veterans of Foreign Wars, who officially disapproved of the Bonus Army, and through them he appealed to every local post to do everything possible to keep men from starting out. He showed himself something of a statesman when he implored leaders in both Houses to vote promptly on a bonus bill. He begged governors of near-by States to prevent the passage of the marchers. To the men already in Washington he gave food collected from private citizens in the District (nothing came from the Federal Government) and with them he made an agreement that there should be no panhandling, no disorderly conduct, and no liquor. The tiny contingent of Communists were isolated by the veterans themselves and when a conservative group tried to rush a Red speaker, Glassford defended this outcast of the outcasts as well. [10]

The marchers were successful in two enterprises from the start: they remained orderly, and by quiet representations, they persuaded the House to disinter the bonus bill. The difficulties they faced were serious, for the greater the concen-

[9] He even took charge of finances for the men.

[10] This record is all the more remarkable because the past year had established another tradition, the law at the end of the night-stick in New York and the tear-gas bomb and the revolver shot in Detroit. The number of army marchers rose to a minimum of 8,000, a maximum of 15,000; General Glassford believes that no more than 300 Communists were ever in the city. The Communists were enthusiastic for the march and about half a dozen of their delegates, sent to encourage the others, were arrested.

tration in Washington, the more menacing the army became to itself, for lack of food, medical attention, and sanitation. In addition to pup tents, the men put up shacks made of packing cases, loose lumber, and whatever other building materials they could find; they followed the army plan of company streets and tried to build proper latrines, but the problem of sewage defeated them and the smoke from improvised hearths could not keep away the swarms of flies which hovered over the encampment. Public officials, zealous for their work, predicted epidemics and reported that they had spotted cases of contagious disease, but the carriers had escaped. New arrivals were examined (for proof of honorable discharge from the army as well as for health) and placed in an isolated part of the camp for a short time, and an inadequate hospital was established. Food came from friends, from Washingtonians, from families left behind, and a great gift of five thousand dollars was sent by Father Charles Coughlin of Detroit, who praised the army on the radio.

To accomplish their official aim, the marchers had to persuade two thirds of both Houses, since a veto from the President was certain. They could hardly do this by physical intimidation; politically they counted only as representatives and they could not claim to represent all of the three million five hundred thousand veterans of the war, and not even all of the members of the American Legion; certainly the million veterans who had not taken advantage of the loan law passed in the previous session could not be considered fighters for the bonus, and from time to time posts of the Legion voted enthusiastically to support the President against the unauthorized lobbying of the marchers. The usual explanation is that the veterans were organized, so that if they represented a twentieth of the voting population and their wives and close friends another twentieth, they were the ten per cent. margin by which many an election was won or lost. Against this compact force was only a scattered public opinion; no Congressman could be *sure* that all the bankers and manufacturers of his district would vote for him because he opposed the bonus; but he could be sure, on the contrary, that every bonus seeker and every man influenced by a bonus seeker would vote against the Congressman who voted against the bonus; to lose ten per cent. and see it move to the column of a rival meant a twenty per cent. difference in the final vote, and no Congressman, in theory, could face it.

Organization counted, but I think what Congress felt was that the campers, now parading before the Capitol, now giving statements to the press, now singing and shouting in the legislative halls, represented not merely the veterans, but the unemployed, not a million or two, but seven million or perhaps ten, with their enfranchised wives.[11] In the opinion of conservative economists the demands of the veterans were hostile to the recovery of the rest of the unemployed, for two billion dollars appropriated to pay them would have to be taken from some other enterprise or be created by fiat money which would certainly wreck the credit of the country, reducing employment still further and putting off any prospective jobs farther

---

[11] The story of Walter W. Waters, commander of the force, is told by *Time:* "Tall, lean, sunburned, Waters first saw service on the Mexican border. Then he went overseas as sergeant. . . . Mustered out, he married a blonde slip of a girl from Valparaiso, Ind., took her to Oregon, where he worked as superintendent of a canning factory, had a house of his own, a car, two little daughters. Eighteen months ago he lost his job. His small savings melted. He led the B.E.F.'s first contingent. . . . Now in command of 15,000 men, he became the sober, strict executive. . . . He directed the . . . lobbyists, organized newcomers, arranged for food and shelter, maintained camp order . . ."

If Congressmen felt the leader typical of the men, they must have known that it was not the service record, but the breakdown of Waters' private life which made him significant, and that if no veterans existed, the same man or his equal would have been leading another army for a similar purpose to Washington.

than any jobless man could see, unless he looked beyond the grave and saw his children growing up beggars in a ruined world. Yet the jobless were not hostile to the Bonus Army and many of them must have felt that this handful, pursuing a special end of its own, spoke for them all. Sensitive to this voice, the House passed the bonus bill by a safe majority; the next afternoon and evening, elated with victory which seemed a sure indication of complete triumph (although the majority lacked much of the two thirds necessary to override a veto) the veterans took up their places around the Capitol and waited for news. It came decisively: the Senate had defeated the bill by 62 to 18. The ten thousand men stood and without any trace of rancor or irony sang "My Country, 'tis of Thee." [12]

The bonus army stayed in Washington and continued to demonstrate; the leaders said they would stay until hell froze or they got their cash, but the atmosphere was overcharged with other emotions. The men stayed because they could not go, and had no wish to go, anywhere else; they demonstrated because Congress was still in session and they felt they had been denied their rights. Actually, their work as veterans was over; they had compelled Congress to debate their claims and to record itself in a vote. They stayed on as a fragmentary, organized unit of the army of the disinherited in America. On the Fourth of July they allowed themselves a symbolic action: they demonstrated on the steps of the Capitol — and the Capitol was empty.

At the suggestion of the President, who had until now ignored the Bonus Army, Congress offered to lend the men money to go home, the sum to be taken out of the final payment of the bonus in 1945; some accepted. In the encampment, a small rebellion against the dictatorship of Waters broke out, and in crushing it, by skillful oratory and maneuvers, Waters made

[12] A few months earlier, the crew of a British war vessel sang "God Save the King" and mutinied.

THE CAMP AT ANACOSTIA PARK BURNING

(*The Glare Was so Bright that It Registered on the Plate in the Time between the Opening of the Camera's Shutter and the Illumination of the Flash-light*)

himself absolute master of the army which, though dwindling, still held some six thousand men whom Waters encouraged by telling them they were twenty thousand. Another army of five hundred arrived from the Pacific to solemnize the end of Congress by taking up a death watch around the Capitol plaza during the final sessions. Vice President Curtis, annoyed or frightened or eager to show authority, or merely confused in mind, summoned marines from the Navy Yard; General Glassford had them returning in a quarter of an hour and, losing his temper for the first time in two months, shouted, "I'm fed up with hysterical meddlers." The Communists grew more active; the demonstrators began to overflow the steps of the Capitol, Waters was arrested for a short time, and again the army sang "America." When the news came that Congress had adjourned, a handful of men started down Pennsylvania Avenue to picket the White House; a vast and disproportionate display of police force followed, and the White House was not molested.

On the 28th of July, the Bonus Expeditionary Force was driven out of Washington by Federal troops. Two veterans were killed in an earlier battle with the police of Washington; a sick baby, gassed during the raid of the troops, died in hospital. The encampment at Anacostia was burned by the troops.

The events of that day remain disputed; investigations have been made and the Attorney-General of the United States has issued a report; General Glassford has given his side of the case, with discreet care for the dignity of the Executive.[13] The central issue of the dispute is whether it was necessary to call out the army; a minor issue is whether the veterans were rich, respectable, and law-abiding citizens. On the first, testimony lies in the tabulation of incidents:

[13] Until he was deprived of office, when he became a bit franker.

The veterans' headquarters were not at the Anacostia Camp, but in a group of buildings, half demolished, on Pennsylvania Avenue, at Third Street (*i.e.*, within three blocks of the Capitol). The ground is owned by the Treasury and "in the latter part of June, the Treasury Department commenced to press for possession of some of the property occupied by the bonus marchers and which was urgently needed [14] to carry on its program of public improvements. . . ." (The Attorney-General's report.)

In July the leaders of the Bonus Army first refused to leave the buildings, then asked for tentage and other equipment elsewhere; this the Treasury had no authority to grant. At the same time, General Glassford, dealing with the same men, had come to an agreement — that they should leave for another camp, two miles from the Anacostia bridge.

On the morning of the 28th of July, representatives of the Treasury took possession of one of the buildings. Most of the squatters moved out, a few had to be jostled, but no disorder occurred.

By noon about two thousand men from the camp at Anacostia had drifted in; according to the Attorney-General they had been listening to "incendiary speeches"; others say they had come in to see what was going on at headquarters.

"Finally the mob of bonus marchers again attacked the police with clubs and bricks in their hands." (Attorney-General's report.) Another version is that a few men tried to reënter the almost vacated buildings, carrying an American flag; police resisted their entry; a brick was hurled and a fight began.

The mob pressed in; the police began beating them back with their sticks. Eight hundred policemen were summoned

[14] As late as November 1, 1932, nothing of consequence had been done on the site which was not even cleared.

by a riot call. General Glassford, knocked down, rose again
and begged for order. Inside the building two officers were
trapped; the fighting men tried to get them; the policemen
fired, one man fell dead, two others were wounded.[15]

These are the preliminaries, for there is general agreement
that after the death of the ex-soldier, the fight drew to an
end. General Glassford dismissed his forces, the battle was
over.

"The situation grew steadily worse," says the official report,
which also asserts that General Glassford "stated that the situation was out of his control and that the police could no longer
hold the bonus marchers in check. He was asked the direct
question whether he thought it was necessary to secure the
assistance of Federal troops, to which he replied in the affirma-
tive."

The Commissioners also quote a recommendation "that
preparations be made . . . to declare an emergency . . . to
provide for the use of the National Guard, or to place into
effect the 'white plan.' " The "white plan" is "the official
designation in the War Department of the plan to be followed
by the regular army in the quelling of serious internal dis-
orders." This would prove that the General saw the possibility

[15] The direct attack on the police and the death of the two veterans
may be taken as the justification of calling out the Federal troops,
on the ground that the police could no longer keep order. For that
reason, the report of Paul Y. Anderson on this incident of the day's
struggle is important. "The trouble was resumed," he wrote in the
Nation, "with more serious consequences two hours later, when a
policeman attempted to bar several veterans from a building which,
in fact, had not been prohibited to them. They rushed him and he
shot. A fellow officer coming to his assistance was hit with a missile
and likewise opened fire. Still others joined in. Glassford, on the second floor of the same building, commanded his men to stop shooting,
and the policeman who had fired the first shot and who apparently
was hysterical, whirled and aimed his revolver at the chief. . . ."

that at some future time the army might be called upon. It is not the same thing as actually calling the army at that time.

The General's own testimony is given in the interview already quoted:

"But . . . you didn't ask, did you, to have the Army come in . . . to evict the bonus seekers?"

"No, I did not."

"You do not believe that it was necessary to order the troops out in order to evacuate the bonus seekers?"

"I have several times stated that I did not consider it necessary."

The Commissioners of the District sent a request to the President and the President ordered Secretary of War Patrick J. Hurley to send troops from Fort Myer.

Between seven hundred and fifty and one thousand men, infantry supported by cavalry and tanks, armed as usual, but employing chiefly tear-gas bombs, moved in on the encampment; the veterans dispersed before the marching men — the first display of armed force by the United States Army since the end of the war in Siberia, the first use of new style tanks, the first time soldiers had used gas masks in warfare in their own country. Neither the newspaper accounts at the time nor the official report issued later suggest any resistance on the part of the marchers, nor any special reason for the use of tear gas; the official report says there were no casualties after the troops arrived, but reporters for both the *Nation* and the *New Republic* insist that there were.[16]

"After the troops arrived," the official report goes on, "fire broke out among the old shacks occupied by bonus marchers

[16] The Washington papers carried a list of casualties the next morning.

THE RIOT IN WASHINGTON

The Lead Pipe Held by the Veteran Fell, a Moment after the Picture was Taken, on the Head of the District Police Officer

. . . where the rioting occurred, and later at the big camp . . . on the Anacostia River, from which the bulk of the rioters had come to attack the police. The cause of the fire in the Pennsylvania area is not known. The troops had no orders to set any fires. . . . While the troops were waiting (at the Anacostia River camp) fires set by the retiring bonus marchers broke out. . . ." George Rothwell Brown, correspondent of the *New York American,* says that "fire in the Pennsylvania Avenue area was started by the soldiers", that he himself saw the soldiers going about, applying the torch and that fire engines drawn up near-by were not used, the firemen standing at hand, watching the blaze. The burning of the larger camp was generally ascribed to the troops.

General MacArthur, who had led the troops, declared that if the marchers had been allowed to remain in Washington, "another week might have meant that the Government was in peril." Secretary of War Hurley said, "It was a great victory." The President said, "A challenge to the authority of the United States Government has been met, swiftly and firmly. . . ." And, much later, publicly thanked God there was still a government in Washington which knew how to handle a mob.

The Bonus Expeditionary Force began to retrace its steps, the States which had trucked them south and east now had trucks ready for the north and west. At junctions leading to important cities, and especially at crossing with eastbound roads, troopers manipulated the governing lights, so that the cars kept speeding in the required direction. More than five thousand of the marchers made camp in Johnstown, Pennsylvania, whence they were shipped, but westward only, by the Baltimore and Ohio Railroad; a few hundred men were sent east, through some arrangement between the mayor of Johnstown, its richer citizens, and the Pennsylvania Railroad; a few of them "marched on" New York.[17] The twenty thousand men who at one time and another had been part of the army disappeared, falling back into the anonymous, unorganized army of the unemployed in cities or joining the growing number of wanderers who, by autumn, were all over the West, — two million men moving along the roads.

Inglorious as the story is, the end is worse because it is petty. Almost as soon as the army had evicted the marchers, the President wrote to a post of the American Legion that he was under the impression that "less than half of them ever served under the American flag." Secretary Hurley gave the figure at sixty-six per cent.; from sources close to the President came repeated assurances that a large body of Communists had been active in deliberate preparation of the riots; but after the evictions, every one of the actual Communists arrested was freed for lack of evidence.

At the request of the President, a grand jury was summoned in the District; the Attorney-General set one of his assistants in charge of the inquiry and, according to Paul Y. Anderson, in the *Nation,* "the presiding justice, in his instructions from the bench, went to the incredible extreme of expressing a 'hope'

---

[17] Shortly after the Bonus Army disbanded, a group of squatters took possession of a strip of land near Riverside Drive, in New York, and in spite of protests were allowed to stay. Another more impressive group came together in Central Park where a reservoir had been drained. Out of rubble and bricks and whatever lumber they could find, they built habitations, and some of them showed that the builders had been excellent craftsmen in the days of their prosperity. They were not violent, they were hardly radicals; few of them were going to vote for Norman Thomas, perhaps one in twenty for Foster. One man said, "I have got lots of friends that are worse off than I am. They haven't even got a home." One said, "Will Hoover drive me out of here?", and on being reassured murmured, "Well, he drove me out of Washington." One man sat with his face in his hands, unwilling to meet the curious and curiously indifferent stares of Sunday promenaders.

that the grand jurors would find that 'the mob guilty of actual violence included a few ex-service men, and was made up mainly of Communists and other disorderly elements.' " The Grand Jury refused and, neglecting the Communists altogether, indicted three men, all of whom had done duty overseas, one with the Distinguished Service Cross "for heroism in rescuing wounded comrades under fire." As the American Legion was preparing its convention, the Attorney-General's Report, from which I have quoted, was published; in nearly every important point of fact, its evidence was disputed. But it emphasized another point: that many of the men were "criminals and radicals." Casting an average, the report suggested that one out of every four men had a police record; but the list of crimes included "disorderly conduct and vagrancy", "traffic and motor vehicle laws", minor theft, and "suspicion and investigation"; Mr. Floyd Gibbons figured that for serious crime, the record of President Harding's Cabinet was proportionately higher than that of the Bonus Army.

The Attorney-General's report was the final word out of Washington; it may have deterred the American Legion from passing a vote of censure on the commander in chief of the United States Army.[18] But the Legion voted, ten to one, and in spite of two stinging messages from the President, for immediate payment of the bonus.

For the first time in American history, Federal troops had been summoned by the President to attack American citizens in the capital of the country. For the first time since the Civil

[18] Censure was passed by the Bonus Expeditionary Force in a convention held at Johnstown. The President received delegates, but refused to accept the letter containing the sentence, "We . . . censure you and those of your administration who took part in the forceful eviction of the B.E.F. from Washington" on the ground that it constituted an insult to presidential dignity. This was in October and the B.E.F. was almost entirely forgotten; the eviction was hardly mentioned by the principal campaigners on either side.

War they had made war, although without bloodshed, against American citizens who were not striking and not interfering with the processes of industry. It was something new and ominous in American history and perhaps the most ominous circumstance was that most Americans were not aware of what had happened.

CHAPTER THIRTEEN

Low Point: the Reaction

THE last two chapters dealt with five major subjects which occupied the American people from the last quarter of 1931 to the middle of 1932; this chapter and the next take up their mental and moral parallels; the five points were:

Unemployment

The Dole

Deflation

Counter-deflation

The Bonus and the Bonus Army

It was not an exclusive preoccupation by any means; there were times when people thought little of these serious questions, as when they encountered the three successive shocks of the Lindbergh case, the kidnaping, the false ransom, and the discovery of the murdered child; [1] or when a record-breaking flight or an exceptionally brutal gangster murder imposed itself between them and the constant worries of their economic miseries; or when Mr. Floyd Gibbons battled in vain to make the United States declare war on Hawaii; or when Mayor Walker of New York matched his private life with any man's and resigned his public office; or when prohibition promised to be the major issue of the campaign; or when a play or a

---

[1] The great, and dangerous, moments in a country's history are when all the people think the same thoughts. In his flight and in his great misfortunes, Lindbergh was the central figure of two such moments.

movie or a magazine story made them forgetful of personal problems; or when personal problems passed beyond the influence of wages and jobs and prices. Yet the first thing to note in this period is that interest in economics grew steadily, so that people definitely wanted to know about its complexities and talked of them with vehemence and passion. The depression was a universal subject; no matter at what distant point one began, conversation led back to it, and conversation about it was more personal and more absorbing than conversation on any other topic. When Mr. Walter Lippmann began his work for the *New York Herald Tribune*, about a dozen newspapers took his articles; before a year was out his syndicate went to over a hundred, giving his articles on economic problems a wider circulation than that of most gossip writers and humorists. Books on every aspect of the crisis were published and sold and read; more than a hundred books of Five-Year Plans for America were listed in the library of Columbia University; the stage, always laggard, had a few plays reflecting the depression; the movies, always timid, caught up with the popular scepticism about Washington; the radio, apparently saving itself for the campaign, contributed little, but the radio still thought of itself as the garrulous friend who drops in when the family is in carpet slippers and wants recreation.[2] "Washington Merry-Go-Round", which mingled a touch of scandal with a savage criticism of the politico-economic minds of the capitol, became a best-seller; the newspapers of the country gave their headlines to economic discussions.[3] But the greatest symptom of the consuming interest was the change in approach. Instead of "When is it going to end?" or "When will prosperity

[2] Yet when the March of Time period was discontinued, the protest was great, and this excellent survey of world affairs was restored in time for the campaign.

[3] The distinguished *New York World* disappeared; on the other hand, the *New York Evening Graphic*, a cheap tabloid, disappeared. The moral is confused.

come back?", the question turned to, "What is going to happen?" It may have had the accent of despair, but it was an enlightened despair; it looked not to the past, but to the future.

I noted before that in this period relief for unemployment, as conceived by the authorities, changed from making jobs to making joblessness bearable. If jobs were to be found, private citizens must find them; at the end of the period the President hotly attacked the idea that the Government could do what the citizen could not and, reversing himself, denounced public works as a delusion, an expensive way of putting very few people to work. The effect on the average man was serious: he began to think that unemployment was inevitable and perhaps permanent. He knew, at any rate, that nothing would be done to put men to work and foresaw that jobless men would walk the streets and the country roads for years to come. Until now he had hoped for an act of authority, if not an act of God, the development of some scheme which would make work and, as a consequence, bring back prosperity; now he knew that prosperity would have to come and, long after, men would be absorbed into industry again. The reversal of direction was difficult, it caused a profound nervous dislocation; we had grown accustomed to looking eastward for the rising sun and now had to turn our eyes westward because we had been specifically told that no sun would rise for us in the old appointed place. I do not think that many people blamed the President for all the good words he had said about Federal projects, or great employers for all the promises they had made; we had passed beyond rancor and cynicism and felt that our leaders had been as much misled as ourselves. But if we did not blame, we wondered what would happen next. It had been impressed on us so often that the man with the job was the foundation of prosperity and that getting jobs, even artificially made jobs, would restore good times, that when this promise, the only one we could easily understand, was unfulfilled, we had nowhere to go for consolation. Everything we did hereafter was shaped and colored by our disappointment; something ingrained in our habits had been taken from us and some of the shoring which held up the American tradition had crumbled away. Six months earlier we had met and faced the thought that America was no longer the country in which every man who wanted a job could get one; we considered it a temporary lapse in the perfection of our arrangements. Now we were threatened with permanent unemployment and knew ourselves socially unprepared to meet it.

For years liberals had been explaining the system of labor exchanges and unemployment insurance and crying in the wilderness of shops and factories; they told us that a million men, perhaps two, were always looking for work and that we wasted national wealth by letting them wander haphazard, never at the place when workers were needed, always flocking in too great numbers to places already staffed. The prophets made no impression, because the proportion of jobless was small and because the wage of the worker was high. It seemed superfluous to erect a huge machine for insuring employment which most of us vaguely assumed was guaranteed to us in the Constitution; and as for paying men when they were out of work, it was absurd, because we always fell back on the great sheets of Help Wanted ads., the long rosters of the big factories — "any man who wants a job can get it."

We faced the dole, then, with all our old emotions against it and only one uneasy little feeling in its favor, — the feeling that something had to be done. It need hardly be said that the permanence of unemployment was never stressed in Congress; only the immediate need. No politician could come before the American people and tell them that now and for ten years or for ever, they would have to take care of five to ten million men; but when all the politicians openly gave up the struggle against unemployment and when the dominant theme moved from reëmployment to refinancing, an unuttered suspicion began to lodge in the American mind. It made people not entirely receptive to the dole, but indifferent to its social dangers. They were seldom called on to express an opinion; one can judge only by scattered instances. When Mr. Burns, the head of the Association of Community Chests, was asked whether those helped by his organization would resent the dole, he answered, with some pathos, that they did not care where aid came from, if only it came. The people of the State of New York never rose against the concealed dole put into motion by Governor Roosevelt; nor was aid from cities (often lumped with aid from charity drives) ever rejected. The moment the Federal dole was voted for distribution by the States, appeals came in promptly and urgently. The citizens of Pennsylvania did not ask their governor to lower his voice when he violently berated the President and the Reconstruction Finance Corporation for delaying a relief loan. It is extremely doubtful whether the individual receivers of Federal money felt themselves more humiliated and demoralized than beggars on the streets.

Yet these negatives do not offer evidence for any generalization. The charity drives in the winter of 1932 were all disturbed by the recurrent talk of a Federal dole, but large sums were collected, and if the People's Lobby thought that the dole was a temporary expedient to head off a premature revolution, givers of charity spoke freely of their contributions as "Bolshevist insurance"; the money was given, but the sense of menace was not lacking, and the process of combing out people who had not given, the practice of publishing names and amounts, were all forms of social pressure which many people resented. In cities with central organizations or community chests, the position was easier than in New York, where the mail of every person in the telephone book might carry three or five appeals each day for months. It was becoming harder

and harder to gather in money, and although the prime difficulty was that with each half year the number of those who
could afford to give was diminished, collectors for charity
met again and again people who felt that private charity was
not enough and that the whole problem must ultimately be
taken out of their hands.

It is interesting to note the character of the appeals. The
President's Organization on Unemployed Relief, led by
Walter S. Gifford and Owen D. Young, issued a series of adver-
tisements in October and November of 1931. The first read:

FORWARD!

Between October 19th and November 25th, America
will feel the thrill of a great spiritual experience. In those
few weeks millions of dollars will be raised in cities and
towns throughout the land, and the fear of cold and
hunger will be banished from the hearts of thousands.

Be sure that you do your part. Give to the funds that
will be raised in your community. Give liberally.

And know that your gift will bless yourself. It will
lift your own spirit. More than anything else you can do,[4]
it will help to end the depression and lay the firm foundation for better times.

The next advertisement carried the picture of a dark, well-
coiffed, handsome and serious youngish woman, with the text:

Tonight . . . say *this* to your wife . . . then look into
her eyes!

"I gave a lot more than we had planned . . . are you
angry?"

If you should tell her that you merely "contributed"
— that you gave no more than you really felt obliged to —

_____
[4] More than creating jobs?

her eyes will tell you nothing. But deep down in her woman's heart, she will feel just a little disappointed — a tiny bit ashamed.

But tonight — *confess* to her that you have dug into the very bottom of your pocket — that you gave perhaps a little *more* than you can afford — that you opened not just your purse, but your heart as well.

In her eyes you'll see neither reproach nor anger. . . .

No — when you tell her that you have given somewhat *more* than you had planned, you will see no censure in her eyes. But *love!*

In a separate box on this page, readers were urged to contribute to their local organizations: "there is no national fund."

The third advertisement repeated some of the arguments of the first. But it emphasized:

MORALE!

It wins wars.
It beats depressions.
It lays the firm foundations of prosperity.

And further, referring to the four weeks of the drive: "Just one month, and we shall have met the worst threat the Depression can offer: and we shall have won."

The mingling of various elements in these appeals is skillful; but the emphasis is fundamentally false. I pass the question of probability; whether "the passion between the sexes" [5] can be aroused by a display of charity, I myself doubt, but do not press the point. The economic principle announced in the advertisements was wrong because the Government of the United States had in effect decided to let unemployment slide

[5] The definition of love in Johnson's Dictionary.

into the bottomless pit. It was, at the very moment of these officially authorized appeals, looking for a solution of our difficulties in other directions; it certainly did not believe that the suffering of the jobless was "the worst threat the Depression can offer." But the combination of spiritual phraseology, social and personal pressure, and hint of menace were, within reasonable limits, successful.

The charity system had broken down, internally; it kept on functioning by more and more applications of electric shocks, which gave a kind of galvanic energy to the drives, simulating the action of healthy life. It was, as Henry Ford bravely said, a detestable system, most detestable in this, he did not add, that it gave to the rich a feeling of moral superiority when they were only returning a tiny fraction of the great sums they had received from the vast uncomplaining anonymous charity of the poor. The rich, with pomp and publicity, gave a little food, a little shelter, and some cast-off clothes; but the poor in their charity provided the luxurious beds and the great cuisines and the noble yachts and above all the ease of life which comes only when the pressure of wanting money is removed. The charity of the poor was hidden under difficult names, as unearned increment or excess profits, but to the poor themselves their charity meant extra hours of labor or months of walking the streets or insufficient food or wages below the level of decent living; in the great machinery of society these things were worked over into profit and so into luxurious living, of which charity was a part; and came back to the poor, sadly diminished, as a little less food and shelter and clothes than they had had before. It was one thing when the rich gave a little to be spared the sight of crawling misery before their doors; it was another when, instead of rescuing the few accidental misfits of the system, they were called upon to save the millions who had made the whole system possible. The foundation of charity had been a moral feeling; when it became an economic principle, it collapsed.

I have described one earlier phase of the depression in the terms of an actuality taking the place of an illusion and it may be that the whole of it, however much longer it runs, will be the process by which we arrive at the contemplation of things as they are. No realist observer of the capitalist system had ever been so dazzled by the sweetness of charity as not to recognize its true function; many of the critics of charity were, in fact, so impressed by its economic value in keeping alive a large number of potential strike breakers, that they forgot both the actual kindness of the giver and the sense of power which giving brought to him. The accepted theory of benevolence remained, however, untouched until 1932; it was the greatest of Christian virtues, the sweet flower of wealth. (Even the poor kept up the illusion by their prayers and their thanksgiving.) The advertisements I have just quoted, and thousands of editorials and radio appeals [6] spread the new gospel of charity as an economic duty, and the only fault to find with the economics of Messrs. Gifford and Young was that they overemphasized charity as a solvent of the depression; their recognition of it as a business factor was admirable.

The new charity is so new that its implications can only be guessed. That people will be reluctant to give seems only natural; the greater menace may be in the reluctance of other people to take. The gift is losing its cover of friendliness, its real or pretended recognition of brotherhood, and becomes a part of the social plan, a tithe forced from all who prosper

[6] J. P. Morgan made his first speech on the air in aid of the charity drives in March, 1932. He said, "My radio friends . . . we have reached a point where the aid of governments or the gifts of individuals, no matter how generous, are insufficient to meet the conditions which have come upon us. So we must all do our bit." The thought is as confused as the language, but both point to an economic obligation as the necessary support, or substitute, for the moral one.

as surely as taxes are forced from them; presently the receivers may proceed as taxers often do, from little to more, from more to much, from much to all — to the bugaboo of all who are taxed, which is confiscation. This is, frankly, guesswork and would fall outside the limits of this book were it not for one condition: that in 1932 people felt certain of having a large part of our ten million unemployed on their hands for at least five years. Economists said that recovery might take a generation, that twenty years would pass before industry could reabsorb all those it had cast out; but human beings do not habitually look twenty years ahead and five years, which is long for most men and women, represents, to all intents and purposes, a small eternity on earth. The full awareness of the time it would take came a little later when "signs of recovery" were widely heralded and it was seen that a gain in employment of a fraction of one per cent. was considered important; recovery, like disaster, could snowball up, but if industry took back two per cent. of the unemployed a month, the process would still take nearly five years; so that those who gave could no longer believe that they were helping the poor through temporary straits; with each gift they had to reckon on the same or greater gifts the next year and to feel the threat behind the appeal.

The day after this was written, the newspapers carried a summary of the speech delivered in New York by Harvey D. Gibson, who spoke in his two qualities of banker and relief worker. He was therefore in a favorable position to indicate the connection between charity and economics, and he did so frankly. The credit of the City of New York, he explained, was impaired; slashes in the budget must be made or the bankers would refuse loans which the city desperately needs. Therefore the city cannot appropriate enough for relief and in consequence private citizens must contribute generously; or, in other words, private charity is required to save the credit of the city, since with fifteen million dollars from private sources for relief, the city budget can be balanced to the satisfaction of the bankers.

What the unemployed felt, when they began to suspect that they were in for five years of misery, has not been recorded. The language of the American Federation of Labor and of the railway Brotherhoods is unequivocal, but it comes from the strongest, the most highly organized section of labor. I have already quoted the Brotherhoods. The more conservative American Federation of Labor did not shout down its president, William Green, when he said: "I warn the people who are exploiting the workers that they can only drive them so far before they will turn on them and destroy them. They are taking no account of the history of nations in which governments have been overturned. Revolutions grow out of the depths of hunger." This is a touch of Marxian doctrine and distinctly a Marxian habit of mind, startling because the Federation is the greatest enemy of Socialism in America. There is a special menace in the appeal to history, not only because revolutionaries are excessively fond of making the appeal, but because until now America has been thought of as the exceptional country, rendered immune by the perfection of its government and social system from the perils of the past, including the peril of permanent unemployment. The ten million battered men who had no organization to utter their thoughts and to give them a fraternal hand could not have felt less belligerent, unless all power to feel had been drained out of them by the very healing processes of time on which so many leaders relied to end the depression. (Indeed it often seemed that this is precisely what they meant: the death of the unemployed taking place perhaps a decade before the death of society was due.) I shall come presently to strange symptoms of a new attitude of mind among the scattered and disinherited — in a chapter devoted to riot and violence and open pilfering. I anticipate the details to say that a new idea of Rights began, in 1932, to enter the mind of the unemployed. It was pressure from below; and charity as a system lay between that pressure and the pressure from those above, who saw themselves made the perpetual guardians of the poor.

In January, 1932, Franklin D. Roosevelt said, "The American system of economics and government is everlasting."

At about the same time a journalist suggested that it was useless to wait for the return of prosperity; prosperity, he said, is here — and all we have to do is get used to it. He meant, I take it, that the process of deflation had reached a level satisfactory to those who profited by it and who would use all the power at their command to see that the advantages they had gained were not lost by the dangerous and un-American novelty of inflation. He was wrong; but he was right for the succeeding half year, which is above the legal requirement for journalists.

For some reason, deflation carries with it a strong overtone of Protestant morality, the morality of the commercial system in which we had been reared and which we deserted after the war. It implies paying one's way, saving, never borrowing, living within one's income and, although it profits enormously by credit, it can only forgive the debtor by never forgiving any portion of his debt. I regret to say that I found little evidence that the Americans were enjoying their experience in the realm of deflation. We are, I am afraid, a boom people.

Even the figures of losses were boom figures. A brokerage house estimated that the Vanderbilts had lost in the shrinkage of railroad stocks alone, some forty million dollars and Arthur Curtiss James, nine millions; John T. Flynn, biographer of John D. Rockefeller, estimated that the Rockefeller fortune had shrunk to one fifth (and returned to one third) its prepanic size, so that in spite of buying "sound common stocks" in the first week of depression, the family of the genius of oil and organization may have lost nearly half a billion dollars.

What the common man lost with the loss of these fortunes was only a dream, but it was a serviceable dream which had kept him happy for years, — the dream of incalculable wealth, waste, and luxury. Radicals had jeered for a generation at the idea that every man in America could become rich and protested, with figures, that very few did; the common man cared little for figures and averages. He was living at the end of the Algerian epoch and the newspapers still were full of stories of young men who rose from office boy to corporation president; the stories occurred more often in obituary notices than in notices of election, but they kept the tradition alive long after the custom was dead. The years of the war and again the years before the crash had turned up so many new millionaires that even economists began to believe that moderate wealth might be the portion of any man and that the way to turn moderate wealth into Occidental splendor was open, although it was as narrow as Wall Street. To hundreds of thousands, the question of what to do with a million dollars was not abstract; it was a preparation for the more or less immediate future, and people answered it with more enthusiasm than they did the other favorite question of the Sunday papers: What would you do if you had only a year to live? The problem of the million dollars seemed so much more reasonable, the likelihood of having it so much greater than the possibility of dying.

When we saw great fortunes shrinking and heard of yachts for sale and great houses abandoned, we knew in our hearts that we must forsake the waking dream of luxury. We might still hope to beat off the sheriff and keep up our installments and perhaps, late in life, buy a little house in the country or rent a little flat in the city; but the Park Avenue-Ritz-transatlantic-liveried-custom-built-lighting-cigars-with-gold-notes ideal had vanished, taking with it Monte Carlo [7] and Antibes and champagne and great white mistresses with marble limbs and all that we had thought of as wealth and care-free spending from the days of the Renaissance to the days of Palm Beach. I do not think it was an edifying dream, but it was a happy one; and to change the dream of a nation in three years is a serious business.

Beside this dream there existed, for millions, an extremely practical opportunity: to work for the government, — city, state, or Federal. A healthy man might become a policeman, a contractor could get a city job, an intellectual could be a teacher or librarian, a friend of a ward boss could be a janitor; for the roving disposition there were the army, the navy, and the railway and air mail service; for the sedentary, thousands of civil service jobs. They were not extravagantly paid, but they were "steady." Now "government" was going broke as in Chicago, facing a deficit as in Washington, cutting down pay wherever possible, taking on no new men. What security could there be in life if the whole support and structure of our daily existence was decaying before our eyes? And, practically, where could we get jobs, if city and State and nation had none to give?

In Chicago, James D. O'Reilly, a municipal employee, saw his home auctioned off because he had failed to pay city taxes of $34; the city owed him, in unpaid salary, $850.

Chicago is, to be sure, a special case, because in the midst of normal difficulties and political corruption, a tax strike occurred, after a judge had declared illegal the assessment base used the previous year. The tax strike is an open boycott, in-

---

[7] For the first time in half a century the Societé des Bains de Mer (which is the gambling hell of Monte Carlo) failed to pay a dividend in 1932. Previous dividends had risen to twenty per cent. a year and over.

STREET SCENE: NEW YORK CITY

(*Photo by Walker Evans. Lent by Courtesy of N. Y. State Temporary Emergency Relief Administration*)

tended to force the city to put an end to its extravagances.[8]
School teachers, policemen, firemen and other city employees
were unpaid for long periods; at times a kind of local scrip
was issued, accepted by neighborhood grocers and landlords.
The State has supported the city for a long time, issuing war-
rants in anticipation of the ultimate collection of Chicago's
taxes. But if our second largest city had been a commercial
enterprise, its bankruptcy would be an accepted fact.

What this means to the citizen who depends on the city for
water and removal of refuse and protection from thuggery
and fire may be foretold by observing what it has already meant
to the intellectual life of Chicago. I had heard a rumor that
the Public Library of Chicago was not buying new publica-
tions and wrote to the librarian, Mr. C. B. Roden, for confirmation. For purposes of comparison, I asked for the appropriations of previous years. His reply shows that in 1929
Chicago spent about eighty thousand dollars for current newspapers, magazines, and books; the next year about fifty-five
thousand; in 1931, over sixty-two thousand; and in 1932
exactly $2,299. The whole of this last sum went for current
American periodicals. The Chicago Public Library, in a year
of profound interest in the actual problems of the day, spent
not one cent for any foreign periodical; it did not have in
its reading room a single newspaper of any kind; it bought not
one new book, fiction, non-fiction, or juvenile. "In fact,"
writes Mr. Roden, "we stopped buying books in May, 1931.
It should also be pointed out that the above figures represent
new books only and do not include the figures for the huge
annual replacements of books worn out, which normally
amount to three times the expenditure for new books. In 1932
this item was also completely wiped out." That is to say that
Chicago is slowly losing its reference books, the intellectual

---

[8] At the end of 1932, the city threatened to cut off the water supply of those who had not paid their taxes.

arms for meeting the future. Perhaps as a writer and reader of books I take this too seriously; perhaps the Cæsar of Bernard Shaw is right when he rejoices at the burning of the greatest library in Egypt.[9] Perhaps the figures for new fire engines would be more impressive. I note only that the death of an intellectual service may precede the decline of other services, and that the people who can get no new books in Chicago may find themselves, a year later, threatened by epidemics of disease or fire or pillage, because the government of the city is bankrupt. The same threat has been made in Philadelphia and in New York. It has not yet been made against the Federal Government because the Government can still float temporary loans; but the activities of the Government in scientific fields, in protection of the health of children, in publication of the results of researches, in doing anything which is not immediately and urgently necessary, are already being threatened or cut down.

I reserve for a separate list the greater part of the mental and moral deflations which we suffered in this period, and note here only two changes in public opinion which, praiseworthy as they are, show a surprising let down in moral tone: one is the propaganda for the recognition of Russia, the other the movement which culminated in great parades under the banners, "Beer for Taxes."

Of both of these it is correct to say that they reflect a strange inconsistency in the American character; the refusal to treat with Russia may have had an economic basis at the beginning, but after 1925 trade with Russia could have been an important source of wealth for us and the moment the home market closed, at the end of 1929, the opening of the greatest single new market, Russia, became economically desirable.

[9] Certainly the Chicago Library missed some bad books by not buying since 1931; but it also missed some excellent ones and half a dozen essential to the average intelligent man.

Prohibition, likewise, was supported by the heavy industries [10] and by others as light as carbonated waters, for reasons of profit; but in 1930 it was clear that the economic motive favored the restoration of free running beer and some other eminent drinks. Yet the American people, so sternly and so long rebuked for having no interest but profit, kept their attitude, like Mr. Jimmie Durante in an equally perilous encounter, and refused to give up a moral principle in favor of cash. It needed the unbearable pressure of a long crisis to bring them even to the point of reconsideration.

Our attitude toward Russia was, on the side of the Government, purely moral, Mr. Coolidge having refused to "make merchandise of any American principle" in boom times; [11] and on the side of big business, purely practical, for General Motors and Standard Oil and dozens of others traded perilously with the moral lepers of Moscow, while the Austin Company built a city for the making of Ford cars near Nizhni-Novgorod. The American Government had refused even to discuss those Czarist debts which, "repudiated" by the Soviets, gave proof that there could be no straightforward dealings between us; and American business men had had to make

[10] Of steel, I am happy to report that the owner of one of the smaller mills in Pittsburgh, an ardent supporter of the Amendment when it was being passed, hopeful of getting sober and productive men to work on Monday mornings was, in 1931, running a small private brewery to supply his men with beer, preferring that to the rotgut liquor they would otherwise buy; of fizzy drinks, it was reported that the sale of bottled soda did not diminish in a Canadian province when liquor was restored.

[11] Boom times being over, the United States recognized three South American governments founded in violence, one of them only a week after it had assumed power, one in three weeks, one in three months. Secretary Stimson said that he had acted promptly "in order that in the present economic situation our delay may not embarrass the people of these friendly countries." Ex-President Coolidge was even franker; he said, "We have little sympathy with revolution. . . . We have large commercial interests. . . ."

whatever terms they could for payments, since the habitual framework of consular representatives and commercial treaties did not exist to give them fixed methods and protection. The propaganda for recognition of Russia was, oddly enough, feeble until the Government, in 1930, began to apply a series of irritants to Russia, denouncing her for speculating in grain (imputing an intention to ruin America) and making difficulties about shipments of pulp wood. Except for the organizations which lived to attack Russia and lived by attacking her, these pinpricks of the Government were feebly supported and in the reaction the cry for recognition was heard. Yet for most people the old morality held firm; while newspapers and liberal organizations asked for recognition, the change in the public was only negative: people abandoned entirely their hostility to Russia and entered on a period first of indifference and then of admiration. The witch-burning of Representative Hamilton Fish was a parade of ghosts.

The moral deflation lay in this: that even the enthusiasts for recognition placed less emphasis on the American tradition of supporting all movements against tyranny, all efforts to attain freedom (the argument of the first years of Soviet Russia); they did not insist that America should be sympathetic to a great experiment (the argument of the second period when the freedom of new Russia began to seem doubtful); they put forward the sound argument that if we recognized Russia we should get a large share of the trade which was going to Germany and England. In 1932 the motive became even more powerful because of a technological danger: if Russia accepted certain systems of measurement from Germany and Great Britain, it might be impossible for us to supply her with goods for generations, since our systems differed from the European. (For instance, the variation in the gauge on railroad track is serious; if the Russian track differs from ours, American builders of locomotives would have to build new

instruments of precision and new machinery, or readjust those
they already possessed, before they could bid on Russian freight
cars; in finer work the discrepancy would be fatal to our business.) Yet neither of the two great parties came out for recognition of Russia, although neither made it impossible.

In the "beer-for-taxes" propaganda, the moral degeneration
was definite, because in accepting "beer-for-taxes" as a worthy
cause, the wets forfeited their profound moral superiority to
the drys and accepted not only their intolerable principles,
but even their methods. Honorable exceptions remained, those
who fought on for repeal because prohibition was an infringe-
ment of human rights and belittled human dignity; the others
were, without knowing it, following the path of the drys. So
long as the attack on drinking remained a moral movement
(known as Temperance) it was sweet and ineffective, directing itself to the drinker rather than the drink, making each
conversion a personal triumph; that movement was, in the
1890's, converted into the economic drive of Prohibition,
which attacked the drink, not the drinker, and substituted
"pressure politics", propaganda and filing cabinets, for petitions tied in white ribbon. It became a business movement,
supported by big business; and it was successful. The resistance
to Prohibition in America flowered from many roots; the deep
soil of all was resentment against sacrificing a human pleasure
in favor of a financial gain. Before this resistance changed from
a minority to, I say hopefully, a majority movement, it moved
from this fine moral soil to the arid ground of economics, precisely where the Prohibitionists had planted their ignoble banner. It is not remarkable that when the "beer-for-taxes" parades
took place, the loudest of all the manifestations, in New York,
was generally supposed to be largely a political stunt of Mayor
Walker, intended to distract attention from the growing difficulties rising out of his habit of being too friendly with people

to whom his friendship might be advantageous. Yet the impact of these parades and of the millions of little signs on motor cars and of thousands of repetitions in newspapers was felt at the conventions and modification was accepted in principle by both parties.

So that it will be known that the American people gave up the right to drink when they most could afford to drink, and clamored for its restoration when they hadn't, in effect, the price of a bottle of good Burgundy.[12] The fifteen years of Prohibition began with a marked degeneration in taste, carried on with the emergence of a second-rate drink, gin, as the urban alcoholic beverage, and was coming to a rather pleasant level of good wines and excellent foods in metropolitan speakeasies, when the deflation of currency brought about the deflation of moral ideas, and the sacred right to drink was forgotten because the Federal Government faced a deficit. There were those who, indifferent to drink, drank to defy a meddlesome government and an unjust law; it remains to be seen whether they will, when beer, for taxes, has been restored, refuse to drink what is handed to them on so sloppy a platter.

[12] Say, Hospice de Beaune, 1915.

CHAPTER FOURTEEN

LOW POINT: THE RESCUE

WE were somewhere in the lower depths when word came from Russia that all was well with America. Specifically it was in October, 1931, one of the low points in the scale, that Mr. Walter Duranty, interviewing great men in Russia, informed the *New York Times* that these men, who would dearly like to believe that America was tottering into the abyss, could find no support for any such belief. They thought there was life in the old dog yet, that the capitalist system as we used it was good for another run, perhaps for another boom and, in strict obedience to Marxian principles, another disaster. Greatly cheered, America proceeded simultaneously in two directions: toward financial and industrial low points unthought of even six months before and to the serious business of reinflating the collapsed balloon of her credit. The downward momentum we had gained in two years was not checked by such a feeble edifice as the National Credit Corporation; we continued downhill, at a good rate, long after the more powerful Reconstruction Finance Corporation had gone to work at the beginning of 1932; railroads and some banks were snatched out of the way of the avalanche, but it was not until the end of May that, with a resounding crash, we came to a stop. The shock was so great that we had not recovered by the middle of August. That is to say, the financial low point came at the beginning of June, the intellectual low point around July, and the low point of nerves in August.

It was during this time that Americans returning from abroad began to say that we had lost our nerve, because we were whining and Europe was not; and those even more remote expatriates, New Yorkers returning from Hollywood, said the same thing of the East; and it was during this period that we showed signs of losing something more important than our nerve, which is our capacity to spring back when we are bent and particularly to snap back at stupidity and injustice in high places. The criticism from Europe came not from Europeans or, when it did come from them, it embraced their own people in the same question; Americans abroad are for a variety of reasons disqualified, since they seldom can see their own countrymen clearly or know the history of Europe well. (Most of the criticism came from Americans in France, and France in 1931 and 1932 was an expanding country, winning diplomatic victories at every turn, drawing gold from the United States, and enjoying a huge program of public works and public services, which meant a movement of money lively in comparison with the French average. Americans abroad are not usually familiar with the long centuries of poverty and the patient living within narrow margins which are traditional there; nor do they give the right psychological value to the lower expectation of even a prosperous European who knows, for the greater part of his life, how much he will earn, how much he will inherit, and even how much he will leave to his children, the variations he expects or even dreams of being slight in comparison with ours. The history of Europe is what Winwood Reade called it, the martyrdom of man, and it has left to Europe contentments and apathies which Americans have not yet learned to cherish. It was the luck of the Bolshevists that Russians could go through famine and pestilence to make a new world for themselves, because they had gone through pestilence and famine to make the old world of the Czars; and the French peasant or shoemaker fell from no height and into no abyss when business turned downward because the margin above comfort, which made prosperity, was small; and the margin below it, which made hardship, was also small. The psychological contrast was even more striking, for our great expectations had lifted us to a high place; we fell in the dark and when we hung on to a sapling in the night, we did not know whether we had a foot or a thousand feet still to drop before we reached bottom. (I think these differences are true of averages; but when I say "Europeans" I mean, of course, only those Europeans whom I know or of whom I have reasonable information; and the same thing is true of "Americans." I feel with Edmund Burke that you cannot indict a nation, even with a psychological indictment.)

Toward the end of the period considered in this chapter, three events took place, and the fact that they came so close together throws a light on the half year which led up to them. They were:

1. Our maximum loss of gold at the end of May, 1932.
2. The cry for a dictator in June and July.
3. The expulsion of the Bonus Army by the Federal troops in August.

If these three things were all to be marked on a chart covering a long period they would roughly coincide, and they would suggest that the economic low point was the cause of the intellectual low point and the low point in nerves. That spiritual deflation came with the financial deflation of the country has been recorded. But I have carefully refrained from saying that one was caused by the other. According to Karl Marx, it must have been. In one of the earliest assertions of the doctrine which came to be known as the economic interpretation (or the materialist conception) of history, Marx said, ". . . upon the social conditions of existence, as a foundation, there is built a superstructure of diversified and characteristic sentiments, illusions, habits of thought, and outlooks of life in general"; and Marx was acute enough to add that individuals almost always assume that these sentiments and illusions are personal to themselves, unaffected by social forces. Marx, like Freud, puts a scalpel into our hand, and his disciples, like Freud's, blunt its edge when they use it not for dissection, but for destruction.

One of his disciples, Robert Rives La Monte, about twenty-five years ago developed the Marxian principle in an ingenious way. My inclination is to reject the point he made, but I have no reason for doing so. Certainly, when we consider what happened between 1929 and 1932 and then consider what we thought in that period, the connection is too close for us merely to cry "coincidence." La Monte's idea is illuminating because he takes the extreme case. It is not only what we think about college education, marriage and free speech that is affected by our economic situation; the man whom we have considered farthest removed from social pressure, the scientist in his laboratory is, according to La Monte, compelled to think as he thinks by the conditions of life about him. The idea that God made the world by one magnificent exercise of absolute power rose in the days of despots; the idea that the world grew by slow evolution rose with the growth of Democracy. "The form of scientific theories," says La Monte, "has been largely determined by the economic conditions amid which they arose, and . . . their acceptance by large bodies of adherents has depended upon their fitness to meet the desires — desires produced by economic needs — of these adherents."

His examples are well chosen. "When the bourgeosie were fresh from their revolutionary conflict with feudalism — the great French Revolution — and were still extending their dominion, they were iconoclastic and revolutionary in spirit. It was precisely then that the cataclysmic theories of Cuvier in geology and biology became generally accepted theories of science.

"By the middle of the nineteenth century, the bourgeosie were firmly seated in the saddle. . . . They had no more use for revolutionary theories in their business; if changes must come, let them come a step at a time. Thus the conditions for the wide acceptance of evolutionary theories in biology and geology were ripe, so that in spite of the rage of the clergy, nothing could prevent the general conquest of the scientific world by the natural selection of Darwin and Wallace and the uniformitarian geology of Sir Charles Lyell . . . (whose) great reputation raised to a sacred dogma the utterly indefensible doctrine that 'Nature makes no leaps'."

The special character of the period from the end of 1931 to the midsummer of 1932 is this: that we reacted to the thing that was happening, which was deflation, not grimly as we had until the Moratorium, with the feeling that things were getting worse and would continue to get worse because nothing was being done; we knew something was being done and suffered a growing irritation because what was done, in the name of counter-deflation, was so laggard and halting and ineffective. We broke down mentally and nervously because we began to believe that although we had the will to struggle, we had lost the power; we began to fear that we had started our march forward too late.

One symptom of this uneasiness about the future was our eagerness to embrace any scheme which gave escape from the present; we were afraid, so we scolded the familiar processes of business and took to issuing edicts. This was time of waiting for crude oil to go to a dollar a barrel because the governors of Oklahoma and Texas had sent militiamen into the fields to close down the wells, and for the price of cotton to rise because the Farm Board was asking the South to destroy one third of its standing crop, while the growers asked the Board to destroy the crop it had already bought. It was said that Mr. Ford had let it be known that every man employed in his works must have a small garden, under pain of dismissal (and engaged men to dig carrots on his own farms, implemented only with old-fashioned hoes instead of labor-saving machinery). Just as the Bonus Army represented the idea of getting what you want by a show of force, these represented the idea of interrupting the processes of the depression by launching against them the law of the land; if we could not have prosperity by slow improvement, we should have recovery by fiat.

The most fertile field for the imagination of man is that in which he is least at home, namely the field of money. The great accumulations of wealth in America after the Civil War were followed by a number of schemes to undermine the power of these accumulations; the farmer and the small industrialist felt a menace to their security in the vast concentrated financial power along the eastern seaboard and tried to check it by changing the value of currency. The same thing happened after the Great War and again after the great boom. Out of the obscurity into which he sank when Free Silver was defeated, "Coin" Harvey came fitfully into prominence; out of the same obscurity the ratio of sixteen to one emerged to be treated seriously, in one of time's revenges, for a new valuation of silver might bring prosperity to some Americans and facilitate trade with parts of the Far East. And these efforts which reached the public, more or less, were the outstanding few; the waste-paper baskets of every editorial writer in America were filled daily with dozens of other schemes, all of them bent on increasing the velocity of spending by shaving off the value of the dollar which was not spent. The ingenuity of some of the planners was admirable: there were to be dated dollars worth three per cent. less each day, so that at the end of a month they were redeemable at banks for no more than ten cents.

There were dollars with coupons bearing dates, for the same purpose, but giving the effect of adding a little to the value of the dollar if it were spent before the coupon was outdated. There were schemes for special currencies, in bright colors, for use internally, with the usual gold-backed currency for international payments. Ambitious manufacturers got out little pamphlets of their ideas; fanatics, impoverished by the lack of the very money they knew so well how to handle, wrote letters in fine Spencerian script, wavering a little, revealing the years of brooding over wrongs and of waiting for just such an opportunity to be justified. They all seemed mad, but it happens they were all inflationist; and one, at least, of their schemes was put into action, in a small village in Germany which lived on the prosperity of a single factory, where a temporary artificial unit of money saved the entire community from destruction.

These fantasies of economics were efforts to escape from the dead hand of the past; they were meant to interrupt the depression and by their nature they could have made the payment of debt infinitely easier. No one had found a way to reduce the fixed charges of life, the enormous burden of debt; no one, so far as I know, spoke of the necessity until late in the campaign, when Senator Borah openly and Mr. Roosevelt (who was much nearer to responsibility) in vague terms referred to scaling down mortgages or refinancing at lower rates. But one method was found, a method practicable beyond compare, where honor rooted in dishonor stood. It was bankruptcy by proxy, or perhaps it should be called subsidiary bankruptcy, and it could only be enjoyed by those who had so organized themselves in the great days that they could stand the long pull of the bad ones — as if, indeed, they had anticipated the very emergency. To avoid the laws of libel, I shall imagine that shoestrings were sold in chain stores all through the United States and that the manufacturers of shoestrings had formed, for retailing, a second corporation; and that the retailing corpo-

ration had formed a third, a real-estate business, which signed
leases for those costly corner stores some time in 1928 and
signed them, at prevailing high rentals, for ninety-nine years,
which is the business man's equivalent of eternity. These rentals began, in 1931, to be a burdensome fixed charge which
refused to go down with the lowering of prices; everything
else the companies used cost less; their product sold for less;
but they had to pay interest on their loans and rent on their
stores. To suspend the first would mean bankruptcy for the
parent organization, which would be uncomfortable; but when
the landlords refused to "adjust" rentals, the subsidiary real-
estate business which actually signed the leases went bankrupt,
automatically cancelling the obligations; and then the parent
company could form a new real-estate company to sign leases
for the very same desirable corner stores at rentals "more in
keeping with the trend of the times." Two notorious cases occurred in New York; on the real-estate pages of the newspapers, protest was made in special editorials; otherwise this
finesse of business went unrewarded with the praise it deserved.
For it had shown the way to every man; in the future he needed
only a dummy corporation to engage him in any business and
to go bankrupt for him. In the Middle Ages and even later,
Slavic noblemen, too proud to handle financial affairs, had a
sale juif to make them rich; the system, with appropriate variations, had arrived in America.

Something else arrived and it is a matter of taste to decide
which is more admirable, the new skullduggery in business or
the new Fascism which was the reply of big business to the
Communism of the intellectuals and the politics of the politicians. From the beginning of the depression it was felt, by a
few, that the tedious process of open legislation might not be
adequate to the critical needs of the time; the inaction of the
President for six months and the spectacle of Congress delaying

a tariff bill for a year, followed by the hysterical stampede of the House when the bills for reconstruction came up, persuaded some people that Mr. Hoover was not the right man in the White House nor Mr. Garner the right man for the Speaker's chair; others felt that no matter how intelligent, disciplined, and farsighted the successors of Hoover and Garner might be, the system of checks and balances, the long jockeying for political advantage, and the impossibility of taking instant and drastic action under the American form of government, made change of personnel worse than useless; what was wanted was change in the system. The men without property, without a stake in the future of capitalism, without hostages to fortune, might turn to Russia and the dictatorship, through a few intellectuals, of a small class, the proletariat, functioning as State Socialism; the man in possession turned to the other conspicuously successful dictatorship, that of Mussolini, originally undertaken for the rescue of capital and carried on until it had become a dictatorship functioning through State Capitalism.[1]

It is pleasant to note that the impetus in favor of Italianate Fascism in America came originally from the admirers of the Russian system of planning. Mr. Stuart Chase had proposed a group similar to the War Industries Board, and although Mr. Chase emphasized fact-finding and thinking and planning, the idea of a small number of men controlling the present course of our government enchanted the minds of many who would have resented, to the last degree, any such interference with their freedom as a national planning system would involve. The President grew aware of this feeling; he had put himself on record as opposed to planning, but when he asked that relief to the States be canalized through the Reconstruction Finance Federation, a body appointed by himself and responsive to

[1] The Italian Government through its investment in industry, by way of the great banks, is virtually part owner of all the chief industries of the country.

administrative hints, he saw that he was being forced into taking more and more control of the actual daily lives of American citizens and, addressing himself to them, said, "I have no taste for any such emergency powers. . . . We used such emergency powers to win the war; we can use them to fight the depression, the misery and suffering from which are equally great."

Instantly the dopesters in Washington were informing their clientele that rumors of a dictatorship were buzzing in legislative halls and executive corridors, and in the middle of June a memorial signed by eighty-six prominent citizens, including Edsel Ford and the President of the American Federation of Labor and retired rich men and active financiers and industrialists begged the President to bring back the Council of National Defense which won golden opinions during the war. It was an open plea for dictatorship and the President rejected it, naming old and new institutions, from the Cabinet to the Reconstruction Finance Corporation, as sufficient. For the time, the agitation ended.

In September, 1932, Frederic A. Ogg, the editor of the *American Political Science Review,* summarized the propaganda for dictatorship in an article in *Current History,* which provides background for the open memorial of the eighty-six Elders. He notes that fifty representative men confessed to Gordon Selfridge their lack of faith in the success of democracy in America. At a meeting of the League for Independent Political Action in July, "intelligent men" wondered whether this was the last time "we shall be preparing to elect national officers under the Constitution." He says that dictatorship is being furtively discussed in some quarters and openly predicted "by many sober-minded people, including not a few members of Congress." [2] He notes the Fascist tone of Owen D. Young's

[2] The inclusion of Congressmen among sober-minded people is one of the rare compliments paid to them in this time, and is therefore noteworthy.

address at Notre Dame (also in June) and quotes, "When trouble comes we need some one with understanding and with power to marshal all our forces, to direct the course of the avalanche, so that the least damage may be done, and to stop it if possible." Julius E. Barnes of the United States Chamber of Commerce and many others favored variants of the coalition cabinet system rising in power (and evading political control) until a national council of best minds, not necessarily Cabinet members or Congressmen, were in command. Smartness approved of franker dictatorship, *Vanity Fair* crying for "powers the President would enjoy in time of war" and for healthier readers, Bernarr MacFadden wrote, "What we need now is martial law; this is no time for civil law. The President should have dictatorial powers. The edicts of the Constitution do not interfere with a general when he is fighting a battle and the Constitution should not interfere with the remedies which are essential to get us out of this appalling depression." The periodical for which Mr. MacFadden wrote this was called *Liberty*. In *Scribner's*, Henry Hazlitt suggested that we abandon Congress, and elect twelve men to be directors of the nation. Finally, says Mr. Ogg, "Finally there is Fascism pure and simple. . . . It is known that at least two or three [movements] have been organized quietly. . . . May we not witness capture of power — not by gross methods of violence, but by graceful usurpation — by interests that will fasten upon us a Fascist régime? Implicit in proposals noted above is the telltale demand for a 'strong man.' One of the editorials cited was indeed headed, 'Wanted, a Mussolini!' " [3]

Lucky as always, the American people crying for a dictatorship got a taste of it almost at once. The month of May was the blackest financial period of the depression; intellectually the response was the search for the man on horseback which continued into June; the delay in action until August was due

[3] Il Duce dissented, saying, "America does not need a Mussolini!"

to lack of experience. Without overstepping his constitutional powers, the President in August called out Federal troops to recapture Federal property and to put down a riot. It was not, however, the action, but the explanation which carried the hard tone of Fascism to the country. I have already quoted: "A challenge to the authority of the United States Government has been met", but the end of the statement is even more impressive: "Order and tranquillity are the first requisites in the great task of economic reconstruction." This has the true Fascist ring; it was to restore order and tranquillity that Mussolini marched on Rome. (I say this without irony; order and tranquillity actually are the social ends of Fascism and the process of restoring them sometimes involves bloodshed.) Whether the rioting of the Bonus Army constituted a challenge to the authority of the Federal Government is, legally, the only question; and the answer may not be found until it is known whether the use of the Federal Army was arranged at a conference which took place in Washington *before* the riot began and at which high officials of the Government were present. Of an earlier conference (July 26) a record is contained in a letter addressed to Secretary Hurley by Herbert S. Ward, a Washington attorney.

Mr. Ward wrote: "I clearly recall your reply . . . to Captain Carter's tender of the loyal coöperation of the B.E.F. to the effect that there was no condition which would lead you to call upon the B.E.F., or any of its members for any service, as well as Captain Carter's rejoinder that you did not feel that way about it in 1917. I also clearly recall your observation that *the B.E.F. had been a problem to the administration because these men had been absolutely law abiding;* that had they violated the law, or been disorderly, they could have been evicted from the District of Columbia . . . and that the President of the United States, by a scratch of his pen, could declare martial law and use the entire military forces of the United States for that purpose. . . ." [Italics mine.]

The latest reports of General Glassford, also, suggest that the high officials not only planned to put down the riot, but eagerly hoped the riot would take place. The display which accompanied the arrival of the troops, the wait of an hour while an orderly "dashed back to Fort Myer for the tunic, service stripes, and English whipcord breeches of General Mac-Arthur", the exhibitions before the news-reel cameras, the use of cavalry to intimidate the crowds, and the burning of the shacks miles away from the actual scene of the battle, all suggest that the episode was being lifted from a riot in the District to the level of an armed attack upon the Federal Government. That the army was ready was the great lesson of the bonus battle, and Mr. Lawrence Dennis informs me that the readiness goes far indeed, as the army, quite properly, has plans for taking over all the vital arteries of communication (telegraph, telephone, railway, and high roads) in the event of any serious outbreaks of rioters or Communists.

The District of Columbia, being directly ruled by the Federal Government, was not a perfect test case; no usurpation of authority was needed to call out troops. The threat was implicit in the elaboration of military force and came close to the surface in the explanations. Insistence upon the number of radicals and criminals in the encampment warned the American people that radicals might hereafter be permanently classed with thieves, murderers, and rapers; the legality of the entire procedure was made doubtful thereby and many people felt that the President had ordered out the troops because he did not like the veterans and because he wished to drive home his authority.

I cannot testify to the immediate response of the American people. I was at sea when the riot in Washington occurred; three days later, coming home and asking for details to supplement the few lines of wireless on a ship's news bulletin, I found little shock, hardly any excitement. The Bonus Army, I gathered, had begun to bore people who had not been enthusiastic for its purposes to begin with and were annoyed by its persistence after Congress had defeated the bonus payment bill. I heard echoes of radical anger and Fascist approval, in about equal measure. It was, actually, not until September, when the Attorney-General's report was issued, that I noted any impatience with the Government or any sympathy with the veterans. Sympathy did not extend to any feeling that the bonus should have been paid; [4] on the other hand, it was impatience, more than anger, that led people to condemn Mr. Hoover. The special pleadings of the Attorney-General's report was so mercilessly exposed that it added one blunder to another. Liberal editors might protest against the dangerous precedent set by the use of troops; I discerned no wave of emotion whatever.

Yet it was, I believe, the use of the troops which started the Khaki Shirts in America. The haphazard Bonus Army must have suggested to many men, statesmen and racketeers alike, that a more disciplined and more dignified army could be created. One was founded by Walter Waters, when he left Washington with the Bonus Army, and Art J. Smith, an American *condottiere* of the school of Richard Harding Davis and Lee Christmas.[5] It is purely Fascist. When Nathaniel Weyl interviewed high officers of the organization in September he was told that "there isn't going to be any election in November" because the Khaki Shirts were going to invade Washington, beginning November 1, demand the resignation of the Presi-

---

[4] Except for those who would profit by payment, I know only one man who favored the proposal and he was an economist who said grimly that we had to come to inflation and would probably take a vicious way to arrive at it, so the payment of the bonus might as well be made.

[5] It must not be confused with another group, of the same name, with headquarters in Washington, which is anti-militarist, although patriotic, and looks to united political action.

dent, "and seize power." Mr. Weyl, reporting for the *New Republic,* was not alarmed, but interested, for "there are sections in the Middle West where they are taken seriously, and where large portions of the people would welcome a revolutionary march on Washington." In Burlington, Iowa, he was told that perhaps a hundred men a day pass eastward on the Hoover Pullmans, while the freight cars westward are empty. In Des Moines, headquarters was rejoicing in the active coöperation of the Farmers' Union, which had contributed a cow and a half, and local tradesmen had given truckloads of food. At Kansas City (National) Headquarters, estimates of the number of men already enlisted ran high, even to two million; a sober estimate was that a hundred thousand might be gathered for the November march on Washington.[6]

The organization of these men is elaborate; the lesson of the Bonus Expeditionary Force has been taken to heart and there is to be a base of support in each State, a camp in which concentrations may be made, from which local pressure can be directed, and to which crusaders may return. The staffing is elaborate and the directors say they are in friendly communication with many similar organizations throughout the country. They hope to seize power and to restore prosperity; they demand allegiance to the Constitution and forbid all "radical talk." Mr. Weyl's summary of the movement (which upholds heretical opinions on currency, derived largely from Coin Harvey and his school) shows the essentially Fascist inspiration:

"The class basis of this appeal is obviously reactionary. It appeals to the small traders and manufacturers who have seen the origin of their troubles in the rapid deflation of the post-crisis years, and the general tightening of credit which accompanied it. They have felt the pinch in their dealings with the

[6] It did not occur.

banks, and their radicalism extends to a denunciation of the banking system and no farther. For this class, inflation is the ideal solution, a solution in which social and class divisions flourish, a period of prosperity in which the small trader is making money hand over fist out of the lag between wages and the cost of living. It is no accident that Fascism in America as well as in Germany transfers the war of labor against capital into a war against capital and interest."

This is the result of hysteria in high places or, perhaps, of deliberate Fascism, that the most arrogantly loyal of all classes in America, the veterans of the Great War who would not let Kreisler play the violin, were alienated from their allegiance; and that the talk of seizure of power rose in tone and volume not from angry proletarians, but from farmers and shop-keepers and ex-soldiers. It remains to be seen whether those who had spoken so earnestly and warmly of Fascism six months before, had prepared to take over the unstable and tricky army they had helped to bring into existence.

CHAPTER FIFTEEN

REVIVAL MEETINGS

THE Republican platform was that something terrible might happen to the country; the Democratic platform was that it had happened. Exploiting fear on one side and resentment on the other, the parties could have reduced the election to a series of riots; intellectually they kept the level low enough, but until the last few days the dignity of the President and the confidence of Mr. Roosevelt saved the country from a distasteful exhibition. The personal abuse at the end and the recriminations were not edifying, but they had no effect on the election and were soon forgotten.

An English editor wrote before the conventions had adopted their platforms that the campaign would be fought on the issue of deflation against inflation. At the beginning of the campaign he seemed to be entirely wrong; Mr. Roosevelt's first important speech and Mr. Hoover's acceptance both stressed the issue of Prohibition, totally unreal by that time and removed from the country's actual interests. Mr. Hoover, intending at the start to make only a few speeches, let his supporters know that he did not wish the question to be much discussed; it came to life again, flickeringly, but the pressure of events was too heavy; the candidates had to come near, at least, to the problems of the people. In doing so, the incumbent had an advantage in debate, for he could list actual accomplishments and promise to continue the work he had done; the corresponding disadvantage was that he had to defend measures which had not yet proved effective. Of this, strangely, the Democrats took small advantage; they quarreled with the Republicans for credit in passing measures for the recovery of the country, without saying any too clearly that recovery had not been made visible; nor did they bring forth a complete program, but promised instead to care for and protect those whom the Administration had neglected, and seldom challenged the excellence of the actual measures taken. They did not need to exploit discontent; discontent was embracing them as saviors on every side. And the longer they evaded specific promises, the safer they stood.[1]

The distinction of Mr. Hoover lay, as usual, in his stubborn refusal to sacrifice the principles in which he believed. In the heart of the Middle West he had no panacea to offer the farmers, telling them frankly that he would give them no "counterfeit currency", as he called fiat money, or false hopes. He attacked "seductive but unworkable and disastrous theories of government" and, addressing lawyers in Washington, called on all good men to "defend our system of government against reckless assaults by designing persons." The idea that the framework of government was actually jeopardized grew in his mind to unexpected dominance and in New York he accused the Democratic Party of "proposing changes and new deals which would destroy the very foundations of our American system", so that he feared grass would grow in the streets. His conception of the American system comes out clearly in a specific controversy with Mr. Roosevelt. In San Francisco, Mr. Roosevelt said, "Our economic life is dominated by some six hundred odd corporations who control two thirds of American industry. . . . We are steering a steady course toward economic oligarchy if we are not there already." He defended the right of

---

[1] Mr. Roosevelt's enemies held that he had delayed the return of confidence by his tardy and not absolutely decisive statement on the bonus question.

every man to his own property, was "not prepared to say that the system which produces princes of property is wrong", and then, standing at the western outpost of the country, looked back not only over space, but over time, and made this analysis:

"A glance at the situation to-day only too clearly indicates that equality of opportunity, as we have known it, no longer exists. Our industrial plant is built. The problem just now is whether, under existing conditions, it is not overbuilt.

"Our last frontier has long since been reached and there is practically no more free land. . . . There is no safety-valve in the form of a Western prairie to which those [thrown] out of work by the Eastern economic machines can go for a new start. We are not able to invite immigration from Europe to share our endless plenty. . . .

"A mere builder of more industrial plants, a creator of more railroad systems, an organizer of more corporations, is as likely to be a danger as a help.

"The day of the great promoter, or the financial Titan, to whom we granted anything if only he would build or develop, is over. Our task now is not discovery or exploitation of natural resources or necessarily producing more goods. It is the soberer, less drastic business of administering resources and plants already in hand, of seeking to reëstablish foreign markets for our surplus production, of meeting the problems of underconsumption, of adjusting production to consumption, of distributing wealth and products more equitably, of adapting existing economic organizations to the service of the people."

The implications of this analysis are extraordinary. In effect, as Mr. Hoover promptly discovered, the candidate was saying that America no longer meant opportunity and that a new social system would have to be built because the old foundation, of free lands and unlimited expansion, had disappeared.

These are not the terms in which a candidate usually addresses voters; no promise of a rosy future lies in them; and they are, in truth, unique in Mr. Roosevelt's campaign. (As Governor of New York he had said that the American system of government and economics was everlasting, which is in the proper campaigning style; the San Francisco speech sounds more like the work of the realistic economists who were among Mr. Roosevelt's advisers.) Mr. Hoover replied:

"That is the counsel of despair for the future of America. That is not the spirit by which we shall emerge from this depression. That is not the spirit that made this country. If it is true, every American must abandon the road of countless progress and unlimited opportunity. I deny that the promise of American life has been fulfilled, for that means we have begun the decline and fall. No nation can cease to move forward without degeneration of spirit."

He gave a clear, general account of the American system he had defended. It is, he said "the product of our race and of our experience in building a nation to heights unparalleled in the whole history of the world. It is a system peculiar to the American people. It differs essentially from all others in the world. It is an American system.

"It is founded on the conception that only through ordered liberty, through freedom to the individual, and equal opportunity to the individual, will his initiative and enterprise be summoned to spur the march of progress."

And, again:

"It is founded on a conception that in times of emergency, when forces are running beyond control of individuals or other coöperative action, beyond the control of local communities and of States, then the great reserve powers of the Federal Government shall be brought into action to protect the community. But when these forces have ceased, there must be a return of State, local and individual responsibility."

To protect this conception the President said he had found it necessary to curb the extravagances of the Democratic Congress, to stand against the issue of fiat money, to veto the bill putting the Government into the power business, to minimize promises of providing employment for surplus labor and to protect the Supreme Court.

The better part of Mr. Hoover's campaigning was his explanation of the steps taken by the Government to beat off the attacks which domestic mistrust and disruption from abroad had massed against it. In the campaign the virtue of each party was questioned and each imputed to the other a desire to pass unworthy laws; the question was academic. Much of the important legislation passed in 1931 and 1932 was asked for in the President's message; the basic elements in it, the Reconstruction Finance Corporation and the Glass-Steagall bill, had the support of members of both parties. It is more important to note the purposes of the laws and their effect than to make a nice calculation of party credit. It was during the campaign that people began to be aware of the meaning of these laws — and that meaning can be briefly examined.

After it was seen that the Moratorium, in itself, would not create a new financial situation, credits were extended by our Federal Reserve to the central banks of both England and Germany; these were insufficient, and the consequent abandonment of the gold standard in England so disturbed domestic confidence, says the *Business Week,* that "currency hoarding started on a large scale, causing a rapid increase in bank failures, paralyzing the credit structure, and bringing the capital markets to a complete standstill." To remedy this dangerous situation, a bank pool was established with the approval of the government, the National Credit Corporation. This again proved inadequate and the President moved to create the Reconstruction Finance Corporation, with the advice of Secretary Mills and Governor Meyer of the Federal Reserve Bank of New York. Its purpose was "to prevent bank suspensions, railroad receiverships, strengthen insurance and mortgage bond companies and savings banks *by loans from public funds.*" (I have underlined the new element; the National Credit Corporation pooled private funds.) Confidence had to be restored; the tendency of individuals and banks to "distress liquidation", dumping of securities which they could no longer hold, was causing disastrous reductions in the price of both securities and of commodities, and this, going on over a long period, could lead to universal bankruptcy. The Reconstruction Finance Corporation, aided by other agencies of the Government, checked the decline, to a point; confidence, the intangible, was at least no farther away than it had been.

It was at this point that the prospect of a grave deficit and of a large payment to the veterans of the Great War entered, attended by costly relief measures and enthusiastic building programs, all of which Congress considered while it discussed the possibility of cutting loose from the gold standard, not by frank abandonment, but by issuing greenbacks to run concurrently with our sound secured currency. Not only foreigners, but Americans began to withdraw gold from the banks. A budget supposedly balanced was made up; the bonus bill with its direct inflation was rejected; the relief and building programs were cut down, and at the same time the Glass-Steagall bill was passed, strengthening the Federal Reserve by allowing it to use government bonds, instead of commercial paper, as security for its issue of currency. Senator Glass put aside his own objection to the measure, the effect of which, according to Secretary Mills, "was at once to free a vast amount of gold reserves immobilized as security for outstanding . . . notes. The freeing of this reserve put our country immediately in a strong position to meet any demand for gold from abroad."

This summarizes the major program of recovery: special agencies were created for Home Loans, the railroads formed a credit corporation, exceptionally important committees were formed by banks to see that legitimate credit was not withheld from business and to study the rises and falls of commodity prices, foreclosures of mortgages by closed banks were suspended and other banks were asked to postpone the step, special committees were appointed to study spreading of work, and efforts were made to assist farmers to market their crops. The Federal Reserve bought government securities in the hope that banks would thereby feel free to expand their investments and loans, bond pools were formed to support the market, and particularly favorable attention was given to business men who wished to borrow money for replenishing stock and to manufacturers who wished to borrow in order to modernize their equipment.

Many of these activities were not started until August, when the President gathered an impressive number of bankers and industrialists in a conference to which he announced that the fundamental steps, represented by laws passed in the session just ended, had defeated all attacks upon us and, using his favorite simile, called on the country for a further effort since we had won the battle of Château-Thierry but had still to press on to Soissons.

One good reason existed for the awed respect with which this program was treated by both parties: neither had an alternative to suggest. Mr. Roosevelt expressed a vague sympathy with his platform's pledge to refinance mortgages, Mr. Hoover recognized defects in the workings of the Farm Board; neither had any plan of agricultural rehabilitation, even of the scope of the plans which figured so prominently in the preceding campaign. About Russia, no open word was said;[2] nor was the problem of the European debts allowed to figure in the speech-making; Mr. Hoover defended the tariff, but Mr. Roosevelt did not vigorously attack it; and nothing was said, apart from the passage in Mr. Roosevelt's San Francisco speech which I have quoted, to indicate that the candidates had read Justice Brandeis' opinion in the Oklahoma ice case, an opinion which was in dissent, but which pointed to inevitable control of the conditions which cause overproduction while consumption is dwindling. Preoccupied as they were with restoring business, neither candidate and neither party showed any new conception of the status of business, its relation to the State or to the individual citizen, its obligations, or its possibilities.[3]

[2] The rumor was that Mr. Roosevelt favored recognition, but was prevented from saying so by fear of the political effect on the South which would take recognition of Russia as the equivalent of a belief in racial equality, because the candidate for Vice President on the Communist ticket was a Negro. It was no wilder than the other rumors current in the campaign.

[3] It is a little difficult to be sure whether Mr. Roosevelt's statements of principle always implied the creation of new policies. Taken in connection with the San Francisco speech, the following words suggest that one of Mr. Roosevelt's first actions in 1933 must be a special message to Congress asking for the creation of some form of unemployment insurance or some method of direct relief: "As to immediate relief: the first principle is that this nation owes a positive duty that no one shall be permitted to starve. This means that while the immediate responsibility for relief rests with local, public, and private charity, in so far as these are inadequate, the States must carry the burden, but whenever the States are unable adequately to do so, the Federal Government owes the positive duty of stepping into the breach." This was said at the very end of the campaign, and if Mr. Roosevelt recognizes its full import, he should have made it one of the fundamental issues.

On unemployment, Mr. Hoover was the more definite; when Mr. Roosevelt made a large promise of "self-liquidating public works . . . to provide *employment for all surplus labor at all times*", Mr. Hoover said this would force us to abandon every principle of our government and proposed, instead, "returning our people to their normal

They could not fall back into the obscurantism of 1929 and pretend that nothing had happened, but they pretended that we could forget what had happened if we did one of two things: continue one party in power or substitute another with almost identical political and social principles. With nothing, then, to say of the future, they naturally fell back on the reconstruction program and quarreled for the credit of having put it into force.

Success of that program could be easily measured: in terms of men returned to jobs (over the seasonal return), in terms of loans made by banks to float new issues and to start new businesses or expand old ones; in the standing of industry; in the prices of commodities. Actually, both sides watched the Stock Market, which is a reflector, not an index. The market had gone up in the summer; the rally was considerable and people were cheered by it; it went down and up and down again, but not in any spectacular dives. The Democrats, in tradition if not in fact the enemies of finance, suggested that the market was being rigged to frighten voters; actually, the wise men of the market were so soon assured of the result of the election that the whole thing was fairly discounted and the day after the election a small rise followed by a moderate fall occurred; a fairly strong upward movement continued for several days. The other indices showed that after July, the international panic had subsided; it did not show that the measures taken were sufficient to revive domestic prosperity.

The program for recovery was based on the idea that a supply of credit was necessary; and this was sound enough; for the negative, lack of credit, would be fatal not only to our chances

jobs in their normal homes, carrying on their normal functions of living. This can be done only by sound processes of protecting and stimulating recovery of the existing economic system upon which we have builded our progress so far.". . . It was definite because it was, again, a return to the past.

of fighting our way back to prosperity, but even to remaining as little solvent as we were. By helping the railroads, by relieving banks of certain obligations, by saving jeopardized institutions and offering money freely to others which could make loans, by all the provisions of the laws governing the Reconstruction Finance Corporation and the Federal Reserve, the Government had created a deep pool of credit, with clearly marked paths leading to the water line; but the horse would not drink. The pool was still. The creation of credit gave us a static thing and the dynamic, acting, moving spirit was missing.

Actually a smaller sum, moving at a faster rate, would have served the purpose better. What economists call "the velocity (or rate of turnover) of money and bank deposits" is extremely important. "If the amount of money in circulation were doubled," says the *Business Conditions Weekly*, "deposits and velocity remaining the same, purchasing power would be increased twelve and one-half per cent.", whereas if "no increase in either circulation or bank deposits should occur, but . . . both commenced to circulate fifty per cent. more rapidly than they do to-day . . . the increase in purchasing power would amount to no less than fifty per cent." Unfortunately, velocity depends on confidence, since men will prefer to stave off their creditors and postpone their buying as long as they can, if they believe that the balance in their banks is the last money they will have for months.

The defect of static credit without the dynamic push of using it was noted by Senator Carter Glass in an attack on the law bearing his own name. He had insisted, when the bill was before Congress, that it was unnecessary (and dangerous) as the Federal Reserve had adequate credit to meet any demand. On November 2 he asserted that he had been justified, for "but thirty-nine limping banks out of a membership of seventy-six hundred were aided in a comparatively insignificant way." Another commentator, writing anonymously in the *New Republic*, said, at the same time, that the statistics of new issues had been disappointing to the investment bankers, because the capital blockade had continued. Apparently the Government, being outside the circle of profitmaking, was the only possible user of capital. This was observed also by those who wished cities and States to make large loans; the terms were high, the conditions humiliating.

The campaign was conducted in an economic vacuum, from which the candidates occasionally made a sortie to say something relevant. The futility of all the discussions of the reconstruction program was made clear about a week before the election by the brief statement of an economist who, removed to the placid waters of Lake Leman, told a gathering of experts of the League of Nations that "measures in the United States aimed to put more money into circulation, far from raising commodity prices, merely sent more currency down into the cellars of banks, while prices failed to respond." According to the Fisher index, prices which had risen slowly and steadily from June (the low point of the depression) to September, were again declining and for the first week in November were as low as they had been in July, lower than the average of the first six months of the year.

Senator Glass asserted that both the Reconstruction Finance Corporation and the Glass-Steagall bill might have debased the currency if they had been accepted by Congress as originally presented by the Administration, and that Congress wrote in provisions safeguarding our financial structure; the argument of the President was that he had repelled vicious efforts to force fiat money on the country. Both of them rejoiced, then, that inflation had not occurred, meaning inflation of currency; but the Senator pointed out what the President ignored, that inflation (or expansion) of credit had not had the desired effect. The banks were not lending prodigious sums of money to commercial and industrial enterprise and the prices of commodities were not going up sufficiently to justify any enthusiasm.

Mr. H. I. Phillips suggested (in the *New York Sun*) that Mr. Roosevelt got the electoral votes and Mr. Hoover the complaints. Mr. Walter Lippmann found one advantage in the election of the candidate he had supported, that we would have in Washington a government with a direct mandate from the people. The two comments cancel one another, but the humorist seems the clearer-sighted of the two. For Mr. Roosevelt, with a magnificent electoral majority, had received no order from the people to undo the work of Mr. Hoover; he was not told to issue fiat money, or pay the bonus, or check the flow of credit available to strong banks, or remove the great pillar of the Reconstruction Finance Corporation from the support of the weak ones, or institute a dole system, or create even a thorough system of unemployment insurance. The mandate favoring beer for taxes was specific; for the rest, one was going far to assume that Mr. Roosevelt was elected for his party's platform, and that platform was vague enough. It condemned the "disastrous policies pursued by our Government since the World War"; one of these policies, never put into words, was to encourage business to expand even at the expense of the public good; another was to use South America and Europe as a dumping ground for excess funds and to withdraw these funds, regardless of the consequences, whenever higher profit could be found at home; another was to use the tariff to prevent Europe from paying their debts to us by trade, to amass gold, and to insist that Europe pay. On none of these did the platform or the candidate lay stress; and consequently he received a mandate on none. Mr. Lippmann believes that the mandate was given to revise the Republican policies, but qualifies this by saying that the electorate have willed the end without willing the means, that they wished the consequences of the policies of Harding and Coolidge and Hoover to be exorcised, but are not at all convinced that the policies themselves must be abandoned.

To Mr. Roosevelt himself, the election came as a great opportunity for liberals to cling together and to make their liberalism felt. In the sense that anything more enlightened and more humane than reactionary Republicanism must be called liberal, this statement is passable; otherwise it is the greatest (and most welcome) surprise of the campaign.

CHAPTER SIXTEEN

The Great Victim

Like governors, mayors, and radio stars, Presidents of the United States are compelled by tradition to do a number of foolish things, for purposes of publicity. At the request of a Senator or a powerful state politician, Presidents accept a turkey or a stuffed pillow, or shake hands with a delegation of children, or send a message, or somehow express interest in a group, an individual, an idea, otherwise (and often nevertheless) doomed to obscurity. These trivial and meaningless actions waste a little of the President's time, but are otherwise harmless; yet Mr. Hoover, more sensible of the dignity of his office than many who have been more successful in it, drew back; he hated to make a spectacle of himself in public; he did not believe that it was necessary to make half-intelligent people happy in order to govern the country well; and he obviously preferred doing the country's business to being a rival of a radio crooner in public esteem. Yet after the first half of his term was ended, it was necessary to "build him up", as press agents put it, and although he resisted, he was forced at times to yield. One of these occasions brought in the name of Chili Fish. To him, a Seminole Indian living in Oklahoma, the President sent a warrant appointing him, for one day, chief of the Seminole tribe in all the United States, empowering him to sign certain government papers relating to Seminole lands in his State, to transact other tribal business, to collect fifteen dollars in wages and expense money. The episode was not much noticed, except by the sharp-eyed editors of *Time*; it may have consumed two or three of the duller moments of a weekly news reel. The event was of no consequence whatever; I can think of nothing less important. Yet to this last trivial detail the President's ill-luck held: the Seminole Indians of Florida telegraphed that they would not recognize the jurisdiction of Chili Fish. In the swamps of Florida they knew that they were dealing with a man ill-starred, who had come to the narrow place where every movement tripped him and every word was thrown back in his teeth. It is an unhappy position at any time, but Mr. Hoover came to it in the midst of cosmic misfortune; everything was wrong with the world and he could cry with Hamlet, "O, cursed spite, that ever I was born to set it right." Or, thinking about election day, he might have surmised that like one of Napoleon's generals, he would be discharged not because he was incompetent, but because he was unlucky.

He is not the only President who has been turned out after one term, and among his predecessors Grover Cleveland has grown to be more and more a great man in the estimate of biographers and political thinkers. If the quick verdict of a popular election is reversed, the future will stress the ill-luck of Mr. Hoover's assumption of power at a time when the errors of our social system had so accumulated that a cataclysm was inevitable; it will say, perhaps, that no single individual could have governed forces which involved every country on the globe; and that through a period of universal chaos, Mr. Hoover, at least, was guided by definite principles. He reversed himself on matters of minor tactics; but his philosophy of the obligations and the rights of the Federal Government did not fundamentally change. Whether this will be called steadfastness or obstinacy, religious faith or black superstition, will depend largely on the outcome. The final judgment on Mr. Hoover does not depend on what he did, but on what Capitalism in America does. If it recovers, it will owe more to Mr.

Hoover than to any other one man, since Mr. Hoover had every chance to compromise, to weaken the resistance of Capitalism, to make a breach in the wall and let Socialism or Communism through. Raiders broke in, but not by any treachery of his; he fought on. If, however, the system changes in any direction except Fascism, it will be held that Mr. Hoover delayed the natural evolution of the country and, clinging to a useless system, paid for his principles with the misery of millions of his fellow citizens.

He had principles which, unfortunately for him, are easier to put into practice during good times than during bad. The hardest blow of fate was that he was elected by a country which promised him prosperity and which promptly sank itself into the black mire of an industrial crisis. Far in the background of the President's experience lay a time when he had experienced poverty, but he was an exceptionally successful man and professionally he could see no reason why poverty need exist. Through the years of the depression and violently in the campaign, Mr. Hoover's enemies cast back at him the words he had spoken in 1928, his pledge to abolish poverty, as if the pledge were foolish and impossible to fulfill; it was, on the contrary, an honorable pledge and excellent economists agree that there is no excuse for the problem of poverty to dog us any longer. Mr. Hoover's only fault was that he implied that the election of the party of Coolidge, himself, and Reed Smoot would do what it would require structural changes in the whole social system to accomplish. As a New Era man, and an engineer, he knew perfectly that the application of scientific principles to the problems of commerce and industry ought to result in continued and growing wealth. "Our problems of the future," he said, "are problems of construction, of progress."

His campaign had been a song of triumph, praising the material comforts and the spiritual calm of his country; his promise was the promise of Henry IV, but doubled, and it embraced the garage as well as the kitchen. But the promise the country made to Hoover was even more noble. A philosopher of history, as every candidate for President should be, Mr. Hoover must have examined the promise, to see whether it could be fulfilled, and since he had served under Harding and Coolidge, he might have decided that the country's offer was good. For we had suffered and conquered. He must have known that the enormous burden of the war would have to be liquidated: the unfortunate Harding had, to the usual accompaniment of graft and scandals, gone through the depression of 1921, a brief liquidation because we had been only briefly in the war; thereafter we had turned to the economy of isolation and, under the always fortunate Coolidge (how fortunate in his exit from office, who could at that time guess!) we had prospered. Under both we had tried to better our relations with the world outside, and all that remained for a President, an engineer as well as a humanitarian, to do was to consolidate the gains we had made, to bring order into the rank overgrowth of government business, to take soundings at every step, to foresee and avert calamity, and, since calamity was not coming, to turn the use of prosperity to nobler ends. It was the happiness of Mr. Hoover that although he won office at the end of a struggle in which race and religion had become involved, he took office, four months later, with almost universal good wishes. America had found itself as a business civilization and had, at long last, put a business man at its head. His mission was clear; few Presidents have been so conscious of high opportunity; to none, except perhaps Theodore Roosevelt, was so free a hand offered.

He began his career well, not brilliantly, but soundly. The undignified business of distributing patronage and dealing with political bosses had, obviously, irked him from election day to his inauguration, but after that, events moved quietly and government functioned smoothly. There was a little threat when the Senate, in special session, was not sure whether Mr. Andrew Mellon could continue in office from the preceding Administration, without his name being resubmitted; but the President carried his point by the excellent method of not submitting the name and waiting for the Senate to discover that he was legally correct. When Congress came into session, the President was urgent to have a tariff bill passed, disliking delay. He appointed the Wickersham Commission and announced the beginning of the Boulder Dam project; he considered revision of policy affecting public lands, but spoke definitely against releasing any oil fields to private hands; money which might have been spent on battleships was to go into a great system of internal waterways, and the President acted promptly when he heard that manufacturers of steel plates had been attempting to break up conferences for naval disarmament, sending an open warning that he would not be deflected in his course by financial interests; Premier McDonald came and the President took him fishing, and their talk on a log was reduced to the friendliest utterances in favor of disarmament and in disfavor of the unthinkable war between England and America; the President refused to pardon Harry F. Sinclair and condemned the inscription on the library at Louvain by which Whitney Warren hoped to perpetuate hatred of the Germans; the Senate, in an unfriendly gesture, voted to deprive him of the right to change tariff duties; at the celebration of the Edison jubilee, Mr. Edison played his ancient part of "butcher" on a train and Mr. Hoover bought from him a peach; twenty-two days after he became President there was a sharp break in the Stock Market and at the beginning of August the rediscount rate was raised by the Federal Reserve, causing another break August 9; the President told enthusiasts for fishing that "next to prayer, fishing is the most personal relationship of man . . .

the fish will not bite in the presence of the public and the press." [1]

This is neither an imposing nor a contemptible record; it is the complete record of Mr. Hoover's more important moves in the period between his inauguration and the collapse of the market. It indicates little except a cautious approach to fundamental problems, a desire to accumulate facts before formulating policy, a high degree of courage in attacking enemies of society and a certain lack of "clubbiness" which the Senate instantly felt. It was not his fault that when, in the middle of September, 1929, he asked a group of editors of trade papers to tell him about business, he was assured that America was prosperous and must remain so; it was as a routine officer, not as an individual, that he proclaimed Constitution Week and Fire Prevention Week and accepted dogs for the White House; he had not yet got into his stride as President.

It was said by his enemies that Mr. Hoover had made a greater success as a promoter than as an engineer and that his substantial fortune came to him through stock companies; yet it is certain that his cast of mind did not let him pay too much attention to the Stock Market in the first days of the crash; he seriously meant and had seriously good reason for believing that the "fundamental business of the country, that is, the production and distribution of commodities, is on a sound and prosperous basis." It was not a long view nor a philosophic one; but it was not a deliberate falsehood or a baseless guess. It was the statement of an engineer, a man who knew the difference between a mine and a hole in the ground; and accepting his enemies' word for it, let us say it was the statement

---

[1] No doubt true; yet it was again the President's ill-luck that when he went fishing for the news-reel, in the course of the campaign, the fish knew how he felt and audiences beheld their Chief Executive in the fundamentally ridiculous situation of not catching fish when he seemed above all things to want to catch fish — and not be photographed.

also of a promoter who knew, after long experience, that you can skyrocket stocks without increasing the yield of a factory or a mill or a copper mine and, if your factory, field, and mine are good, you can smash stocks to smithereens without impairing their capacity to yield. It was regrettably not the statement of an economist who knows relations and who has discovered that your factory can, but will not be asked to, yield unless there is a purchaser.[2] The technician knew that the machinery was intact for making goods; he did not know that into the machinery for making people want goods and be able to buy goods, a monkey wrench had been thrown.

The President's first actions, after his first statement, were also characteristic. He called upon the people to give thanks for the blessings which God had sent to them and on business men to rectify the error by which those blessings had been derouted from their destination by the crash. He invited prominent men, sound men, good men; he did not invite men of any radical tendency (except Mr. Ford, and Mr. Ford's radicalism the President could understand). He wanted, and got, from them a reasonable program of construction which would give rise to a reasonable confidence in the future. At this point one of the faults of his temperament began to show itself, for the man of scientific training succumbed to the man of stubbornness and pride who inhabited the same body. Hardly a month elapsed before the President announced "most encouraging results." There had been impatience and criticism in the press and the President, according to excellent authority, read (and continues to read) the press hostile to himself; but he is sensitive to criticism, a function of the human mind considered, perhaps, superfluous by engineers whose work is accurate and

[2] In 1932 the same attitude of mind could still be observed in Mr. Hoover's remark that there were better mines in Wisconsin than in all of Soviet Russia; the engineer was technically right, but the statesman failed to explain why no one was working the better mines.

mathematical. At the beginning of the year, then, he told critics to be still by announcing the success of his plans and then released to the newspapers a letter written to a friend in which he spoke of the malice of newspaper headlines and said, "Every man has a few mental hair shirts and Presidents differ only by their larger wardrobe — for certain individuals, newspapers, associations and institutions officiate as haberdashers with a high generosity." In the letter also he defended his habit of appointing commissions and committees and conferences, saying, "The people will take care of progress if the Government can put the signs on the road." The clamor for action did not move him from his firm belief that action must wait for data and for thought.

The President had a deep, almost fanatical belief in America and in that side of America which had grown up in the past forty years, during his own mature life; he believed that America could make its way through difficulties and that the system under which he had grown up was still functioning, so that it need not be scrapped or changed. That is why, having done nothing unusual after a shock in the market so spectacular that it could not fail to impress the world, he felt justified in making, on the 7th day of March, his famous prediction that within sixty days the worst effect of the crash, on employment, would have passed. I have already mentioned the slender facts upon which this statement was made and that, promptly at the expiration of sixty days, the worst had passed, according to the President's mind. I have noted the statement of May as one of the decisive moments of the depression, not only because people were made acutely conscious of the gap between fact and official fiction; the more serious thing was that the President, who had been obstinate in repelling hostile individuals and ideas, seemed willing now to set himself against the course of our depression, defying it to continue after he had done what he had done and said what he had said to make it come to an end. It was, perhaps, the engineer who had predicted; but it was the magician, his trick spoiled, who insisted that the trick had worked. The President's whole attitude toward the results of the depression is colored by his resentment against its defiance of those first orders he issued in November, 1929, and March, 1930, — orders to the clouds to disperse and be gone. Colored, but not determined; the President's course of action was determined by his experience and his philosophy — to an extent rare in the history of the presidency; he had an outlook on life and a belief about America which made it impossible for him to follow any other course than the one, unhappy in its foreseen results for him, which he did follow. Only the method, the daily contacts, the technique, the politics — everything that showed first and that created first impressions — took color from his distaste for the bungling which had brought on the panic and the stubbornness with which the panic resisted his counterattack which, as an engineer, he felt ought to be successful.

The record shows that all the important actions of Mr. Hoover, affecting the crisis, were taken at the beginning and after June 1, 1931. The inaction of a year is one of the bewildering elements in the depression. I have suggested a psychological reason: that the President either thought the worst was over, as he said, or was so resentful at the persistence of bad times that he determined to ignore them. There was, also, a practical reason. In November, 1930, his party was rebuffed by the voters; therefore, from March 4, 1931, to December 7, 1931, the President would have been compelled to summon in special session a Congress which represented dissatisfaction with his policies. (Actual control of the House was unsettled at the time; but as the Democrats had won some fifty Republican seats and lost only one of their own, it could not be hoped that the new Congress would give the President much support.) In such a decisive move as the Moratorium, Mr. Hoover used the telephone, got the support of leaders of both parties, and acted. But for a legislative program, he had to face his difficulties directly in Washington. A chief executive at odds with his Congress is always a disturbing spectacle to the country; it would come soon enough; the President chose not to rush things. He delayed, thereby, the program of reconstruction by many months, running the risk that the program would be nullified by delay. Such far-reaching and slow-moving creations as the Reconstruction Finance Corporation, for instance, could not make their value felt in a short time; had they been set in motion in June of 1931, instead of half a year later, they might have won for the President the little upturn which could return him to office. He disliked the political nagging and bickering he would have to go through; he disliked a Congress which represented a vote of lack of confidence; so he took the risk of delay, and lost.

The President's impatience of Congress is not exceptional. He had seen it act stupidly and even viciously over its tariff bill; he had heard Calvin Coolidge say, "the general reaction at the adjournment of Congress will be one of relief"; he knew that business men feared sessions and hoped for a favorable swing the moment Congress stopped talking; and besides, it is possible that he had a solid intellectual contempt for nine out of ten of its members. When they were, to make matters worse, elected to oppose him, he naturally felt that they could hinder more than they could help. That he could coöperate with them seemed impossible.

He could not, in fact, coöperate with his own party, misunderstandings between him and the Republican leaders were frequent and it sometimes appeared that the President might forgive opposition in an enemy, but never even criticism in a friend. Most of those known as his intimates were friends of the days of Belgian relief; as President he used certain publicists, also friends of earlier days, but attached few people to himself.[3] He was working hard and he was austere; he never had been one of the gang that met and played poker in the days of Harding. The admirable side of his dislike of opposition was shown on occasions. When William Green, speaking for the American Federation of Labor, seemed to be trying to dictate the appointment of a Secretary of Labor, the President took the risk of alienating this powerful group and said that the suggestion "that appointments must come from one organization . . . imposes on me the duty to maintain the principle of open and equal opportunity and freedom in appointments to public office."[4] The persistence of the cries for payment of the bonus also brought the President to a point of direct and persuasive speech. His rebukes were, in fact, stylistically superior to his recommendations, his vetoes more stirring than his messages to Congress; on the negative side he seemed to stand firm and to feel the backing of his people; when he came to urge and commend, he was lacking in warmth, awkward, and feeble.

It is a misfortune for a public man, in the era of publicity, that one characteristic has to be named and attached to him for ever. The strenuous Roosevelt, the genial Taft, the idealistic Wilson, the good pal Harding, the silent Coolidge, all managed to escape unpleasant branding; but the temperamental quality by which the American people came to know Hoover was fatal: he was irritable. He had to do a thousand trivial things, to meet a thousand stupid people; his whole training and experience were against the waste of his time and energy. He would cancel

---

[3] An old story was renewed with the names of Mr. Hoover and Mr. Mellon to give it sharpness, thus: They were walking along the street and Mr. Hoover said, "Lend me a nickel, I want to call up a friend." "Here's a dime, call up all your friends." I have been told that when Mr. Mellon heard this, he shook with unsecretarial mirth.

[4] The principle was excellent and the enunciation of it courageous; but the special case led to the appointment of James N. Doak, who became known as the "Secretary Against Labor."

appointments to meet journalists, or meet them and drum with his fingers impatiently on the arm of his chair, or quarrel with them, because, like Asquith, he wished the press to limit itself to a record of fact. When a newspaperman told him that the American people were more interested in a President's granddaughter than in news of the Moratorium, he said severely that he refused to hold so low an opinion of the American people, implying, I fear, a low opinion of the American Press. In the midst of his triumph over the domestic reception of the Moratorium and of his worries over the French opposition to it, he engaged in a quarrel with the American Press over incidents almost unbelievably trivial. A story had been printed which annoyed him (it implied that in an emergency relating to the Moratorium he had broken local speed laws to return to Washington from his camp) and he determined to put an end to "leakage" of news. The men covering the White House asked for examples of news "leaks" and among those offered was the story of the patching of a curtain in the White House, for the sake of economy, and that the wife of a secretary had fallen off a horse. When a political expert discussed (with much kindness) the possible effects of the Moratorium on Mr. Hoover's prospects of reëlection, he became so angry that he dispatched a long, furious telegram to the United Press, demanding an apology. The United Press must have assumed that on reconsideration the President would regret his haste; in any case, the demand for an apology brought none.

For his resistance to the "humanizing" process of the press agents and political advisers, the President deserves the thanks of all who are weary of seeing great men belittled to make a front-page box on a newspaper. The process consists largely in making a fool out of a public man and is silly and distasteful. Mr. Hoover fought it bitterly and when he was compelled to yield, he remained angry and totally unconvincing. It was heartening to observe his dislike of the news-reel camera which was trained on him as he rode a horse or cast a fly; the misfortune was that when he surrendered to publicity, his efforts were so bungling.

The list of non-political callers at the White House is not impressive; one notes that the President refused to see the mother of Tom Mooney and the representatives of the Bonus Army and turning to those whom he did see, one finds Rudy Vallee. It was in an effort to be chummy, I suppose, that the President told Mr. Vallee to sing a song to cure the depression, as he later told Weber and Fields that what the country needed was a good joke and Christopher Morley that a good poem might help, something like "that poem of Markham's", meaning "The Man with the Hoe." [5] What he said to Ely Culbertson, the bridge expert, is not recorded.

All these trivial incidents indicate that the President had not mastered the technique of easy dealings with men. Whatever he was privately, as President he had no lightness; his mind and his wit both moved slowly; he was psychologically stupid. Nothing glancing or mercurial was in his temperament; he stood still and met every shock, lacking the mental agility to dodge. When he was accused of being an ignoramus in naval matters, he appointed a committee to investigate whether he was an ignoramus or not, and the members of his committee included some of his most devoted adherents. When the Bonus Army came to Washington, he could not treat it as an innocent rabble or as a pathetic chaos of unhappy men; he could not even treat it as a potential danger which could be removed by good politics — such as summoning the leaders, speaking warmly to them, and enlisting their aid on his side. He had to ignore them until he could make them appear a danger to the State and then destroy their power by an action which was forceful, but with the force of jangled nerves, not of judgment.

[5] Fatal ill-luck again. Mr. Markham wrote a poem — not a very good one — and dedicated it to Franklin D. Roosevelt.

The tendency to "ignore" things which are annoying or hostile lies on one side close to the Olympian calm of great men and on the other close to the infantile habit of pretending not to see and refusing to speak to dolls, other children, dogs, or whatever has given offense. Mr. Hoover began his ignoring of opposition in 1928, when he refused to mention the name of his rival in the campaign; he ignored the true direction of the Wickersham Report in his announcement to the press; he ignored other challenges and other demonstrators, as he ignored the Bonus Army. It was as if he was playing some magical game in which if you are sure not to say a certain word or look at a certain object, you will have your wish. The President's tendency to repeat one significant word many times in a single speech, his use of worn-out and sentimental associations of images, also suggest his belief in incantations; at Springfield, Illinois, he rather pitifully tried an even older magic when he reminded the people that Lincoln had been elected on the 8th of November, 1864, and this year the election also fell on the 8th of November. Whenever he touched politics, the mind of the engineer, trained to observe facts and to reject whatever lies outside of fact, deserted him. Fundamentally, I believe that he despised politics.

For three years he gave the impression of fighting always against opposition; he was, in fact, doing his official duty by fighting against the course of events. He resisted deflation; short of the miracle of inflating the moment the market break showed signs of affecting industry, it was the only thing he could do; but deflation went on inexorably. He resisted what seemed to him Socialism, the attempt to make the Federal Government directly responsible for the well-being of the citizen; and Socialism crept in, although he diminished it by accepting its blood brother, State Capitalism. He resisted the tide against Prohibition; he resisted the popular desire to see the Government do something spectacular in the way of spending money;

he resisted the appeals of the veterans; he resisted the American ignorance of and indifference to the European crisis. In the last of these, he proved to himself that a wise leader can more easily overcome than resist; by taking a positive step, he turned his back on his people in the only way a leader can turn his back and survive — he made the people follow him. In all the other major decisions, he was on one side, the people either on the other, or standing by, indifferent to him and his principles. He had no capacity for speaking the public mind, none of reading the public thought, none for giving the public consolation or courage. From the beginning of the crisis, he was always pushed into action; events occurred and plans followed. Except for the Moratorium, the President did not initiate, nor did he dig in advance, the channel through which he wanted events to flow until, under compulsion because another and more dangerous channel might be dug, he designed the reconstruction program of 1931–1932.

He was driven too harshly. With the exception again of the days which followed his announcement of the Moratorium, he had no hours of triumph, none in which he felt the applause and the encouragement of a whole people. So he turned to small victories, announcing the success of the anti-hoarding campaign at the slightest evidence of its effectiveness, presently declaring that we had fought and won the battle of Château-Thierry and must go forward to Soissons.[6] But until the last days of the campaign, he never told why it was worth while

[6] He repeatedly used the figures of speech of war in his description of the depression. It was a skillful association of ideas, for the war was a difficult time which ended happily; it was exciting; and it was the last time the whole nation was united. What Mr. Hoover lacked was precisely what Mr. Wilson had: the capacity to put into memorable language ideals which people imagined they already believed in. Perhaps it is the defect of accurate minds that they cannot make these large and impressive statements; perhaps Mr. Hoover had no noble ideal to give to the people.

going on, and then he fell back upon his promises of 1928, —
comfort and prosperity. They were not enough; they were
ardently desired, but no one seriously believed they could be
restored in the following four years, even under Mr. Hoover.
What was needed was something much more emotional, even
if the emotion were a little tainted; if we were in a war, and
had won a beginning victory, the purposes of the war should
have been reduced to some simple formula, like "the world
made safe for democracy" — in which a great many people
profoundly believed in 1918. The President had no cry to utter, perhaps not believing in cries; he neither repented nor
called others to repentance; he had no eloquence; he made
promises of small things to happen in a short time, but never
suggested what the promise of American life meant to him and
could mean to the American people. Perhaps he was as confused as the rest.[7]

[7] Mr. Roosevelt attempted to sum up the emotion of the discontented people in his phrase about the "new deal" which Mr. Hoover
wittily called a new shuffle. The "new deal" was Mr. Roosevelt's only
reminiscence of his illustrious namesake, and suffered by the comparison. It suggested that the depression and all its woes stemmed
from abuse of privilege, from corruption and bad faith, from the
richness of the rich and the poorness of the poor. The actual situation
made hash of these phrases. It was not a new deal with the old pack
in the old game that was needed, but as Mr. Roosevelt once, and only
once, suggested, a new structure and a new method and a new purpose.

PART TWO: THE LONG RUN

CHAPTER SEVENTEEN

DEBIT ACCOUNT

IN April, 1932, the seniors at New York University estimated that at the end of 1942 they would be earning salaries of five thousand dollars a year; the preceding class had expected an annual income of ten thousand dollars, a decade after leaving college. One class differing little from another, we may write down a deflation of fifty per cent. in the expectations of young men, which, since values did not go down by half in the year 1931–1932, shows only that psychological deflations work more rapidly than economic ones.

I have noted examples of both kinds of deflation in the preceding chapters; they may be summed up in single, parallel statements: from October 4, 1929, to June 30, 1932, we suffered an unexampled decrease in the value of loans and investments, the greatest loss ever recorded in history; and in that period we reluctantly gave up the idea that America was fortune's favorite, that "our government is in its theory perfect, and in its operation it is perfect also", as Edward Everett put it; that we were exempt from all the pains and penalties of existence, the greatest, strongest, happiest, and from everlasting to everlasting, the richest country on earth. These are the broad outlines; to fill them in, for the economic deflation, would require pages of statistics, only a few of which actually had meaning for the common man upon whose mind I am trying to trace their effect. He could not easily conceive of the number eight million in the abstract, but he had a reasonably clear idea of what it meant for eight million men to be out of work, especially since he was perpetually under the threat of making the number eight million and one; he knew that since the stock-market crash, stocks which had been selling at two hundred and fifty dollars had gone down to thirty dollars a share, and that others were being quoted in pennies; he could understand that in 1929 (including the months after the crash) only seventy-two out of nine hundred great corporations had shown a deficit and in 1931 as many as three hundred and fifty of the same nine hundred were in the red, and that the profits of the lucky ones had dwindled from two billion to half a billion, while the losses of the unfortunates had risen from thirty-three million to ten times as much. The figures may have made little impression, but their meaning was visible in bread lines, at hospitals, along every city street and in many farmhouses (where the collapse of wheat was another factor easy to comprehend). Finally the average man knew, with certainty, that nearly everything told him had been misleading and that everything done to save him had been unavailing.

The outline of the parallel deflations in the mind can be filled in with more detail. Some of them refer back directly to business. There was, for instance, an editorial in the *Kiwanis Magazine* on Small Plants:

"The great plant with its efficiency and its labor-saving devices was, until recently, the ideal of every great quantity-producing believer. Deep study is now being made of the advantages of splitting these vast plants into smaller units. . . . Apparently the smaller plants can be more readily and quickly adapted to a rise and fall in volume of production than the large plant. Overhead can be more quickly brought into line with current operations. In larger plants, in large towns, unrest among employees is more quickly aroused than in small plants, in smaller towns, where the average employee owns or rents a home with its gardens or chickens. . . ."

The assumptions behind these arguments are startling: that American industry must be made so flexible that it can adapt itself to sudden shrinkage is in itself a heresy unheard of in the age of permanent prosperity which economists, to the cynical amusement of Carl Snyder, called the New Era. That there can be a fall in volume, when the entire science of salesmanship depends on annual, monthly, almost daily increases in orders, is another unpleasant heresy. The breaking up of large factories into small units marks in itself the abandonment of our pursuit of the greatest on earth, the record-breaker, and the monstrous-superlative.

From the beginning of the depression we resigned ourselves to a loss of population, not by birth-control,[1] but by closing our doors to immigrants. The door had been slowly closing for some time; at the end of 1929, it was slammed. The economic reasons were apparent and we had long ceased to be the haven of the oppressed, the sanctuary of political exiles. Yet the definite exclusion of immigration was a sacrifice not only of an outworn idealism but of a point of pride: we could no longer say that the entire world was streaming in through our ports; a year or two later the number of returning Europeans actually exceeded the number of those who entered on the limited quotas; and if we had cared at all, in our lethargy, we should have had to confess that people found it more pleasurable to live elsewhere.

Economic deflations are promptly seen in size and quantity; even after the process had gone on for a year we were consoled by the President's list of all our numerical superiorities to the rest of the world and by the figures of statisticians who asked us to remember that in deep depression we still constituted roughly half of the economic world, either producing half of the prime commodities or, if we did not produce, consuming

[1] A judge in Long Island City virtually ordered a woman, brought before him on a minor charge, to stop having children. (1932)

half. It is only to superior people that size, in itself, has any
suggestion of vulgarity; to others it is axiomatic that if a thousand cars are good, a million cars are a thousand times better.
On this mathematical basis we had set our pride; and it was
disquieting to hear from a governmental agency that size was
a danger to us and we must destroy wheat, plow under cotton,
shut down oil wells, and go through a general process of
diminution. For us, of all people, to create artificially the
"economics of scarcity", when we had lived for generations in
the belief in plenty, was psychologically ill-advised.

Yet deflation of quantity was only half the story. In the past
decade we had begun to pride ourselves on two other attri-
butes: quality and style. Both now were under attack. I have
already quoted the heart-questionings of manufacturers on
the subject of high-styling.[2] In support of the National Quality Maintenance League, Bergdorf Goodman, of New York,
published an advertisement:

LOST!

The Judgment of Quality

Three generations have passed since ladies spun or wove.
One, at least, since they have sewed. Too far from loom and
needle themselves, women have lost their judgment of quality. Instead, they have trusted to advertisers' claims, superficial appearance, price.

Merchants who should have respected this confidence in
their word have abused it, until to-day it is small wonder that
women hardly know whom to trust. Mere crying of "quality" to-day where "price" was cried yesterday will only add
to that distrust. Honorable stores should take the greatest
care to claim quality only for truly fine merchandise, and

[2] On page 28.

to show their patrons exactly wherein that quality resides. Only thus can the confidence of the feminine buying public be regained.

Bergdorf Goodman is essentially a style and quality store; yet a department store of large turnover and an advertised policy of selling at six per cent. below its competitors (notably those who do not sell exclusively for cash) repeated the argument with the announcement that for an exceptionally important sale, every article had been tested by its own bureau of standards, a precaution necessary, the advertisements implied, because manufacturers had been forced by retailers eager to offer bargains "into the uneviable position of lowering quality in order to reduce prices." It is, to be sure, sound advertising to impute wrongdoing to unnamed, but indicated, rivals; but these advertisements suggest uneasiness and a suspicion that less corruptible business men might take advantage of the economic disaster to throw overboard some of the deadweight of business ethics which their own publicity had imposed upon them.

That business, as a whole, was weakening may be judged from an advertisement published, in August, 1931, by Batton, Barton, Durstine and Osborne, one of the most influential of all agencies of advertising, known for the rigid standards by which it judged the products it agreed to publicize. In a statement headed "On the Level", the heads of the company analyzed certain business habits and declared their position. "It is a grim fact," they said, "that most of us, in the past year, have been jammed up against stark realities in a way that has made it easy to consider the expediency of compromising a bit on the more idealistic phases of square dealing. Nothing really dishonest, of course, but a sort of liberal attitude toward any device which might ease the strain. . . . One can sense in the air a slight tendency to slip.

"We have threshed this matter out among ourselves and have decided upon a simple rule which we mean to stick to, even if things get a bit scratchy in the advertising business. On any important policy move, we are going to ask ourselves, 'Is this something we wouldn't have done in the prosperous year 1929 or which we might be ashamed of in the prosperous year 1932?'

"If it is, it's out."

Things were still a bit scratchy in the advertising and other business in 1932, but optimism does not invalidate the principle. The slight tendency to slip was indeed sensible in the air of commercial enterprise. There were book publishers who issued off-color books, not a new thing, but the publishers were not the usual venders of pornographics; there were final sales of haberdashers on Fifth Avenue which lasted three or four months, with goods especially ordered for the sale and a cut below the standard of the house; there was a new frankness (which might be termed a new vulgarity) in the advertisements [3] and a new tone of snappish anger between rivals, especially in cigarettes. Dishonesty or shady dealing on a larger scale occurred in such enterprises as the bankruptcies referred to in another chapter and in complicated financing through which directors sold their own companies short or unloaded stock which they knew was going to be worthless. They were not frequent enough to justify any blanket charge of corruption in the moral fiber of the country; if general corruption existed, it could only be measured by the comparative calm with which revelations of dishonesty were accepted.

With deflations in morals went deflation of mental values. The colleges were under constant attack from within and with-

[3] The *Saturday Evening Post* finally admitted advertisements for cigarettes, but this hardly comes in the category of the vulgar; social pressure combined in this instance with financial. I am not aware of any marked increase in the advertisements of medicines which are just within the law.

out. Even the public school, the very foundation, one had believed, of the democratic system, was reëxamined and Doctor
Henry Suzzallo, President of the Carnegie Foundation, said
that "it offered the opportunity for the individual to choose
what he believed he wanted and was fitted to do, regardless of
what was necessary to be done, or what there was available to
do. The result was that we prepared twenty thousand persons
to act where there was only need of twenty." The White House
Conference had written into its Children's Charter: "for every
child an education which, through the discovery of and development of his individual abilities, prepares him for life; and
through training and vocational guidance prepares him for a
living which will yield him a maximum of satisfaction"; but
Dr. Suzzallo is the realist and reverses the emphasis, saying in effect what the editor of *Good Housekeeping* said:
"Before making lawyers, doctors, engineers, of our boys, an
educational institution should try to find out whether there
is a reasonable chance of their finding an opportunity to work."
The economic parallel is perfect: find the market before
producing the supply of goods. And since the market for
brute labor is always greater than the market for the mind,
a prominent educator announced that colleges had overreached
themselves in supplying higher education to all and sundry,
spoiling "happy, contented and useful citizens by luring them
into dyspeptic white-collar jobs." (The slur at the secretary,
the bond salesman, and the professional man is the pin point
in the balloon of their inflated prestige of five years ago.)
Doctor Clarence C. Little, once president of University of
Michigan, holds the same opinion of the specialized student:
"Research advances our knowledge of truth, but it does nothing to insure a happier, more human civilization. The tail is
wagging the dog in American education." (Deflation, in a
sense, of our faith in science.) And Dean Lawrence of Minnesota is so bent on discouraging students from going to col-

lege that he accuses high education of "handing out hokum" and roundly declares that the charts proving the higher earning power of college graduates are "unsound and downright untrue."

The economic basis is explicit in an argument made by President James L. McConaughy: "Society will not tax itself to give $1000-a-year education to a 30-cent boy or girl. Colleges which expend annually on each student twice what he pays in tuition will be wise to insure themselves on the value of their investment in students. . . . I sometimes think colleges are too popular to-day. . . ."

The sense of all these belittlings of college education was that the average American young man must moderate his ambitions; he must be content with the job for which a public-school education fitted him and prepare to roll up his sleeves and abjure starched collars; he was not to rise in the world, but to take his place in a world far more rigidly classified than any ever promised to America. The old complaint against the college was that it did not prepare a man for life, with the usual meaning that it did not prepare him to make money instantly; testimony came from some colleges that they were making their courses more practical and from technicians that the mind trained to think was more valuable to them than the man trained to do; the colleges were getting on and when it was discovered that the "contacts" of college life made men superior bond salesmen, the last prejudice was removed. The situation is now reversed. Criticism, to-day, assumes that college does train men for practical work, but adds that the work is lacking, with the implication that the colleges might as well go back to Latin, Greek, and Medieval Logic, and limit themselves to a few students. For the rest, the upward social movement characteristic of America in the last century was to come to an end and the prestige of the professions was to be no more.

A generation ago a new profession was added to the list of
the noble: the profession of business. Yet it was not to business
that the detractors of the older professions could point with
pride, for the idea that business was big in anything but size
was one of the first to be pricked. In the back of the American
mind, ready to come forward at any provocation, lingered the
bogey of the capitalist pirate — a picture drawn by the Popu-
lists, by William Jennings Bryan, and under the name of "the
Interests" by F. Opper in the Hearst papers at the beginning
of the century. As late as 1912 one could think of the predatory
interests as a conspiracy; when they went down with the rest
of us in the universal crash of values, we refused to pay them
that compliment. How could they be conspirators if they could
not even be friends, if steel fought motors and bankers fought
factories? How could they plot, if they could not even think?
How could they be trying to create an invisible government
if they hadn't the foresight to run an efficient business?

It was not all relief to know that a hundred great bankers
and corporation directors were not running the country, for
the corollary was that they were not capable of running it —
and if they were not, who was? I think that little as the American people anticipated disaster, they definitely counted on
business to save them, should disaster come. We might make
fools of ourselves and our politicians might make fools of us;
but business had too great a stake in the future to let either
of us go too far. This, and not a fondness of filing systems and
push-buttons, was the true religion of business which bound
men together. That faith crumpled far more rapidly than most
of the others; we might still believe that business could recover, but it had made the fatal blunder of not being infallible.

When business proved incompetent, people turned to the
very agency they had always accused of extravagance, the
Government, to pull them through; that is, as Mr. Fabian
Franklin pointed out, they turned from all of those who had

labored for profit to the "one great domain that lies outside this circle — a domain in which the motive of activity is not supplied by the prospect of business profit" — the domain of government. Could the deflation of the business ideal be more marked?

Mr. Samuel Untermyer, a lawyer not unfamiliar with the great ones of the business world and with their methods, summed up the ancient tradition and the new scepticism when he said, "In calmly accepting our vast, accumulated, albeit poorly and unjustly distributed wealth, as the reward of superior brains, energy, and industry of the nation, we have utterly lost sight of the fact that it is largely the result of the development of the great natural resources with which bountiful nature started us on our course. . . . It has suited our vanity to delude ourselves in the belief and to take it for granted that we are the architects of our own fortunes." Melvin Traylor and Gerard Swope also came to confession, accusing business men of ignorance and stupidity, of narrow views and greedy hands.

While strong industries begged for the repeal of the Sherman Anti-Trust Laws, the weaker ones, the sufferers, turned against the very principle of "rugged individualism" which was being promulgated as basically American. The *National Petroleum News* spoke of the "destructive character of unrestrained and relentless competition" and an editorial in *Cotton* read: "In the long run, therefore, the industry may look back on the depression as a not unmixed blessing, for having mitigated or even broken the curse of unregulated production. From being in a rut of unbalanced industries, textiles have taken a place in the vanguard of businesses emerging from the depression" — into un-American, controlled, and regulated production.

In March, 1932, the Supreme Court of the United States upheld the principle of rugged individualism and the devil take the foremost, the middleman, and the hindmost, although this was not the language of the Court. The State of Oklahoma had passed a law making the manufacture of ice a public utility, so that producers had to get a certificate of public necessity and convenience before they could establish new factories. The law was tested, came to the highest court, and was held to violate the "due process" clauses of the 5th and 14th Amendments. In practice, no man may be prevented from making ice in Oklahoma, even if his activities are useless to a community and, through competition, ruin both himself and his rivals.

The great interest of the case was, however, the dissent of Mr. Justice Brandeis. As always, he connected the special case with the actual facts of contemporary life, analyzing the depression, stressing "failure to distribute widely the profits of industry", and saying:

"Increasingly doubt is expressed whether it is economically wise, or morally right, that men should be permitted to add to the producing facilities of an industry which is already suffering from overcapacity." He gave, in passing, approval to the idea of a planned economy and denied that the framers of the 14th Amendment intended to leave us helpless "to correct the evils of technological unemployment and excess productive capacity which the march of invention and discovery have entailed. There must be power in the States and the nation to remold through experimentation our economic practices and institutions to meet changing social and economic needs.

"To stay experimentation within the law in things social and economic is a grave responsibility. Denial of the right to such experimentation may be fraught with serious consequences to the nation. It is one of the happy incidents of the Federal system that a single courageous State may, if its citizens choose, serve as a laboratory; and try novel social and economic experiments without risk to the rest of the country. This court has the power to stay such experimentation. We may strike down the statute embodying it on the ground that, in our opinion, it is arbitrary, capricious or unreasonable; for the due process clause has been held applicable to matters of substantive law as well as to matters of procedure. But in the exercise of this power we should ever be on guard, lest we erect our prejudices into legal principles. If we would be guided by the light of reason, we must let our minds be bold."

This opinion was important, psychologically, because it was the noblest call for courage uttered in the depression and because it showed why courage was necessary; we had to confront the fact that the American system of undisciplined freedom of action had become a danger to the community; we had to deflate our ideas about ourselves. The last words — "we must let our minds be bold" — were everywhere quoted with approval, so that we almost forgot, for a time, that it was not the Supreme Court, but a dissenter from its judgment, who had spoken.

Little deflations came with these resounding ones. Mr. Josef Hoffman advised that fewer musicians be encouraged to become soloists, a damper put on the American habit of trying to exceed all others; pictures of knock-down cottages appear in the chic magazines of life in the country; *Vogue* published styles for limited incomes and an essay on the discomforts of being rich; radio split itself into inexpensive units of quarter hours; churchmen deplored the enormous administrative machine they had built up; conductors thought it might be better to play only acceptable music in this sad time; advertisers had no money to buy great testimonials and tried to get them free; the popular magazines came out with 72 or 96 pages instead of 224; Childs' restaurants offered "all you can eat" at a low fixed price; the rewards for solving puzzles and supplying missing lines grew smaller; barter set in.[4]

[4] Divorces were fewer, stocks were sold in mixed lots by the package, and apartment houses, formerly "exclusive", let down the bars. The word "adjust" came to mean "cut down" or "lower."

Had anything fundamental been touched? From my point of view, the unuttered aspirations, even the foolish and vulgar dreams of people, are fundamental; to tamper with them is dangerous; to destroy one series of beliefs and not supply another is fatal. The years from 1929 to 1933 were, for America, a succession of breaking idols and abandoned faiths, some of them the notions of willful children, some deeply ingrained in the character of the nation. It is a long and unhappy list over which I shall pass as quickly as possible.

Fact-finding commissions: the suppression of one report, the shifty handling of another, brought the Wickersham Commission under a cloud.

The Department of State: in spite of denials that the Department did not approve foreign loans, it was known that the Department examined such loans and when it did not object, was considered to have approved.

The Church: the spectacle of a bishop defending himself, none too candidly, when accused of bucket-shop gambling, was not edifying.

The Courts: although Albert B. Fall had been sentenced for receiving a bribe, the giver, Edward L. Doheny, was acquitted. The logic was not clear. The scandals of New York were notorious. It had to be pointed out, at one time, that several judges were honest.

The President: the comparison of his campaign in 1932 with that of 1928 was not encouraging.

The Law: District-Attorney Keyes of Los Angeles was sentenced to St. Quentin for five years for accepting bribes.

The Schools: it was discovered that school-teachers in New York bribed political bosses in order to advance on the waiting lists for appointments.

The Banks: not only for their disastrous failures, but for their debasement of the banking function into security-selling and for permitting kiting and other doubtful practises to favored clients.

The Treasury: the refunds of income tax were always under suspicion — possibly not justified.

Official Statistics: the resignation of Doctor Ray Hall, a trustworthy economist in the Department of Commerce, was not well taken, since Doctor Hall's picture of the depression was more serious than the one the Department wished to circulate; a year later Ethelbert Stewart, Commissioner of Labor Statistics, the man who had refused to supply bankers with the kind of figures they demanded in the dispute over wages, was let out after forty-five years of service. He had refused to corroborate Secretary Doak's optimistic announcements about increasing employment in the spring of 1932. The President might have kept him in office.

Bank Statements: by agreement with the Government, banks placed an artificial value upon certain securities they held. Those who did not know of the agreement assumed that the values were actual.

The Police: both their integrity and humanity were always, in recent years, questioned; but the handling of the Lindbergh case made people wonder whether our entire system of dealing with crime was at all adequate.

Conservatism: the involvement of Lee, Higginson and Company in the Krueger scandal, after its failure to take the most elementary steps to safeguard investors, was a shock to all of New England, making it difficult to believe in the intelligence of business men no matter how easy it was to believe in their honesty.

The Government: the deficit and the flight of gold.

It is clear that not all of these deflations were due to the economic disaster, but they were more keenly felt because the disaster had brought with it a decline in the general faith of Americans. In the years following the war the common emotion was dissipated; when we discovered that the idealism of the war had led to the squabbles in Congress over the League, to the occupation of the Ruhr, to the furious quarrels over war debts, and to the sour, angry, greedy world of the 1920's, we turned our backs on all ideals, and the next common emotion was the natural one of enjoying our prosperity. It was, for practical purposes, an ideal, and it became so mastering that it pushed all others into the discard. So that, when it betrayed us, we had nothing to cling to. The feeling that we had been tricked or imposed upon or deliberately misled was universal. We had been told that the budget had to be balanced, that the dole must not be given and the bonus bill must be rejected because the first duty of a State was to have a balance; and in four months we learned that the deficit on the balanced budget was over half a billion dollars, substantially equal to the deficit of the unbalanced budget a year before. We had seen the sacred institution of the Red Cross mired in politics and science debased to make arguments for administrators. We had seen our country lose rank in the things we cherished most: its enterprise, its courage, its wealth, its power. All that was left was for us to deflate the future.

For a German pessimist to say that "the progress theory of the nineteenth century is buried" was natural enough; but Oswald Spengler is precisely the type for which the Rotarian had the greatest contempt. Mr. Roe Fulkerson, however, wrote in the *Kiwanis Magazine:* "There will never be another fifty years in history which can hold a candle to the last fifty. . . . I am not the least bit envious of these twenty-one-year-old boys just breaking into life. Poor chaps, they came along after everything had happened." All the blessings of engineering and research were belittled and the return to simpler forms was preached; Doctor Kenneth Mees, Director of Research for the Eastman Kodak Company said, "In some respects the life of the future will be closer to the life of the past than it will be to the life of to-day"; the life of the past was suggested by news of barter taking the place of buying and selling, marking the breakdown of our medium of exchange, and it was not surprising to learn that in the State of Washington, wooden money had been issued and used in local stores.

To be sure, the major interest of Americans was for several months in 1931 the breach of promise suit in the broadcasts of Amos 'n' Andy — and that too occasioned a loss of faith, since it all turned out to be a dream.

The effect of these shocks, seemed, at first, to be good. We were getting at the truth and the truth would, following its nature, make us free. The depression was our coming-of-age. Very little that occurred in the presidential campaign showed intellectual or spiritual maturity and while it went on new illusions were successfully created. The political situation in New York City might be taken as an example of the sweet uses of deflation. A committee of investigation had pushed Mayor Walker so hard that he had finally to appear before Governor Roosevelt to answer charges; this committee was led by Samuel Seabury, but the political head was a Republican named Hofstadter. The Mayor was, his friends said, persecuted for political reasons; there was danger that his backers, Tammany Hall, would knife Roosevelt at the polls if the Governor removed the Mayor. Walker resigned and his place was taken by an apparently honest man, Joseph V. McKee, whose first work in office was a thorough exposure of waste and a great slash in the city's expenses. The object lesson was clear.

Instantly Mr. Hofstadter was nominated for a judgeship by an agreement between Tammany and the Republicans; Mayor McKee was prevented either from continuing in office after January 1 or running for election; a good Tammany man was nominated against a Republican nonentity; and the budget was restored to its pristine luxuriousness. The bargaining judge, the Tammany mayor were duly elected. Nothing had changed

except for the worse; the cynicism of the politicians was justified by the apathy of the people. Throughout the country the
same political parties nominated the same candidates for office;
no new principles were announced; the tonic effect of knowing the truth had not worked.

It had not worked because with the breakdown of our economic life, we had no sense of national destiny. It was not
enough to know that we were always to be rich and lead the
world in comfort, and the inadequacy of the motive was, of
course, most apparent when it was proved that it had led us
astray. We had for twenty years been throwing overboard the
burden of libertarian ideals; we were not the country of free
speech or free press or free assembly; we were not the country
of the rights of labor; we were not free of religious prejudice;
we were not interested in social justice; we upheld no strict
morality; it did not shock us to read that a few hundred thousand people controlled nearly all the wealth in the land or that
less than a hundred controlled the country's industry and
finance and policies; we heard of starvation wages and child
labor and barbarous cruelty in chain gangs as if these were
natural episodes in the brilliant news reel of our lives. So long
as they passed quickly, they did not matter.

We had no direction, no deep feeling of why we were a
nation, no feeling that we really were a nation. The only call
we had heard was to stand steadfast and to give, so that the
Government would not have to give. It roused no emotion, not
even anger. When an obscure mid-Western weekly suggested
that it would be a good thing to string up a few of the men
who had betrayed us, the Post Office Department denied it the
use of the mails: neither the exhortation nor the display of
tyranny moved us to more than a faint interest.

The country had been saved. The financial crisis, as Mr.
Lippmann said, was surmounted in June. Mr. Coolidge believed that the social fabric was untouched. To set against

them the story of hunger and hopelessness of these three years
would be to meet thought with emotion, and I shall not do
it, although the President and Congress are as accountable for
human misery as a general is accountable for the loss of life in
a campaign: they must show that the loss, minimum and inevitable, was justified. What remains to be proved is that the
country actually was saved, that its character was not weak-
ened and its capacity to live and grow not corrupted beyond
redemption.

CHAPTER EIGHTEEN

WHEN BLOOD IS THEIR ARGUMENT

ON the whole, the Communists have been disappointed in the course of the American depression, possibly because their "ideology" requires them to judge all the signs of unrest by Russian standards. There have, in fact, been only five mass movements, the rioting in England, Arkansas, which was followed in July, 1931, by a march of three hundred jobless men on the food shops of Henryetta, Oklahoma; the riot at the Ford plant in Dearborn; the march of the bonus men; the farmers' strikes and the migrations of the homeless. The violence in the mines of West Virginia and the occasional outbreaks in Connecticut and Pennsylvania and High Point, North Carolina, were purely industrial disputes which give little light on the depression. But these five are the creations of our own special period. And the first thing to note about them is that with the exception of the Ford riot which came after a Communist rally addressed by William Z. Foster, all of them are the work of respectable and even reactionary citizens, farmers, veterans and the dispossessed of the middle class. Perhaps that is why they are not interesting to Communists who want a proletarian revolution or none at all.

Mr. Oakley Johnson has written a factual account of the riot at Dearborn for the *New Republic*:

"About 3,000 participants in an unemployed demonstration on Monday, March 7, marched with police permission along

Fort Street from downtown Detroit to the Dearborn city limits. They were walking in orderly formation, four abreast, singing or joking, carrying banners. A few hundred women were among them. They stopped just before reaching Dearborn and were addressed by Alfred Goetz, who instructed them to remain orderly, to use no violence and to maintain 'proletarian discipline.' At the Dearborn limits they turned into Miller Road and were met by about fifty Dearborn police, who ordered them to turn back. No parade permit had been issued in Dearborn, in accordance with local policy toward radical demonstrations, although in Detroit the permit, under Mayor Murphy's liberal policy, had been freely granted. The marchers insisted on going ahead. The police threw tear-gas bombs, using up, according to one report, tear gas worth $1,750. Maddened by the gas, the crowd picked up stones and threw them at the police. The police retreated, made another stand, retreated again. Finally the police used their guns, killing one and wounding some others. Then Harry H. Bennett, chief of Ford's private police, drove his car into the crowd and fired either his revolver or his tear-gas gun at the demonstrators. He was hit by a rock, and was taken back toward factory gate number three by the police, who then, in conjunction with plain-clothes men in Ford's employ, opened up with their revolvers, wounding others. The crowd, several hundred feet from the gate, were then on the point of retreating, when the police and plain-clothes men opened fire again with a machine gun, killing three more and wounding over a score. The crowd broke and ran. The workers carried off some of their wounded fellow marchers, leaving the dead and others of the wounded lying in the road."

Nothing in the newspaper accounts of the riot suggests any unfairness in Mr. Johnson's story. Back of it lies the pathetic faith of the American people in Mr. Ford's magic. He had an-

AT DEARBORN, MICH.

The Bombs are Tear Gas.   In the Riot for Jobs at the Ford Plant, Four Men Were Killed and
Fifty Wounded

nounced a few weeks before that "we are going to risk everything we have got to create useful work for just as many people
as possible." And this statement, like all of those issuing from
Detroit, brought the job-hungry from all parts of the country
trailing into the city. Mr. Ford's capacity to affect the lives of
hundreds of thousands of workers has been proved again and
again; when he shut down his main factory to prepare for a
new model, the city of Detroit was in despair and was in
despair again when the announcement that work was to be
resumed brought thousands of drifters in to take jobs which
thousands of old employees were still clamoring to get.

The shooting at Dearborn was an anachronism; it was the
reëmergence of the private constabulary which had made the
Homestead strike infamous; and like Andrew Carnegie, Mr.
Ford may have had deep regrets; but so far as I know, he gave
them no public utterance.

It was, however, the first time since the sailing of the Peace
Ship that Mr. Ford did not have the universal sympathy of
the American people.[1]

He lacked particularly the sympathy of Detroiters. Mr.
Johnson says:

"The majority of Detroiters support Murphy and hate Ford.
Barbers, waitresses, clerks, most white-collar workers — not
radical in any sense — say such things as, 'I wish they'd tear
down his whole factory. Maybe *that* would give the unemployed a job, building it up again'."

On the other hand, a branch of the American Legion in
Detroit offered its services to the Ford Motor Company "in
any official emergency" and one of the prosecutors in charge

[1] When he said that history is bunk, the American people, convinced they had no lesson to learn from history, and that if necessary
they would confound every axiom of history, loudly cheered.

of the investigation of the riot said, "I wish they'd killed a few more of those damned rioters."

It was a demonstration, not a strike; it was an appeal not for higher wages or better working conditions, but for jobs. The legal wrong of the marchers parading without a permit, and the legal right, if there was one, of the Ford police to fire are matters for the Civil Liberties Union and the courts to dispute; significance lies only in the purpose of the manifestation. In Arkansas and Oklahoma men rioted for food; in Dearborn for jobs. The next act of violence was even more ominous. It came from the farmers in the Middle West and its object was repudiation of debt.

The farmers' strike actually began in May, when Milo Reno, once President of the Iowa Farmers' Union, began organizing a Farmers' Holiday Association. In the middle of July it was powerful enough to attempt a blockade of Sioux City. The method was as simple as that of the Minutemen; it was direct action, and like the riot at Dearborn was out of date; but it was out of date by a wider margin and went back not to the days of dominant industry, but almost to the days of 1776. The farmers patrolled the highways leading into Sioux City and they were armed, but not with shotguns; they had pitchforks to puncture tires and stones for smashing windshields, but they were not prepared for further violence. Two thousand of them picketed the roads, sometimes throwing a barricade of logs or ropes across or stretching barbed wire or throwing down boards with nails in them; their first object was to gain time for argument. If the argument did not work, they held the vender helpless while they poured out his cream or threw his produce into the roadside. The purpose was simply to put up the price of farm produce to the point where it reached what the farmers called the cost of production. It is doubtful whether their books were so well kept that they knew the cost of production; what they wanted was to make a little money. In Sioux City itself the farmers attacked the stock-yards, after twenty trucks of livestock had escaped the pickets. From Des Moines a hundred leaders of the movement set out to spread the strike, threatening neighboring States and intending to proceed west and east until a solid block from the Rockies to the Alleghenies was withholding all food from market.

Mr. Wayne Gard reports in the *Nation* the words of a farmer:

"I own a farm near Boone. My share of the oats crop from twenty-four acres on this farm was $40. My taxes on this same land amounted to $44.16. Before prices took a jump, I could buy a 400-pound packing sow for 90 cents a hundred, or $3.60. At the same time, I went to a meat market and priced a 20-pound smoked ham. It was $3.20. I told them to go to hell; I'd buy a whole hog and cut off a ham."

The pickets on the roads let dairy products through for the hospitals and even donated several thousand gallons of milk to the unemployed; sometimes sheriffs and their deputies were sympathetic. Governor Olson of Minnesota called on the heads of other States to join him in support of the farmers, announcing that he would be willing even to declare martial law if necessary to help them.

But the governors of the States did not even approach the real problem of the farmer. That was done for them by Senator Borah, who said on the 1st of October:

"The foreclosures against farmers are going to reach the point . . . when these debtors in sheer despair will adopt a method which will be an unhappy incident for all of us."

And he proposed to "adjust private debts to conform to the change in money values" after official inflation — in short, Senator Borah proposed to scale down either the amount of a mortgage or rate of interest. And although the picketers along the Iowa roads may have thought that all they wanted was thirty-five cents a dozen for eggs and ninety-two cents a bushel for corn, what they really wanted was to be relieved of their debts. They had pledged themselves to fight off the sheriff with his foreclosure.

In the manifesto of the farmers, accepted by men from the Dakotas, Illinois, Minnesota and Nebraska, there was a promise of further violence: "We pledge ourselves to protect one another in the actual possession of our necessary homes, livestock and machinery as against all claimants." It is not very clear, but the claimants alluded to must have been the holders of mortgages. The farm strike was not a success, prices did not go up and the movement did not spread sufficiently. It was not, in fact, directed against the consumers of food, and hardly against the middleman, except when the middleman was a corporation; it was directed against the Farm Board, the holders of mortgages and the American economic system.

Every observer of the Iowa strike commented on two things. The first was the open expression of the farmers' feeling that in the boom years every one had taken what he wanted and now the farmer was going to get what he wanted. The second was the connection between the farmers' strike and the bank holidays. The idea of these came, I believe, from the mayor of a small Ohio town who, foreseeing panic when the principal bank failed, got all the business men of the town to agree to close up shop, except for vital necessities, for a week. The effects in allaying panic were so good that banks which were merely threatened adopted the system, and the moment they feared a run, would ask a local authority to declare a week's business holiday. Finance is more refined than agriculture; there was no violence; but business men got together in groups, like sellers of Liberty Bonds during the war, and using the same kinds of social pressure, persuaded depositors to sign agreements allowing the banks to use money on deposit, and pledging themselves to withdraw only a small percentage. Mr. Donald R. Murphy says in the *New Republic*, "In the cases where farmers have refused to sign, and banks have reopened, the banks have refused to let the non-signers have their money." It is not remarkable that the farmers have turned the trick against the banks when one considers that the banks were often the holders of mortgages.

The farmers' strike took a political turn when President Hoover went to Iowa to make an address. The *New York Herald Tribune* reporter wrote:

"One watched the truck loads of 'insolvent farmers' arrive at the rallying spots . . . with mingled emotions. Here was genuine misery going on parade; here was village or prairie smartness, also on parade and quite definitely exploiting misery; here were men shivering in the cold fall wind, wearing nothing but a suit of overalls and a pair of shoes, no socks and no underwear, and with blue skin showing through the rents and above the broken shoes. Here were stout, frankly dirty fellows, warmly if roughly clad, cursing Mr. Hoover and Wall Street.

"These noisy men were the organizers, the drivers, Milo Reno's county lieutenants, Smith Wildman Brookhart's prairie rabble-rousers.

"Here also were decent men, fearfully poverty-stricken, poorly clad in patched shirts, patched overalls, patched overcoat or no overcoat at all. They were here in the hope that this demonstration would bring them some sort of relief. And making up the balance of the assemblage were hundreds of youths from the back ways, as poor as their elders, but too young for tragedy to cheat them out of a good time."

From Mr. Hoover, however, the farmers did not expect and did not get the promise they needed; Mr. Roosevelt made a somewhat equivocal statement about mortgages. The farmers, at least, had brought a basic problem into politics.

In his account of his first meeting with the Bonus Army, General Glassford says that he noticed a banner demanding, "Give us the Bonus or a Job." By the time the army dispersed in the middle of August, the Children's Bureau of the Department of Labor had discovered that two hundred thousand children were wandering across the country, seeking neither a bonus nor a job, but food. The first report of this phenomenon came from Mr. Harry Ferguson of the United Press, who said that this "hungry horde" was "comparable only to the so-called 'wild children' of Russia." They were only the camp followers of a larger army, estimated in millions, of "white-collar bums" with whom railroads and cities chiefly in the South and Southwest were attempting to cope. Through El Paso forty-five thousand had passed in six months. Through Kansas City fifteen hundred were passing each day. The Bureau quoted railroad men as saying "that the policy is to remove the transients from the trains. But the last year we have been unable to do so because the numbers are so large."

The City of Detroit was one of the first to create an effective program of relief, the result of which was that hundreds, and perhaps thousands of jobless men made their way from less indulgent cities to take what Detroit had to offer. I have already noted the ineffectiveness of the program in checking unemployment. No matter how much was spent, no matter how many men were put to work, the number of the jobless rose. Between 1931 and 1932 twenty thousand families — nearly half — were dropped from the list of those entitled to municipal relief. By July of 1932 the head of the Welfare Commission an-

PERSUASION IN THE WEST

The Principal Highway Leading to Sioux City Blockaded by Striking Farmers

nounced that the number of families which could be helped
were dropped from the maximum of forty-five thousand to
only six thousand. Mr. Mauritz A. Hallgren reported to the
Nation:

"Petty thievery is increasing. Windows of small retail shops
are smashed at night and relieved of their goods. Children from
the poorer districts have taken to snatching bundles from
customers coming out of grocery stores. They run off to barren
homes with their booty, or eat it themselves in out-of-the-way
alleys. More frequently, grown men, usually in twos and threes,
enter chain stores, order all the food they can possibly carry,
and then walk quietly out without paying. Every newspaper
in town knows of this practice and knows that it is spreading,
but none mentions it in print. The Press excuses itself on the
ground that these occurrences are not a matter of public record. And the chain-store managers refuse to report such incidents to the police lest the resultant publicity encourage the
practice."

If the number of men engaged in all of these movements
were added together and perhaps multiplied by ten to allow
for those we know nothing of, our total would still be unim-
pressive as a record of violent or illegal resistance. Europeans
have indeed commented on the docility of the American people and the phenomenon of our depression which struck them
most was the absence of the phenomenon they expect at home
in similar circumstances — that is, the rise of a great popular
movement expressing itself either in politics or in direct action.
That ten million people could be out of work and not combine
to riot or to vote does seem extraordinary; it is, perhaps, a
tribute to the skill with which the employing class dominated
the minds of the workers in the ten years before the crash.
The power of labor, organized or not, seems to have diminished;
for one thing you cannot go on strike ten months after a fac-

tory has been closed; for another, it is not good policy to call a thousand men out on a strike when ten thousand are crying for their jobs. The Communist Party has gained recruits. In the summer of 1931 I heard Mr. Foster say that the actual number of party members had increased by thirty-three per cent. since the beginning of the year, and he added that a great many of the new members had been Ku Klux Klanners two years earlier. Yet the Communist Party, with its principle of a small and highly disciplined organization, cannot take in millions of workers; and the Industrial Workers of the World, which might have, is, in practice, dead.

There are, however, a few indications that the unemployed are slowly becoming conscious of their economic necessities and of their political power. Of the latter the most impressive manifestation is the Chicago Workers' Committee on Unemployment, which expected to have one hundred thousand members by November, and which has already become influential in dealing with problems of relief in Chicago. When it appeared that the emergency relief stations would be closed on June 4th, the Workers Committee appealed both to the mayor and to the bankers who could save the situation, and directly to the people over the radio, and so were successful at least in postponing the complete collapse of municipal relief.

Even more important is the Unemployed Citizens' League of Seattle, which has fifty thousand members, all of them penniless, and all "carrying on much of the business of relief without the use of money." Mr. Bruce Bliven, editor of the *New Republic*, informs me that the experiment in Seattle has already been copied in many other cities. How it works is best explained in an editorial in the *New Republic*:

"The membership fee in the League is two days' work a week, but only about one half the members are contributing this much, the others being without skill in the League's enterprises. Every member is given food and other necessities for himself and his family, share and share alike. The League is conducting a clothing factory, a shoe factory and a coal mine. It is operating numerous farms and livestock ranches, as well as garages, barber shops and other businesses. It has even taken over apartment houses in the city, putting them into repair in exchange for a lease of a specified period, during which members of the League can occupy the apartments rent free.

"All these enterprises have been inaugurated practically without the use of working capital. Farmers, unable to earn a living on their land, have turned it over to the League and have become members, receiving for their families the same maintenance that others get. Trucks have been donated by business firms unable, because of the depression, to make use of them; and the coal mine and the factories have been obtained on the same basis. The State of Washington has loaned much land, some of it in timber; and workers are carried from and to Seattle each day in the borrowed trucks."

In the *New York Times Magazine* of October 30, 1932, Mr. Arthur Krock recorded a conversation with a hotel clerk in Seattle:

"It's pretty bad out here, though they do say that some of the 60,000 people who are being taken care of at the commissaries ride up there in cars and complain when it's stew instead of steak they get. Sometimes I think this depression, so far as the Coast is concerned, is like our clock time. We're three hours later than the East and we're just feeling this depression hard. It hasn't been good out here for a long while, but lately it's seemed worse. We can tell it quick in the hotel business."

The hotel clerk was apparently unaware of the greater fluidity of the West and its greater willingness to make social experiments. The self-supporting workers may be crushed when they come to trade with the outer world; they have not solved the problem of the depression. But they have indicated what organization can do.

Every one of these phenomena seems more important to me than a staged riot of Communists in Union Square in New York. And the last three I have named, the revolt of the farmers, the wanderings of men and children across the States and the direct action of the hungry in the West, show resistances and desperations which are profoundly important. They are not the methods of revolution but they may be revolutions themselves. In his vigorous book on the technique of the *coup d'état*, Malaparte says:

"Neither the Governments nor the Catilines — this much is clear — have ever seriously studied whether there is a modern science of *coup d'état* or what its general rules are. While the Catilines pursue their revolutionary tactics, the Governments continue to oppose them by defensive police measures, thus showing their absolute ignorance of the elementary principles of conquering and defending the modern State."

The defensive police measures of which Malaparte speaks are used, in times of stress, as much to protect the governing class (Society, the existing order, the State) from the rights of minorities as from the wrongs; in America, the police are the only defense against the first ten amendments to the Constitution which make up the Bill of Rights. Protection of these rights, and especially of free speech, free press, and free assembly, has fallen into private hands, upheld by the American Civil Liberties Union.

Since mass protests have been coming from farmers and

loyal American citizens, as well as from Communists, it might seem reasonable to suppose that the general feeling about demonstrations would become more tolerant. I suggested this to Mr. Roger Baldwin, the director of the Union, and he wrote me as follows:

"I do not think that the more recent exhibitions of hostility to the Administration by veterans and farmers will make it any easier for radicals. On the contrary, these people, following methods suspected of being radical, make every effort to dissociate themselves from the 'Reds.' The Bonus Army expelled them. The farmers will have nothing to do with them. Therefore, pressure comes against the radicals, not only from those who uphold the present order, but from those who are on their own part agitating against it. This history, as you well know, is repeated in other countries."

The year June, 1931, to June, 1932, however, suggests that while sympathy with radicals may not grow with the depression, the police power is being more wisely exercised. In New York City, Chief of Police Mulrooney, acting in sympathy with Mayor McKee, virtually put an end to police violence and gave full liberty to Communists to assemble and speak in Union Square; the result was that Communism did not figure in the papers for several months, and it appears that the only people who were disappointed were the Communists themselves and the Tammany candidate for Mayor, Surrogate O'Brien, who, certain of election, announced that he would put an end to all Communist demonstrations as soon as he was in office. (He also spoke in favor of a "kiddie" in every home.)

From a report issued by the Civil Liberties Union itself I find that correspondents of the Union in forty-three States were asked to report on the situation:

"Most of them reported comparatively little resistance which would arouse repression, and most thought that tolerance for minority movements had increased. Some reported the situation as markedly better, due, they all said, to the fear of authorities of inciting trouble if they interfered with demonstrations of despairing workers out of jobs. Reports from every State except three agreed in describing repression of civil liberties as either less or unchanged. The three States reporting conditions worse were Kentucky, Michigan and Texas. The attitude of the press on the whole has been remarkably better all over the country in condemning interference with civil liberty, and in insisting upon the rights of people with a grievance to be heard."

The Union's summary of the year is interesting:

"Despite the wholesale unemployment in the growing economic depression and the despair of millions who live on uncertain charity, public resistance has been remarkably slight — confounding the prophecies of police and radicals alike. No food riots have taken place. Strikes against wage cuts and street demonstrations by the unemployed have been numerous, but disorder has been only occasional. Police officials have been nervously watchful and in many cases have broken out into open attacks.

"But the record of meetings prohibited or broken up or of serious prosecutions for agitation shows no increase over recent years. Indeed, the figures show less than in the early part of 1930, when the Communist-led unemployment demonstrations began."

There is always the possibility that it would have been better for our nerves if we had rioted a little.

The spearhead of an American revolution may be a compact and disciplined Communist Party; but the spirit of revolution in the conservative farmer and the loyal citizen is more important. The Mississippi Bubble burst when an indignant Frenchwoman, a flower seller or a concierge, standing in the crowd outside John Law's office clamoring for redemption of bonds, threw the paper which had been worth one hundred livres on the ground and spat upon it. The Russian Revolution, as Trotzky tells us, was an assured fact when a Cossack winked at a striker in the streets of Petrograd. The harried clerks in the chain store who dare not call the police may be performing a similar and symbolic function.

CHAPTER NINETEEN

THE WORD OF GOD

THE Monday-morning papers in most of the large cities in America have a page, or a part of a page, which is not often carefully read and which can hardly be called a circulation-builder in comparison with comic strips. It is devoted entirely to reports of Sunday sermons, and one notices that the number of columns given to these is greater in those newspapers which have a quality circulation. I take one of these (the *New York Herald Tribune*, October 10, 1932) as perhaps an average representing the thought and feeling of religious leaders about a depression which by that time had lasted nearly three years. It should be remembered that, as a general rule, only the more intelligent or the more prominent preachers are reported.

The Reverend Doctor Norman Vincent Peale said:

"New York to-day stands in the same need of regeneration through Christianity as the Rome of St. Paul's time.

"I say to this city and to my generation that you will never be good and wholesome, you will never realize the things of which you are capable, until you incorporate into your social, municipal and personal life the principles of Jesus Christ. There is a close similarity between that Rome and this America. We worship the things of the flesh, we have a naïve confidence in the efficacy of force, and Rome had all these. We must be regenerated."

The Reverend Doctor Don O. Shelton said:

"When Tammany's twenty thousand delegates . . . by acclamation selected the one suggested to them for nomination as mayor, a unity of action was exhibited probably unprecedented in political history. It was another demonstration of the fact that often the children of this world are shrewder than the children of light."

Rabbi Rosenblum said:

"Instead of depending upon voluntary contributions to the Gibson fund, I propose that every citizen who has employment should be required by ordinance to pay an emergency bread tax for the jobless. The amounts would depend upon what each person earns, but every one in the city, from the bootblack to the banker, should give something every week until the crisis is over.

"To-day there are nearly twelve hundred thousand persons out of work in our city, which means that three or four times that number, or at least half the population of New York, are on the danger line. Fifty thousand children are in need of feeding. What are the synagogues going to do about it? We cannot keep alive on prayers. We must give them bread. It is well enough for those who come to our synagogues to fast. Most of them fast by choice, but it will be a sacrilege if out of our worship there does not come the urge to keep the other half from starving."

The similarity of our plight to that of Rome was noted also by Doctor Ralph W. Sockman, who said:

"If the Roman empire grew decadent, it neglected the Forum, with its coöperative citizenship, for the Coliseum, with its circuses designed for the entertainment of spectators. One wonders if American life is going to follow the same trend. Are we going to become a nation of spectators regaled by professional entertainers, politicians, athletes and even preachers? There are signs pointing that way."

In a direct analysis of the depression Doctor J. Stanley Durkee said the economic crisis was due to the world's lack of faith, and added:

"It is the breaking down of godly faith which has brought New York to the very verge of disaster and makes us all wonder if we have the moral strength to hold the load of this mighty government in city, State and nation."

Doctor Henry Sloane Coffin expressed the hope that "the mad decade of prosperity would never be repeated" and remarked that the prayers of those who had never prayed before should not be taken as proof of a renewed faith, for, "What these people are praying for is a return to the 1929 prosperity with its leanness of soul and its terrible moral bankruptcy. If they were sincere, they would pray for the morning when some measure of economic security will be guaranteed to every worker."

Reverend Doctor Harry Emerson Fosdick, from the pulpit of what is generally known as the Rockefeller Church, said:

"This is a world where in the long run we cannot keep for ourselves anything we desire unless we share it with the whole body of the people. If we wish health for ourselves and our families we must share it. An epidemic knows no boundaries and scarlet fever is no respecter of social classes. There is no assurance of health for any one unless there is assurance of health for every one."

In its report, the Laymen's Foreign Missions Inquiry said that heathen lands were absorbing a disconcerting consciousness of the defects of Western culture, and suggested that it may be an aftermath of the war, or perhaps the depression; the inquiry recommends that "for the sake of securing for Christianity a fair hearing, it is necessary to separate it, as far as possible, from our history and our promoting agencies and to present it in its universal capacity."

The dissatisfaction of churches with themselves is marked; the churches did not win back converts by the hundreds of thousands, as they had during the war; they were missing a great opportunity and it was clear that the fault had occurred long ago, for while business men were clasping their hands and calling upon Heaven to testify to their devotion to Service, the Church, broadly speaking, had the secret of sound economics in its keeping, a secret not precisely inviolate, since Jesus had made it public twenty centuries ago, and the Church had repeated and reaffirmed it a thousand times until in the days of the great boom the Church went into business itself and forgot its principles. It is, in a word, that the laborer is worthy of his hire and that he who came only at the last hour shall receive as much as he who worked through the heat of the day, and even that man shall not live by bread alone. The most penetrating and the most unanswerable criticism of the economics of the New Era is that capital did not pay to labor enough in wages to enable labor to buy what capital and labor had produced; and this is the principle which Christianity has been proclaiming, with a profound moral and spiritual meaning, for centuries. The terms in which Pius XI expressed his view of the depression on Christmas Eve, 1930, are not those of the Communist or the capitalist, but Mr. Lawrence Dennis is probably justified in thinking that the Pope has shown himself a better critic of our system than those who profit by it and those who suffer by it, not to mention those whose profession it is to criticize it. The Pope, opposing "unbridled competition which is dangerous to financial and economic conditions", asked for "an adjustment" which is not the downward revision of the great corporations, but one which "without upsetting the order established by Divine Providence, would make fraternal collaboration possible and effective among the classes of the people." Forty years earlier Leo XIII, in the famous encyclical Rerum Novarum, rejected Socialism and put the Catholic Church on the side of trades unions, the eight-hour day, minimum wage laws and old-age pensions; recalling this radical departure of the conservative Church, Pius XI spoke through a microphone of gold and silver, and said to the world which had fought against every one of these reforms, "It is . . . absolutely necessary to re-construct the whole economic system by bringing it back to the requirements of social justice so as to insure a more able distribution of the united proceeds of capital and labor. Thus will be achieved that uplifting of the proletariat which Leo XIII so ardently desired. . . . In the present order this can be accomplished only by a fair and just wage. . . ."

The Protestant churches were in a more difficult position, for Protestantism had become desperately involved with the theory of profit.[1]

Some power not in man which makes for righteousness had to be found to take the place of the absolute rule of the Catholic hierarchy; for several centuries after the Reformation the power of kings was sufficient. But Protestantism makes for independence and so for democracy,

---

[1] No one can say this without instant mention of the name of R. H. Tawney and his book "Religion and the Rise of Capitalism." When I was making a study of American revivalism in the 19th century I was impressed by the steady decline in intellect and the steady rise of the feeling that God could be glorified by size and numbers. To this and to other obscurities, Tawney's pioneer work gives a clue.

and it is notable that the industrial system flourished in the most democratic of European countries and rose to its height in a country dedicated to the principle that all men are born free and equal. The idea that the capitalist system is the direct work of God had been implied even when it had not been definitely proclaimed as it was by "Divine Right" Baer; our capitalists "under God" could do no other than they did, and since the system was divinely created, the man who took most advantage of it contributed most to the glory of God. That Jesus was sceptical of the rich man's capacity to get into Heaven was brushed aside even in 1932, when a minister of a Protestant Episcopal church, Reverend William S. Blackshear, said:

"Christ was happy to be at the banquets of the rich. It was at such a place that the woman broke the vial of costly ointment and anointed His feet. There were those who cried out for the improvident and rebuked the woman, saying that this should have been converted into cash and given to the poor. It was then that Christ spoke on the economic plan, 'The poor ye have always with you'."

Yet Protestantism as a whole was compelled to consider the difficulties of the system which it had in part created. The first comments of the Protestant churches on the crash in Wall Street were not different from the comments of laymen, except in the choice of words; there had been excesses and we were reaping a whirlwind. The capitalist system was invited to turn its thoughts to higher things.[2]

By the middle of 1931, the Young Men's Christian Asso-

[2] The head of the National Association of Manufacturers told the Methodist Federation of Social Service that in his own factory he had done so even before, instituting a morning prayer exercise, with the result that "workers are producing far more goods than before the prayer system was started."

ciation and the Young Women's Christian Association were both busy repudiating the report of a commission they had sponsored which was definitely Socialistic in tone, asking, among other things, for unemployment insurance, social ownership of public utilities, natural resources and basic industries, as well as increased taxes on inheritance, income, and excess profits. A few months later the Federal Council of Churches of Christ, which had condemned our generation because it "insisted on the rights of property to dividends but . . . concerned itself too little with the right of workers", gave in to the popular enthusiasm for planning and said, "Our economic life now seems to be without a chart." It condemned the faulty distribution of wealth and the system by which in bad times those who had created wealth were treated as hangers-on and social liabilities; it asked for employment insurance, other benefits, and "a Christian motive of service." Shortly thereafter the bishops of the Protestant Episcopal Church, also enthusiastic for planning, turned on the system and called it by name. "An acquisitive society," they said, "stands bewildered in the presence of a crisis precipitated . . . by the competitive profit-seeking principles upon which, it has hitherto been assumed, general prosperity is based. . . . The profit-seeking motive must give way to that of service. . . ." The bishops spoke of the paradox of plenty, the starving men and the overflowing warehouses and said that "the conception of society as made up of . . . independent individuals . . . is as faulty from the point of view of economic realism as it is from the standpoint of Christian idealism. Our traditional philosophy of rugged individualism must be modified. . . ." [3]

[3] George W. Wickersham, a deputy to the general convention where this pastoral letter was read, brought in a minority report saying, "I think it would be a sad day when the American people abandon the principles on which they have grown to greatness." He recognized

In May, 1932, the general conference of the Methodist Episcopal Church heard Bishop William F. Anderson begin with an attack on the rich for trying to "shift the burden of taxation from their own shoulders to the backs of the poor", by repealing the 18th Amendment. He also said that "industry has, as a rule, given labor a grudging, insufficient wage, keeping it down . . . while at the same time huge fortunes have been amassed for the favored owners of the resources of production." The Bishop disapproved of turning the worker off to starve or beg "after giving his labor for miserable financial results."

Shortly after England went off the gold standard, the archbishops of York and Canterbury allowed a special prayer for these times which ran, "Because we have indulged in national arrogance and satisfaction in our power over others rather than in our ability to serve them, forgive us our trespasses." The prayer was not binding and the vicars in many communities refused to read it out. But twenty-six Protestant churches in America, refusing to be consoled by assurances that the economic problem had been solved, either by the Republican Administration or the Democratic Congress, called upon twenty-three million Americans "to give themselves by an act of will, personally and corporately, in penitence and prayer to Almighty God", in order to end the depression. It is easy to be flippant and cynical; the week of October 2d was set for this penitential exercise, and the week of October 9th and the weeks which followed not only failed to show an alteration

the importance of the pronouncement and objected to being bound by it. The bishops, it may be noted, were on the side of the economists who believed that the régime of food, exercise, undiscipline and throwing one's weight about, which is appropriate to adolescence, may be dangerous for maturity and middle age, and that America had certainly reached maturity. Mr. Wickersham would not dissociate; because he had been a youth in the last stages of America's infancy, he insisted that nothing should be changed now, although one ventures to assume that he had himself abandoned the principles on which he had grown to greatness.

in the economic position; they showed no alteration of mental or moral or spiritual attitude.[4]

Yet cynicism is out of place. The most powerful directors of the dominant churches of America were now condemning the history of America over the last twenty years. To religious sceptics the emphasis on divine forgiveness and the suggestion that a return to the Church would be effective in an economic crisis are absurd. The importance of the call to prayer, as of all the other manifestations of dissatisfaction, lies only in that it is a cry of repentance from the Church itself. The heads of the Protestant churches said:

"We address you on urgent business. The Church and the nation face a grave and serious situation. There is on every hand physical and mental suffering. This condition has long continued and no one can point the way of escape. Our best men are powerless before the devastating effects of commercial distrust and moral confusion. While we long for the return of prosperity, we pray rather for the correction of those causes of distress without which prosperity may prove to be other than a blessing. . . .

"We have worshiped at the shrines of false gods — the false god of mammon, money, things; the false god of power, production, bigness; the false god of nationalism, individualism, social injustice; the false god of pleasure, amusement, disregard for things and times sacred; the false god of success, high living, careless thinking; the false god of magic, reaping where we had not sowed, profiting where we had not toiled.

[4] They showed to an observer not peculiarly concerned with the results of the election a measurable degeneration, for the campaign of 1932 was, considering the magnitude of the issues involved, the most deplorable exhibition of loose thinking, evasive politics and nasty personal attacks in a generation. I do not think that in these respects it was any worse than most campaigns, but few campaigns came at so critical a point in the history of the nation.

"The Church dares not stand aside and whisper peace either
to itself or to the nation, when there is no peace. Only a
national turning to God in repentance and moral restitution,
seeking His divine forgiveness, will restore the spiritual health
of our people. . . ."

There remains only the question of the ineffectiveness of the
Church's condemnation of the profit system and I have suggested a reason for it. Roughly speaking, the churches had
believed what Mr. Ford believed in 1914, when he established
a minimum wage of five dollars per day, not only for work
which was, in the common terms, worth five dollars, but for
work which he could have had done at a dollar and a half and
two dollars a day. It is oddly enough a principle which runs
not only through religion and sound economics but through
the personal relations of civilized beings as well — to give more
than one has to give. When the Players have come to Elsinore
and the Player King has spoken of Hecuba, Hamlet asks Polonius to see the Players well bestowed. "My lord," says Polonius,
"I will use them according to their desert." And Hamlet cries
out as a noble gentleman, "God's bodikins, man, much better.
. . . Use them after your own honour and dignity: The less
they deserve, the more merit is in your bounty. Take them in."
It is a generous improvement on the old principle of Saint-
Simon, "From each according to his ability, to each according
to his need"; it is an offense to the Communist and the egali-
tarian because it implies that one has the power to give or to
withhold; but it is a better system than the usual one of
giving as little as possible. In modern economy it is fundamental; a capitalist must give more than he has to and more
than he wants to, so that the worker need never stop buying
and capitalism can insure itself against disaster.

The Church, then, was grounded in good economics, but
just as it failed to denounce the war, it failed to dissociate

itself from the boom except when it felt that motor cars and golf were taking people away from the church buildings. It employed the methods of high-pressure salesmanship and it set in important positions those who could talk business to business men, the hearty man-to-man talk, or the snobbish social talk, or whatever it was that would bring contributions. The campaign for the completion of the Cathedral of St. John the Divine, "House of Prayer for all People", was at least as good as the campaign for cigarettes and razor blades.

When the smash came, it was discovered that somewhere in the nineteen hundreds the Church had cast off the lifeboat. Obviously if churchmen had sat in the lifeboat when the great ocean liner of prosperity plunged from port to port, they would have cut a ridiculous figure; but they would have been in a better position to effect a rescue.

It had been my intention to make this chapter a record of the feebleness and futility of churchly utterances during the depression. There were enough of them. But comparing them with the utterances of statesmen, industrialists and bankers, I find them not perceptibly worse. The language sounds a little more antiquated, but there is no special reason why the Church, which is supposed to deal with eternal things, should be particularly up-to-date. I doubt whether any churchman has said anything as stupid as the day-to-day comment on the depression of our trusted leaders and our experienced and disappointed business men.

CHAPTER TWENTY

SOME SPECIAL PROBLEMS

IN preparing this book, I have naturally come across problems for which my equipment was inadequate and some, I suppose, which I was temperamentally unfitted to understand. The tremendous mental excitement which the depression has generated has, however, created a vast literature, and much of this is so clear that anybody who can read English can find himself at least a guide.[1]

But once I found myself in the odd situation of having asked a question which apparently no one else had asked and no one could answer. I suppose that because it is my own question I attach an excessive importance to it. In the end it irritated me so that I am afraid my own guess at the answer is the result of exasperation rather than of sound thinking. The question is: How many separate individuals actually speculated in the market in the six months preceding the crash of October 19–November 1, 1929?

There are two usual answers to this question, and the first is, "We were all in the market"; the second is, "Between fifteen and twenty million people." I am compelled to reject both of these answers, the first one as an example of extraordinary loose thinking and the second as an example of loose guessing.

[1] My indebtedness to John Maynard Keynes, Walter Lippmann, Stuart Chase, Carl Snyder, M. J. Bonn, Henry Pratt Fairchild, W. E. Woodward, Lawrence Dennis, Donald B. Woodward, Marc A. Rose and W. B. Donham is enormous.

My conviction is that the number of people in the market was probably in the neighborhood of a million, and in order to protect whatever reputation I may have for sanity I double it and add half again and set the figure at two and a half million, being particularly pleased with this number because it is just about the number of enrolled members of the Communist Party in Russia. This comparison suggests the importance of the problem. We have always rejected the idea that Russia is governed by or for itself because, obviously, it is governed by a small oligarchy controlled by a very tiny proportion of the total population; and if the number of people speculating in the market was just about as small a proportion of the population of America, we are compelled to revise our ideas in the field of morals and, I suspect, in the field of economics.

I maintain that our entire attitude toward the depression was colored by the repeated assertions that the speculative mania was actually universal. There was the idea that we — not many of us, but all of us — were tainted with a peculiar guilt because we had all been gambling; there was the idea again that the banking world might be innocent or the industrial world or the commercial world or the political world, because all of these had been trampled down in the mad rush of all of us toward Broad and Wall streets; there is the idea that it was good for us to suffer for our sins; there is the idea expressed by ex-President Coolidge that nothing ought to be done for us because those who "made losses" should suffer them. It was impossible to attach guilt to any individual or any group of individuals if we were all guilty; and it was not necessary for those in power to do anything special to rescue us, since they were fundamentally more innocent than we were.[2]

My point here is that there were innocent people and that they suffered as much as the guilty — and I am using these

[2] The Coolidge argument in favor of Mr. Hoover. See page 14.

terms in the sense of innocent of speculation and guilty of speculation, without any special moral feeling about speculation itself. I know that when Mr. Coolidge said we were all in the market, and when Mr. Hoover said it, and when a great many other people said it, they did not mean that 122,775,046 individuals had marginal accounts with brokers; but the psychological effect of what they said was precisely that. Therefore I begin my calculations by a series of subtractions from this figure. (It is actually the population of the United States on the 1st of April, 1930, but the variation from October, 1929, cannot be great.)

I deny first that the two thousand blind deaf mutes in the United States were all in the market; I doubt whether the forty-four thousand deaf mutes were all in the market; as one of the great pleasures of being in the market was following the ticker tape or reading the stock-market reports in the newspapers, I suspect that some, at least, of the fifty thousand blind in America were not in the market. There were eleven and a half million children under five years of age and twenty-four and a half million aged five to fourteen years, and I think that if they were in the market they must have been represented by trust companies and were not, as Jonathan Edwards might have suspected, little sinners possessed by the devil of gambling; we live in an era of precocity, so I will assume that half of the children approaching maturity (fifteen to nineteen years old) were in the market which leaves five million who were not — roughly a total of over forty million individuals to be subtracted from the gross total — that is to say, one third of us were certainly not speculating. I do not think that the two hundred and sixty thousand patients in state hospitals for mental diseases were competent to conduct the business of stock speculation, although the antics of those who did suggested that they had better be in hospitals. There were one hundred thousand men and women in prison during this period and their cells were not equipped with tickers. There were sixty thousand feeble-minded and epileptic men and women in state institutions — a kindly supervision prevented them from following the rational into the market. I have no figures for the number of people in poorhouses during these boom years, but there were a few and I think they did not speculate.

And now we turn to another set of figures with the warning that there may be some overlapping. Over fifty million Americans were classified by the census as living in rural territory, but of these only thirty million lived on farms. Omitting one third of this number as under twenty-one and therefore already counted in this calculation, we have twenty million people, the majority of whom by all accounts were not making enough to live on; the plight of the farmer had been serious for years before the election of 1928 and was a major issue in that election; one of the first things to which President Hoover turned was the method of rescuing agriculture. I cannot think that all the men and women who were struggling desperately to make a living, and who had mortgaged their farms, and who could not buy seed and machinery, took the spectacular way of the Stock Market as a relief from their burdens. But assuming that half of the farmers were either moderately prosperous or willing to gamble, I put down ten million as the number of those who were not and did not. This net figure is to be added then to the forty million children and adolescents, giving us a minimum of fifty million people not in the market.

Take now another group of figures. About fifty million people "had money" in 1929 — that is to say, they drew wages, clipped coupons, earned salaries and otherwise received money which they spent. Four out of five of this number received less than two thousand dollars a year, or forty dollars a week. Inasmuch as there were forty million of them, the total sum of their income was enormous — nearly fifty billion dollars (but note that that makes the average twelve hundred and fifty dollars a year, or twenty-five dollars a week for forty million people). I have the greatest admiration for those who pluckily managed to live on small incomes, an admiration tempered by my own memories of the unpleasantness of living in that way; but I do not attribute to men earning twenty-five or thirty-five dollars a week, each with a wife and two children to support, the reckless and romantic dash which would bring them into speculation in the stock market. If they had two dollars a week to spare they may have put in a building and loan association, they may have invested it, they may have put it in a savings bank; I do not think that they were in Wall Street. If we move to a slightly higher bracket, we find that ninety-eight per cent. of the individuals who earned money in 1929 got less than five thousand dollars a year, or, say, one hundred dollars a week. That is a rather large income, but with motor cars and radios to be bought and turned in, and rents to pay, I doubt whether one hundred dollars a week for a family of a wife and three children living in a city apartment left a great deal of loose cash for speculation. However, let us take merely the forty-five million people who received less than three thousand dollars a year, and if we assume that one third of them did speculate, that gives us thirty million who did not. This is not a figure which can be added to the fifty million we already have, as the overlap must be great, but it can be added (although I do not yet say that it should be) to the seventy million people who are not listed as having any income at all (children, other dependents and wives earning no income, I suppose, make up the bulk of this number). This would give us the really impressive total of one hundred million people who, by luck or under compulsion, were not speculating. It fits in fairly well with another. There were in 1930 about thirty million families in the United States, an average of four persons to a family. The week after the market crash, Assistant Secretary of Commerce Julius Klein said, as I have noted, that only four per cent. of the families in the United States were affected, which would mean something over a million families and something over five million people altogether. I have no way of knowing how Mr. Klein arrived at this figure and can hardly bring myself to believe that he is a reliable guide; but the other statistics come close to proving his point. Note that the figure gave the number of families affected; again making a deduction for children and dependents, it seems probable that the actual number of speculators could not have been more than two and a half million.

For the year of the great crash four million people (three per cent. of the population) filed income tax returns, and of these returns only two and a half million were taxable. This was the year in which the American people said it had been caught short in the market and October was the month when they were sold out. The income tax returns listed the number of people who admitted that they made a profit or complained that they suffered a loss by selling real estate, stocks and bonds.[3]

The total number of those who reported gains in the year of the great smash was above three hundred thousand. And the total number of those who reported losses was less than eighty thousand. Commenting on these figures, J. Edward Meeker, the economist of the New York Stock Exchange, wrote me, "Only those individuals would report who closed their commitments out at a profit or at a loss. Many people actually took up their stock outright and probably still have it, so that these figures again do not accurately reflect the total number of individuals in the market. In addition, the question of bonds and real estate of course is unfortunately included in these same total figures." There are, of course, the unfortunate ones

[3] ". . . other than taxed as capital net gain (or loss) from sale of assets held more than two years." This is the technical phrase which separates speculative losses and gains from others.

who continued to put up margin and sold out later, but the figures for 1930 are not yet available. Obviously nothing definite can be derived from this number alone, but it is interesting to note that in the previous year, before the violent excess of the bull market began, the number of people who profited in the same category was three hundred and forty-four thousand — that is to say, it was greater than the number of those who made a profit in the boom year. What impresses me is that four million people filed income tax returns and that less than one tenth of them showed either profit or loss in the stock market in their returns.

At the same time we know that there were about three and a half million stockholders in American corporations in 1929; the number increased by forty per cent. or so to 5,848,000 in 1932. Assuming that eighty per cent. of the people who bought stock for investment also bought stocks for speculation, we arrive again at the figure of about two and a half million.

One final set of figures: According to the survey made by the *Business Week* forty-five million people whose income was less than three thousand dollars a year actually spent "for consumption, savings and taxes" eight billion dollars more than their income. The "excess of spending over income", says the *Business Week*, "makes the paradox of prosperity"; but when it is brought down to the level of those whose income is less than sixty dollars a week it leaves very little margin for speculation.

The biggest day in the crash was the sale of some sixteen million shares of stock. It was reported that members were selling in lots of fifty and one hundred thousand and the same individual might have made three or four such sales. But if we take an average of a thousand shares for each sale, it would indicate that there were sixteen thousand transactions involving in each a buyer and seller, or thirty-two thousand people.

Assuming that one thousand shares is too high for the average lot, we multiply by five and say that the total number of sales involved one hundred and sixty thousand people, on the assumption that the average block of stocks sold at the height of the panic was only two hundred shares. The selling of odd lots is very difficult to trace; on the other hand, there are professional security dealers who, as Mr. Meeker says, "might not have any prominent position in securities but simply trade in and out", and their enormous activities in large lots might perhaps make an average for the number of small traders who dealt in odd lots.

It is said that the great campaigns for selling the Liberty Loans during the war made the American people "bond-conscious" and that from bonds they proceeded to the purchase of common stocks. It is quite true that the number of actual owners of stocks increased tremendously between the war and the crash, and also increased after the crash. This implies that before the war we were certainly not all in the market, and the testimony of brokers all proves this. Stock-market speculation was, in the first fifteen years of this century, the privilege of a few misguided and dangerous individuals who were envied or hated by the rest of the country. The figures, therefore, for this period, may give us a point of departure. In August, 1900, the average number of transactions on the Stock Exchange was, roughly, 150,000; this was a low point and the following peak in April, 1901, was 1,800,000. The next low was September, 1903, with 430,000 shares and the next high was November, 1904, with 1,300,000 shares; in June and November, 1908, the variation was between 260,000 and 1,000,-000. In February, 1915, less than 120,000 transactions were made daily, and in November of the following year, the average was 1,480,000. In 1929, when we were all in the market before the crash, 5,000,000 transactions a day was considered high; the average for the nine months preceding the crash is just under four million shares a day, or less than three times as many transactions as occurred in the high point in November, 1916. If this were an accurate measure, it would suggest that only three times as many people were involved.

The head of a prominent organization which studies the stock market for professional purposes (Mr. Luther Blake, of *Standard Statistics*) suggested to me that while few figures are available it might be assumed that between fifteen and twenty million people "were interested in the market" and economists of various brokerage houses have told me the same thing. One of them writes, "According to the 'World Almanac' about forty-nine million people were gainfully employed in the United States in 1930. I suppose you could make a rough guess that fifty per cent. or sixty per cent. of this number were interested in speculative ventures of one kind or another." Since thirty-six per cent. of this number earned less than twenty dollars a week, eighty per cent. less than forty dollars a week, and ninety-five per cent. less than one hundred dollars a week, I think the figures of the economist are enthusiastic. On the other hand a great statistician guessed — and warned me that he was guessing — that a maximum of four hundred thousand people were in the market in 1929. If interest means mental interest, there can be no question that the greater figure is right, but if we assume that the head of a family was the only one in the family who actually was in the market, even this figure brings the number of speculators down to five million.

Obsessed with this question, I put it to every one I met in the course of three months, and naturally got a variety of points of view. The most common piece of information I received was that butlers and maids and chauffeurs were all in the market; a noted editor told me that often when he walked home from his office late at night he would see taxi drivers reading the stock reports and discussing sensational rises. From the testimony of others I should judge that every

man or woman in domestic service in New York had taken a
flier in the market. Inasmuch as there were twelve million
families in the United States who had a radio in 1929, we might
assume one third of these had a servant (although I doubt this
very much.) That would give us four million servants available for speculation. But I do not think that this enters into
actual statistics. Certainly domestic servants, with their food
and lodging provided, might speculate; but a large number of
them were as likely to have invested; I have heard of those
who were most unwillingly in the market since they invested,
without any intention to speculate, in real-estate bonds, the
promotors of which were speculating and went bankrupt.

I have set my figure at two and a half million and now
doubling it again and saying that there were perhaps five million people actually speculating in 1929, I note that this means
one person in every twenty-five; that is to say, when we were
all in the market *twenty-four out of twenty-five were not*
in the market. If my first guess is right, the number goes up
to forty-nine out of fifty. In either case, every moral and
economic assumption based on the idea that the whole of
America not only approved of speculation but actually was
engaged in speculation must be discarded.

I have suggested at the very beginning of this survey that
there was a classic explanation, most of which was classic only
in the cruel sense of the word, which makes classic synonymous
with dead. There rose in the course of the depression a whole
series of new explanations delivered by economists without
political affiliations and of a realistic turn of mind, and among
these there were three items which constantly recurred; that
there had been overproduction, that lack of planning (which
is the adjustment of production to consumption) was at
fault, and that the manipulation of money was the only solution of the persistent recurrence of depressions. These have

become almost classic in the sense that they are widely accepted, and I suppose that a generation from now they will
be attacked in turn as the theory of automatic business cycles
is now attacked. Of these the most interesting is the problem
of overproduction and it is also the easiest to become confused
about. The man who loves quiet naturally thought that there
were too many radios, and the man who wished to drive
slowly through charming roads thought there were too many
motor cars. Later, manufacturers who had to spend a higher
and higher proportion of their profits on the business of selling may have thought that other manufacturers were producing too many washing machines and oil burners and electric
toasters; but it was not until an enormous quantity of goods
began choking the warehouses because the retailers were not
drawing them out, because the consumer was not asking for
them, that overproduction as a thing in itself began to be felt.
That is to say, overproduction is purely relative to the power
to consume. Mr. Santayana once said that to the believer in
certain forms of absolute philosophy it is not enough that
liquor intoxicates man; he must believe that the whisky
stands dead drunk in its bottle. So the believer in overproduction sometimes speaks as if there was a natural and normal
amount of production beyond which everything is "over."
In a sense the first part of this is true: not that a certain rate
of production is morally right, but that a certain rate of increase in basic production happens to have existed for the last
fifty years. This great contribution of America to the science
of statistics was suggested some twelve years ago by Carl
Snyder, who recalls with indulgence (or perhaps it is his usual
cynicism) that the trained masters of statistics to whom he
suggested the possibility of charting this rate, all looked upon
him as slightly mad. In the last decade, however, Mr. Snyder
has developed his theory and brought forth his figures so that
now it is generally accepted that regardless of booms and

panics, and regardless of the seismographic ups and downs of charts, there is a fairly constant growth in physical production. The growth is slackening slightly at the present time, but roughly our basic production increases about four per cent. a year. That is to say, that although copper may produce ten times as much in one year as the next, and farm products may vary only a trifle, and steel may go down when copper goes up, if you consider all basic production over a long period, you will find that it doubles itself in about twenty-five years — that every year four per cent. more is produced than the year before.

"We now know," says Mr. Snyder, "that we have made no unparalleled gain in efficiency, either during the war or since. The impression of increased efficiency seems the illusion of every period of marked industrial expansion, and [is] directly the product of our incorrigible thirst for bunk. The rate of our industrial growth, the gain from one decade to the next, seems not materially to have changed within the last sixty or eighty years. So far as the evidence is attainable, this rate of growth seems not to have varied widely from a long-term steady average of about four per cent. per annum. In periods of boom it is a little higher; in the ensuing depression, a little less. We have been steadily growing richer and more efficient for at least a full century, and, taken over the larger intervals, at apparently an almost unchanging rate."

These words were spoken in March, 1929, and are, therefore, without prejudice; after the crash, when the cry of overproduction rose, Mr. Snyder made another survey of the "almost ineradicable belief that the five or ten years preceding the crash . . . were a period of unusual, if not unprecedented, industrial expansion." He had been told that the usual measures failed to take in newer industries; he therefore took in newer industries, and his measure of production in five years of the "new era" includes data "on some two hundred different series, ranging all the way from broad, inclusive series, like car loadings and the larger crops, to bathtubs and radiators, or from locomotives to spinach." It was obvious that the rates of increase in certain industries were enormous — two hundred per cent. for rayon, one hundred per cent. for gasoline, eighty per cent. for trucks; but against these there stood considerable and important decreases in shipbuilding, in radiators, in bathtubs and, at the very bottom, locomotives which declined nearly sixty per cent. in this period. I will not go through the methods by which these various statistics were brought together. Mr. Snyder's conclusion is: *"What they all showed was an average for the five-year period of twelve to fourteen per cent. That is an average rate of increase of a little over two and a half per cent. per annum."* This is not a measure of trade and it does not "measure the undoubtedly large increase in 'services' of every type, and notably of manicurists, marcel-wavers, radio crooners, real-estate agents, bond salesmen, and a wide variety of occupations that make their appearance and are a characteristic indicator of every boom."

It does show that a gain in one direction may be counteracted by a loss in another (motor trucks, for example, and freight cars). It checks popular misconceptions. There is, for example, the enormous, as Mr. Snyder calls it, "the fabulous" increase in cigarette smoking; but in five years the total gain in the actual production in tobacco leaf was only sixteen per cent. — about three per cent. a year. Mr. Snyder wants to know what would be a normal rate of growth in basic production if in a boom period of tremendous financial and economic activity the rate is only two and a half per cent. a year.

The importance of Mr. Snyder's principle is that it finally destroys the idea of the business cycle — the idea, that is, of a depression which has to come at a stated interval of time. The invariable sign of an approaching depression is a fall in the price of commodities. Heretofore these falls have been contributed to the direct workings of the law of supply and demand. But if supply is constantly increasing over a long period and demand can be whipped up by high-pressure salesmanship, the law itself begins to be questionable. Mr. Snyder sums up his conclusion briefly:

"The evidence seems clear that for the maintenance of business stability and the maximum of production, employment and general well-being, credit must expand at close to the same rate as the normal or long-term rate of growth of trade itself; that is, in this country, in recent years, at about four per cent. per annum.

"An excess of credit above this normal rate of growth appears to mean excessive speculation, inflation, and their attendant evils. A deficit seems to spell an arrest of growth, unemployment, strikes, and depression. And these are essential, perhaps *the* essential, features of what we call business cycles.

"If this be true, the only rational answer we can give to the question as to the future of the business cycle is that it is largely a problem of the effective or rational management of the credit supply. As I see it, it is essentially an engineering problem. . . ."

An engineer employed by the American Telephone and Telegraph Company told me that this corporation knew with considerable assurance how many telephones would be in use ten years from now, how much replacement would have to be made of materials, and how many new inventions could be absorbed. The budget of the corporation accounts for all these long views of the future. For a whole country the problem might be infinitely greater, but Mr. Snyder believes that if the essential factor is controlled, that is, the supply of credit, all the others can be successfully managed.

At various points after the middle of 1930, it was said that the depression had struck bottom; that there was no place to go but up. The arguments were:

1. Stocks were as much below their actual worth as they had been above their actual worth at the peak. Between June 27 and October 5, 1931, almost all the services guiding investors advised buying. Between March 8 and July 8, 1932, when the stocks in the Dow-Jones Index dropped more than fifty per cent., several of these services also advised buying. The qualifying phrase "for investment", "for dividends", "for the long pull", often appeared, and the basis of this was that a stock bought at fifty would pay twelve per cent. on the investment if it paid a moderate six per cent. dividend. As many stocks were selling in the twenties the prospect of twenty-four per cent. dividend was really enchanting, and there would have been a boom in the market if any one thought that they ever would pay dividends at all. Actually, there were several flurries in which the market went up considerably, so that speculators often made money and the "value" of stocks went up by the billions. The tendency of the same stocks to go down again should not have affected the buyers, because they were theoretically investing for dividends in the years to come.

2. Another indication that bottom had been reached was the exhaustion of all raw materials and of manufactured goods held in warehouses. This should have been a matter of statistics exclusively, but prejudice seemed to have crept in. The announcement that we had all worn out our shoes and exhausted our pleasure in our motor cars, and cleared out the granaries was premature. Or perhaps they did not take into account the fact that penniless men do not buy shoes. On one specific problem I have been told that a group of specialists believed we would promptly have to return to the production of iron in 1932, where another and, as it turned out, more accurate group, figured that we could continue with the stock on hand until the middle of 1934.

3. We had struck bottom psychologically. On this there was neither argument nor data.

There is a faulty assumption in all of these beliefs that is curiously like the assumption at the beginning of the crash — that nothing serious had happened. United States Steel would resume, just as the Republican Party would resume, just as the sun would rise next day. It was implicit in the President's assurances that in the next twenty years we should build more houses and more motor cars. It was, of course, fundamentally based on the idea that our civilization had not crashed. Another assumption is that prosperity is the normal thing and depression is the exception — an assumption colored by our desires, very similar to the assumption that peace is the normal thing and war the exception, although it can perfectly well be maintained that peace is only an exceptional interval for the preparation of further wars, and booms are only exceptional periods preparing for further depressions. For psychological reasons, however, it is desirable that the idea of striking bottom should be more closely examined than it has been. It is an image connected with "the healing process of time", a phrase so often used that one would think old age, which is time enough, healed itself. Not only the President but dozens of other leaders, upholders of the American system as well as experimenters, have in desperation fallen back on the idea that when things have become worse for a certain time, they are bound to be better. Whenever a more radical program has been suggested, conversatives have resorted to "time", preferring healing to drastic surgery. They have always closed their eyes to the alternative, which is the bottomless pit or, in financial terms, bankruptcy; in social terms, anarchy.

In the last month of writing this book, I have spoken to many economists and found not one who believed in this healing process. Some of them believed that the avalanche could be resisted and some were doubtful. But not one countenanced the idea that automatically a lapse of time would cure ills brought on by the actions of human beings. There is no healing process, and what is more, there is no bottom. There was no reason at the beginning of 1932 that stocks should go up or men be taken back into factories, merely because stocks had gone down far enough and enough men had been laid off; there is no reason at the moment of writing. The downward process of deflation has to be checked by specific action; it will not check itself. Those with the power to check it must decide that it must be checked and how it shall be checked, because there is nothing in the process of destruction which acts as a brake upon it. Accustomed to looking at stock-market charts, people have assumed that there is a bottom line. However, they themselves have seen stocks disappear entirely from the market list and go into oblivion. The assumption that depressions cure themselves is a pleasant one for those who are incapable or unwilling to face the difficult job of finding and applying the cure.

There is no bottom line and in a sense there is no normal line. If the reconstruction program was put into effect at the beginning of 1932, it means only that the President and the Congress had decided things had gone far enough — enough speculators had been punished, enough flimsy businesses had gone to the wall, enough bad debts had been written off — but what constituted enough was decided by them. It was not, for example, decided by men who had been out of work for two and a half years.

With no clear idea of how the depression would end, the common man and the expert were equally vague about the meaning of the revival of good times.

Ideas of how prosperity would return changed with every postponement of the happy day. I judge that in the first year of the depression people expected to unfold their morning newspaper and see a seven-column headline in extremely large black type: "PROSPERITY RETURNS!" It was only in 1932

that we began to think that the process of recovery itself would
be long, difficult and full of special problems. The reason we
began to think so was that there was a rally in the summer
of 1932 and we found that our standards of measurement had
changed. Roughly, we were using low points as a norm instead
of high points.[4]

President Hoover had always skillfully used the figures of
1925 and 1926 when he wished to make comparisons. But in
the minds of most people, stocks were to be measured by the
15th of October, 1929, and general prosperity by the average
of April to September of 1929. In 1932, when stocks went
up a few points, people spoke of a thirty-three per cent. increase although, increase and all, stocks were still fifty per cent.
lower than they had been in 1931. The typical headline (The
New York World Telegram, August 23, 1932) was:

"COST OF LIVING DEFINITELY SHOOTS UPWARD;
LABOR BUREAU REPORTS .006 RISE IN WEEK."

The same thing was true of increases in employment; even the
customary seasonal rise which created a tiny increase was considered of exceptional importance.

The headline I have quoted was over a story which revealed
a great many of the difficulties of recovery. One paragraph
read, "Grocers said here to-day that they planned to put increases into effect on goods for which they had to pay greater
wholesale prices"; and another, "Employment decreased 4%
in manufacturing industries in July . . . and manufacturing
pay rolls were 7.9% less than in June. Of the sixteen major
industrial groups included in these figures, four showed increases in employment . . . (of these) two reported declining pay rolls at the same time that the number of employed increased. The remaining twelve groups showed declines in both

[4] Wall mottoes appeared in offices with the words, "Whew! That
was some depression, wasn't it?"

employment and wage totals." The changing standard was shown by the record that wholesale prices of farm products mounted from 47.9 to 49.4 compared with the 1926 average of 100.

A period of inflation which is also a period of the rising cost of living is theoretically advantageous to a man who has no fixed income; there are more jobs and he gets more money. But in practice, retail prices are always put up a little faster than wages, just as they always stay up a little longer than wages. Food prices, for instance, rose in forty-three out of fifty-one cities in July, while pay rolls were still decreasing six per cent. There seems to be a flaw somewhere in the working of the economic law.

The psychological effect of rejoicing in the fact that one hundred thousand men have returned to work when ten million are still out of work is the danger which liberals warned against. They thought that it would be even harder to put through a program of social relief during the upward swing than it had been during the decline. They suspected that employers who were still unreconciled to the moderate power of the American Federation of Labor would take advantage of the existence of millions of jobless men to break up the power of organized labor and perhaps to return to the old economy of low wages. In the fight over the wage rate the bankers, rapidly becoming a controlling factor in industry, had turned their backs on the principle that high wages meant prosperity; it was reasonable to expect that they would use their advantage in keeping labor perpetually under the threat of the great reserve of the unemployed.

The image of the corner remained in the public mind. Long after they had learned to scoff at the idea that prosperity, like Botticelli's "Spring" or a dancing figure in chiffon from a cartoon, would ever come around it, they thought of themselves as rounding the corner and coming out of the shadow. For that it was only necessary to sniff a brisker air or to know that the Duponts or the Detroit motor factories or textiles were receiving rush orders. It was not necessary to consider what the rate of recovery might be. Impressed by Mr. Carl Snyder's figure of the steady four per cent. increase in basic production, I asked men who knew about such things whether that rate would correspond to the rate of recovery — the black inference being that it would, for example, take us twenty-five years to reabsorb the ten or twelve million jobless and to return to, let us say, the average prosperous levels of 1926. They assured me that the rate of recovery after a slump is rapid and far above the average rate. The quick panic and sharp decline of 1921 was held by the great bankers and manufacturers of the time to be only the prelude to a long period of hard times; they said with some sense that we would have to liquidate the war and they did not suspect that liquidation could be postponed eight years. Yet, the depression ran an odd course; there was a rally in autumn and then a drop to the lowest point, after which all the indicators moved upward for the entire year of 1922, and before that year was over general business was "in excellent shape" and presently a shortage of freight cars was impending. Conditions of 1932 are not those of 1922; it is, for one thing, a three-year depression and not a one-year depression that has to be overcome. If it is overcome at all, the upward swing will be rapid and will be accelerated by the impatience of the American people as well as by their natural boom psychology. Yet at its best, recovery will be a long, and for many people, a dreary time; unless proper inflation should occur, the poor will struggle on in a world of rising cost of living and labor will seek jobs which do not exist. Awareness of the long road still to go certainly changed the position of the American Federation, which rejected all idea of insurance against unemployment in the first years of the depression, and now, facing its own weakness in the years to come, has definitely declared for such insurance.

The relations between America and Europe have been scantily treated in this record of the depression; they represent the most complex of the special problems of the time and the one on which light and leadership, that desirable combination, are conspicuously divided. I have left many things out for lack of special knowledge, but one thing, on which general information is enough, must not be omitted. It is that during the depression we tried hard to withdraw more and more from Europe; we entered conferences and appointed observers and entertained prime ministers and quarreled about war debts; under the compulsion of circumstances we acted internationally when we proposed the Moratorium; but we wanted to be left alone.

One reason was the official explanation that our ills had been blown across the ocean from Europe, like a plague carried by westerly winds. If Europe was the center of infection, we had two ways of saving ourselves: by isolating ourselves and by curing Europe. We tried the first with our tariff, then wavered and tried the second with the Moratorium, and reverted to the first, late in 1932, with our demand for payment of the war debts. Regrettably, the policy of isolation is hostile to the policy of cure, and the attempt to combine them rose from panic more than from principle. The European countries which naturally retaliated against our tariff and at the same time tried to embrace us in their economy, suffered from the same indecision. In each, the struggle between a national and an international policy was going on; the most elaborate organization of countries acting together had been erected and the most profound impulse toward isolation grew up to check it. In every country there were political leaders who looked toward Geneva and economists who were sure that the era of interaction had ended and that each country must be self-contained to the highest possible degree. Our country, with its official tradition, fell naturally into isolation.

It was remarked, however, that much as we blamed Europe for the events of 1929, the second blow in 1930, the approaching bankruptcies of 1931, we never were encouraged to thank Europe for any part in our rally of 1932. The conversations between President Hoover and M. Laval could not be binding, but they implied that the United States would listen with more sympathy to proposals from Europe if Europe arranged its own affairs and took the initiative into her hands. At the Lausanne Conference, this was done, although not in the way most agreeable to us. In a sense, England and France dismissed reparations, by scaling them down to about one cent on the dollar; but the condition, that reparations be scaled down in proportion to cancellations by the United States, was reinforced by an agreement on the "United Front" which the American Government found unacceptable. Since reparations had seemed at the beginning to be punitive indemnities and were not looked on with enthusiasm by the American people, the Lausanne accord was important chiefly as an admission, from Germany's creditors, that Germany could not be expected to pay more than a nominal sum.

Yet Europe seemed, at last, to have achieved peace; a way was open. The emotional effect was good. American industries could not call back millions of workers because of an emotional effect, but American spirits rose and the stock-market index rose. It cannot be said absolutely that the improvement in America, the most marked since 1929, was caused entirely by the European settlement, for at the same time Congress adjourned and the reconstruction program had gone into its stride; negatively, it can be said that the results of Lausanne did not check the upward swing.

The presumption in the agreement at Lausanne was that America could be persuaded to play an international part; but the presidential campaign, which might have given the successful candidate a specific direction, was fought on the as-

sumption of isolation. France and England had agreed not to
bring up the subject of war debts; the candidates had other
and safer things to emphasize. Promptly, after the election,
Europe approached America. Even if Mr. Hoover had wished
to function as a mere forerunner of Mr. Roosevelt, he would
have had no clear mandate.

The prime difficulty is that the structure of the world is
changing and no one seems to know in what direction. The
world may be turning toward economic isolation or economic
internationalism; or part of the world may be tending to one,
part to the other. The uneasiness of the American situation lies
in this: that we have been politically isolationist while we have
been economically international. We have, in the past, counted
on exporting certain farm products and manufactures; we
have counted on certain habits of finance, centered in London;
we have not learned to do without the one or to supplant the
other. In 1932 we made a great effort to raise the level of commodity prices, by domestic means; in the three full months of
the campaign we pretended that the level could rise, no matter
what happened in Europe. Yet the price of wheat continues to
be affected internationally by the pound, and the relation between these two nullified a great part of our domestic effort.
The price level which rose, sank again. The corresponding figures are illuminating.

I take the beginning and the middle of each month and
quote the nearest whole number. On the first of August wheat
sold as high as 55 cents, the pound stood as high as $3.52 (the
lows were one cent less in each case). On the fifteenth, wheat
was at 56, the pound at $3.48. In September the figures were
57 and 53 for wheat, $3.47 and $3.48 for the pound — a complete lack of correspondence for the fifteen days; but the trend
was more marked when the variations of the pound were
greater, for in October wheat began at 54 cents and went to
49, and the pound went from $3.46 to $3.45, and then slumped

with exceptional rapidity so that it was at $3.31 at the beginning of November and $3.16 at the end, wheat moving down more slowly, but steadily from 44 to 42. In the whole period wheat fell from 55 cents to 42, the pound from $3.52 to $3.16.

I have been told that the world will never stay prosperous over a long period until it has an international central bank controlling credit (which implies the deposit of each nation's gold, if the gold standard is held, in a central place); it has also been said, urgently and even violently in the past few years, that every nation must learn to live by itself, counting on no exports beyond those which would pay for the few commodities it could not possibly raise itself. Between these extremes, the world to-day wavers. The decision is of vast importance, because the whole system of finance, industry, and agriculture must be changed in accordance with the choice. So far, we have tried to make the best of both. We have neither evolved a domestic economy by which we can subsist without the rest of the world, nor a national consciousness which would allow us to live with the rest of the world. The discomfort of our position is that while we may recover enough material strength to try one way or the other, we are intellectually prepared for neither.

CHAPTER TWENTY-ONE

The Saviors of Civilization

AMONG the fatalities of the depression were the capitalists and the intellectuals. Long separated one from the other, each fell for lack of support. It is remarkable that after the first six months or so, hardly an authoritative word was spoken in defense of the capitalist system, and the baffled financier had to pick crumbs of comfort from such radical realists as Maynard Keynes and Stuart Chase. On the other hand, one trembles to think what would have happened to a large number of intellectuals if the Communist experiment in Russia had failed before 1929; the flight to Moscow was so headlong that if Moscow had not existed one imagines intellectuals would have drowned themselves fanatically off the shores of the Atlantic.

The actual number of writers and artists who cried their devotion to Communism is not large. It includes, however, Theodore Dreiser, who had become the great Cham of letters with "An American Tragedy" and turned to active support of labor and radical movements, and Mr. Edmund Wilson, in my opinion the finest critic of our immediate time, who turned from the symbolists and the Parnassians to write "The American Jitters", from analyses of Marcel Proust to praise of William Z. Foster; Mr. V. F. Calverton, a less perceptive and more thoroughly Marxian critic, listed among the important writers John Dos Passos, Michael Gold and Charles Yale Harrison who, he said, "have seized leadership in the creative field."

And there are other critics who support these novelists. A proletarian theater exists in New York and proletarian fiction and poetry is being written. Naturally writers interest writers, so the appearance of editors of the *New Republic* and reviewers for the *Nation* and individuals like Sherwood Anderson and Dreiser among the Communists makes news. The Communist writers think of themselves as the Encyclopedists of our time, forerunners of our revolution, as Diderot and d'Alembert were of the French Revolution. The Voltaire has not yet appeared.

It strikes me as important, not that a few excellent writers have become Communists but that a great number of excellent writers have obviously begun to feel a certain insignificance in their work. "Now," they say, "is there nothing serious in mortality" except the doctrines of Marx. Naturally interested in the creative life, they have been at odds with a productive and acquisitive society; but when that society broke down they did not turn to the creative life, but to another system of production which they felt was neither grasping nor greedy. I know enough of these men to be sure that they did not embrace Communism as young English politicians did, in the hope of being among the rulers. They embraced it because Communism seemed to them to give the promise of a free and expanding life. It was as if they were willing to give up their creativeness and their freedom in order to insure it for others.

Yet this is in part a kind of depression pessimism. Just as Oswald Spengler had preached to us after the downfall of Germany the religion of becoming mechanics in an age of mechanism, on the theory that the present was no time for artists and poets, so the intellectual victims of the depression preached to us a profound devotion to economic problems because this was no time for the parasitic activities of art. It was amusing to read in the *Nation* certain reviews of books, informed and just, with foreknowledge from the signature that the last paragraph would point out the defect that the author had not accepted the Marxian interpretation of history. It was not so amusing to learn that every writer who had not gone over to Communism was considered not only a renegade to the freedom of the mind, but a paid slave of capitalism.[1] It was not expected of a great scientist that he should give up his laboratory in order to build barricades in the streets; Einstein might continue his abstract speculations, Stravinsky might continue to compose, Picasso to paint, but the indifference of Mr. Joseph Hergesheimer and Miss Ellen Glasgow to the economic problems was seriously held against them. Intellectuals were putting their minds at the service of an order of society; they were definitely doing what they had often been told to do — they were "getting in touch with life"; but the touch was a hostile one. I do not recall any novelist who put himself at the service of the existing system, either to defend it or to improve it. The silence of Sinclair Lewis is as impressive as the outburst of Theodore Dreiser.

One can hardly blame the writers, because the conductors of the capitalist system in America showed little inclination to self-improvement. Distinguished men of letters endorsed the candidacy of Norman Thomas because the Socialist Party, adapting itself more and more to American conditions, seemed to them the most effective protest against the meaningless politics of the two older parties, and at the same time stood definitely for modification of capitalism. But few intellectuals could bring themselves to believe that the election of either Mr. Hoover or Mr. Roosevelt could mean very much to America.

The surprising thing is that the capitalist system had so few hired men among the litterateurs. According to the Marxians, the arts subconsciously serve the economic system; but in a moment of crisis one would assume that the service would

[1] Pardon my glove.

be a little bit more active and open. As in the French Revolution, the rich have taken pleasure in supporting their enemies — Mr. Otto H. Kahn's gifts to the radical theater were as well known as his support of the great artistic prop and failure of capitalism, grand opera. It became, in fact, clear that the American capitalist had been extraordinarily stupid. In twenty years he had witnessed a fermentation of intellect and a growth of criticism which colored books and plays, and even popular newspapers; but it had never occurred to him that these things might be a danger to the source of his wealth. (Perhaps he relied on the calming influence of a movie and a radio.) Nine out of ten plays which dealt in any serious way with marriage defamed that harrassed institution. Nine out of ten plays exhibiting a business man made fun of him.[2] Mr. Booth Tarkington fought loyally for the plutocrat, but it was a rear-guard action. If radical economics were put down when the *Freeman* failed, they spread into the book reviews of the *Herald Tribune*. Everywhere intellectuals were at work sapping. When the crisis came, the capitalist was cold and friendless. He turned to the economists who had hymned his praises, but they were abashed and a new modesty crept into their pronouncements.

The capitalist was not as good a conspirator as one had hoped. He rallied no intellectual forces to his support. A few did discuss the crisis; a few cried for a dictator; for the rest, either conviction was lacking or the old money devils had lost their cunning and did not know how to handle the simplest forms of publicity.[3] It seems as if they themselves felt that their func-

[2] Twenty years ago they attacked him as a villain.

[3] Mr. Henry Ford is a conspicuous exception. Nearly everything he said from 1929 to 1932 was memorable and the interview with him in the *Pictorial Review* in October, 1932, was entirely remarkable. Among other things, he said, "This is not a cycle of hard times from which we shall return to build bigger panics. This is not a period of depression to be tided over until good times come back. This is not a

tion had been fulfilled and all they wanted was to live out the remaining years of their lives without losing all their money. They seemed to disbelieve as profoundly in the future as the intellectuals themselves. It was fatal for the capitalists because their whole system was based on investment which looks toward the future; in the past two decades it had shored up the edifice of capitalism with science and technology, both of them depending not on the immediate moment but on the long run. The great corporations have created research laboratories, letting men work on problems for years in the general belief that the discovery of scientific truth would ultimately redound to their profit. But if they no longer believed in their own ultimate existence, what was there left for them to do?

It had been characteristic of many generations of Americans to believe that the world was born when they were born, that America had no past. The laments of writers who crept away to Europe in search of a tradition, and the impatience of the engineer at the bungling of his predecessors, were evidences of the same feeling, — that our world began yesterday. But in all this time no one in America doubted that the future belonged to us, and there was something unmanly in the prompt enthusiasm with which we leaped overboard the moment the ship struck a reef. Three years after the market crash a number of banks joined to protect the financial system; by that time the intellectuals had either joined Moscow or retired each to his solitary tower. The capitalists and the intellectuals were both being highly romantic in the sense that neither was willing to contemplate things as they are.

Under the profound disinclination to contemplate the future, under the Bourbonism of the Republicans, the liberalism of some Democrats, and the turn to Moscow of the Com-

'clean-up' by which the rich profit and the poor lose. This is not a breakage which can be patched up so that we resume our reckless course again. This is the ending of an era."

munists, lay a common uneasiness — a fear not often expressed, that "civilization is doomed." This is the price we pay for having read history, that we are self-conscious; we note that civilizations have broken down before and Flinders Petrie has told us that at least one civilization which vanished was as rich and complex and intelligent as our own. To two types of mind the thought of a Communist revolution in America was virtually equivalent to the breakdown of civilization: to the capitalist and to the technological expert; to the first because his fortune and his prestige would go, to the second because he could estimate the cost of an interruption in the fundamental activities of a highly complex industrial civilization. Once in a great while a Communist suggested that the proletariat could take control of America without plunging the country into chaos; but in general the adhesion of the Communist Party not only to Marxian doctrine but to the methods of Russia suggested that the violent intention of the dominant class to keep its power would be met by a violent fury on the part of their enemies to gain power. "The masses," said Leon Trotzky, "come into a revolution not with a proper plan of social reconstruction, but with a sharp feeling that they cannot endure the old régime."

If the lesson of the Russian Revolution was learned by the American Communists, the capture of power here would mean in the first instance the capture of a few fundamental services — communications, above all. But communications (radio, telegraph, telephone and post) are infinitely more complicated in America than in Europe; moreover, there is no doubt that the Federal army has its plans either to capture communications or to employ a subsidiary system of its own, in case it ever loses control. Transport is another key to successful revolution, and here, too, the vast disorganized trucking system of America would have to be taken as well as the railroads. The established government would be in a position to fight unless the psychological lethargy of the ruling class in America develops into locomotor ataxia; and there is no reason to believe that the governing class will not fight desperately to protect itself. In the struggle we might learn how delicately our system is balanced. Mr. Stuart Chase estimates that if two hundred thousand trained technicians "were blotted out of existence to-morrow, the social and industrial life of the nation would be paralyzed. Mines, factories and public utilities would cease production. Food supplies would accumulate remote from the great markets. Babies would die while men and women fought for bread and meat. It would take not months, but years to train the men necessary to restore the constant reliable flow of commerce.

"By themselves alone," Chase continues, "the technicians can, in a few weeks, effectually incapacitate the country's productive industry. . . . No one who will dispassionately consider the technical character of this industrial system will fail to recognize that fact. Mr. Veblen estimates the number of men necessary to do this at 'no more than a minute fraction of one per cent. of the population.'

"An engineer once told me how something in the order of one hundred key men, operating its veins of water, power, gas, sewage disposal, milk supply, communication, could bring the life of a great city to an end — almost as neatly as though its every crevice had been soaked with poison gas. . . . The machine has presented us with a central nervous system, protected with no spinal vertebræ, lying almost naked for the cutting. If for one reason or another, the severance is made, we face a terrifying, perhaps a mortal, crisis. All previous cultures have got along with hardly any central nervous system at all; they could be destroyed only village by village, for each was largely self-sustaining."

All revolutions are transfers in power, and whether outside of the army any ruling class in America has made any plan

for preventing a transfer in power is doubtful, more doubtful now since we have seen that the ruling class is incapable
even of planning to prevent its own disruption and of uniting
to reform its lines after a defeat. The defensive tactics of the
men in possession of America have been a trivial and displeas-
ing extension of the police power. The country born in revolution seems to imagine that it could head off revolution by
rapping a few heads with a policeman's stick. The long miserable story of injustice in factories and mines, the throwing over
of almost every principle of civil liberty, the cynical faith in
the shotgun and in the corrupt court, are evidences of an
appalling ignorance of the course of history. I do not disbelieve in the use of force and corruption; they have certainly
suppressed revolts in their time. I doubt only whether they
are adequate to protect a system so overgrown, and apparently
so rigid, as our own.

To most people the death of a civilization means the destruction of the few institutions by which they live; no doubt
Russian *émigrés* consider that the United Socialist Soviet Republics have fallen back into barbarism because churches have
been dynamited and a royal palace is a summer home for
proletarians. To Americans the destruction of the capitalist
system would be an equivalent of the death of society, and it
would therefore be interesting to discover whether any symptoms of the collapse of capitalism have occurred. As I have
said, trust and hope in the future is the fundamental characteristic of capitalism: Money spent to build a factory to-day
will bring returns for forty years; bonds bought to-day will
pay dividends almost to the end of time; one hundred dollars
loaned to-day will bring interest until the loan is paid and
then will bring back one hundred dollars; devoted work at
a machine will make a man a foreman three years from now;
savings placed in a bank will be safe and assure an independent

old age. Confidence in these things is more important than the immediate comforts which the capitalist system has promised, and temporarily this confidence does not exist.

The symbol of the capitalist system is money, and since the war money has become flighty; it is not a fixed power but a variable. Germany, Russia, France, Italy and England have in various ways confessed their lack of faith in money itself, and in the United States, the priests of money have been compelled to utter various incantations and black threats in order to preserve the potency of their symbol. From time to time little items have appeared in newspapers suggesting that in isolated communities the money system has broken down and barter, which is considered a symptom of semi-barbarism, has taken its place. The negotiations between Brazil and the United States for the exchange of quantities of wheat for quantities of coffee were another indication that the medium of exchange was faulty.

The capitalist system is an invention of modern times. Mr. Maynard Keynes has pointed out that Sir Francis Drake, after his career of piracy (or purifying the seas) gave enough money to Queen Elizabeth for her to pay the national debt and have two hundred thousand dollars to invest; she did invest it in the East, and the sum of two hundred thousand dollars at compound interest from her time to ours is about twenty billion dollars, which is, roughly, the total foreign investment of Great Britain in our time. The British investment grew not only by compound interest, but by the extension of field which came from discovery and invention; the full development of capitalism, the arrival of the capitalist as the dominant social and political figure came with the industrial revolution and with the industrial revolution came its great dangers. Mr. Carl Snyder notes that this country became subject to severe financial disturbances after the canal and the railroad had appeared on the scene, and of course our present depression may be considered a parallel, with motor transport taking the place of railroad transport. The railroad, the transatlantic steamer, the highly equipped army used in the penetration and civilization of colonies have all made it possible to sell goods over a wider area to more people; this "demand" made necessary the invention and the manufacture of enormous machines; machines require capital — that is to say, investment; but they also give scope to human inventiveness which is not as steady in its activities as compound interest. Mr. Howard Scott has pointed out that the first dynamo ever made by the General Electric Company for the Insull Power Utilities in Chicago was built in 1903. In 1909, although it was still functioning perfectly, it had become obsolete; new types of dynamos were producing so much more profitably that this dynamo was removed and now stands in the company's yards in Schenectady as a museum piece. Yet the bonds which financed the purchase of this dynamo have still some eighty years to run, and if the Insull properties were solvent, they would still have to pay. The machine was meant to function in the future; the payment of it was postponed for the future. When the machine ceases to be profitable, bankruptcy alone can relieve its owner from the burden of debt.

So far, the social revolution through which we are passing has attacked the debt and not the machine. We have had no machine wreckers at the gates of the factories; the crowds at the gates were only too anxious to get a chance to use the machine. But the civilization based on the machine can be wrecked just as surely if confidence in the future of the machine is destroyed. At the present moment (the end of 1932) it is freely stated that half of the factories and the equipment for manufacture in the United States is obsolete, but there is no flow of money to finance new ones. A profound uncertainty has touched the investor. In his own lifetime he has seen the vast network of railroads upon which the prosperity of the country depended growing profitless; he may have suspected, in fact, that the entire depression can be figured as the last move in the triumph of the motor car over the railroad. And if he is asked to invest in the motor car he knows already that the aëroplane may take its place in another generation. What stock and what promise to pay in a hundred years can be of value? What research and what scientific enterprise should be encouraged? Into what obscurity will pure and applied science both begin to disappear?

I have noted elsewhere the growing suspicion of education in itself, but on the whole I found little evidence of the arts and sciences descending into the night of the Dark Ages. Obviously, hard-pressed municipalities will be compelled to cut down their appropriations for schools, and the first interests to be sacrificed will be the less practical ones and the less popular ones, those which, having little immediate result, look to the long future.

The American Public Health Association is already concerned over increased demands upon doctors in the public employ, and its field director has said, "We have had to lop off many activities essential to health . . . those which have been most seriously affected are child welfare and public health nursing, which are the most vitally important of all." The public health officer, with a diminished staff, will have to limit himself to preventing epidemics by protecting the supply of water and food; heads of public health may find that the removal of garbage and sewage exhausts their appropriations. Should the deficiency of the police system be impaired for similar reasons, at a time when theft and robbery are bound to increase, a return to the kind of barbarism in which every man protects himself would not be far distant. The other great protector of human rights has already been jeopardized. In May's Landing, New Jersey, "lack of funds to pay jurors has forced postponement of the hearing of civil suits scheduled for trial by jury at the fall term of Atlantic City courts", and a large number of criminal cases were deferred for the same reason.

The disaster of the Chicago Public Library I have already mentioned; the struggles of municipal orchestras all over the country have been desperate; the theater in New York, which seemed in 1928 and 1929 to have beaten off the attack of the moving pictures, succumbed to the combined attack of the talkies and the depression. I suspect that the art museums are not very happy; colleges with great foundations and large investments in superior securities can still carry on, but it has been noted that the older chairs (in the dead languages and literature) have the more solid endowments, and those dealing with modern problems are likely to be the first to be abandoned. Yet of all of these evidences of disaster none moves me more than two accounts from opposite ends of the country. In Los Angeles the county zoo has been put on the auction block; in Philadelphia no money was available to feed the thirty-three hundred animals in the Zoölogical Gardens, and the director faces the necessity of putting the animals to death; whether the devoted children of Philadelphia can, by their gifts of pennies, save their zoo is doubtful, but civilization may still be saved, for a Philadelphia showman has offered to take the zoo over and make it into a three-ring circus.

The birth rate fell in 1931 seventeen per cent. below the rate of 1921, ten per cent. lower than that of 1926. If the next hundred years are to mark the slow decline or the catastrophic disappearance of our civilization, going out with a bang or a whimper, at least there will be fewer human beings alive to enjoy the spectacle.

CHAPTER TWENTY-TWO

COMMENTARY

ASKED, many years later, what he had done during the French Revolution, the Abbé Sieyès replied, "I lived through it."

THE END

INDEX

72/95